# Everyday Cooking
## with Dr. Dean Ornish

ALSO BY DEAN ORNISH, M.D.

*Stress, Diet & Your Heart*

*Dr. Dean Ornish's Program for Reversing Heart Disease*

*Eat More, Weigh Less*

# Everyday Cooking with Dr. Dean Ornish

## 150 Easy, Low-Fat, High-Flavor Recipes

## Dean Ornish, M.D.

### with Janet Fletcher, Jean-Marc Fullsack, and Helen Roe, M.S., R.D.

HarperCollins*Publishers*

Grateful acknowledgment is made for permission to reprint the following copyrighted material:

The chart "Comparing Legumes" on pages 42–43. Reprinted by permission from *The Wellness Encyclopedia of Food and Nutrition*, © Health Letter Associates, 1992.

The chart "Nutritional Content of Breads" on pages 53–54. Reprinted by permission from *The Wellness Encyclopedia*, © Health Letter Associates, 1991.

The article "Dark Leafy Greens" on pages 182–183. Reprinted by permission from the *University of California at Berkeley Wellness Letter*, © Health Letter Associates, 1995.

HarperCollins books may be purchased for educational, business, or sales promotional use. For information please write: Special Markets Department, HarperCollins Publishers, Inc., 10 East 53rd Street, New York, NY 10022.

FIRST EDITION

*Designed by Jessica Shatan*

---

Library of Congress Cataloging-in-Publication Data

Ornish, Dean.
    Everyday cooking with Dr. Dean Ornish : 150 easy, low-fat, high-flavor recipes / by Dean Ornish. — 1st ed.
        p.   cm.
    Includes index.
    ISBN 0-06-017314-9
    1. Vegetarian cookery. 2. Low-fat diet—Recipes. 3. Quick and easy cookery.
4. Nutrition. I. Title.
TX837.O74    1996
641.5′636—dc20                                                     95-47392

---

96 97 98 99 00 ❖/RRD 10 9 8 7 6 5 4 3 2 1

*The book is dedicated to*
*President William Jefferson Clinton and Hillary Rodham Clinton.*

*May God grant you the wisdom, courage, and compassion*
*needed to lead our country during these transformative times.*

# Contents

# Acknowledgments

Writing the acknowledgments section is my favorite part of any book. It gives me the opportunity to reflect with gratitude on the many people who have been involved in the creation of this book and the success of the research and hospital programs upon which it is based. It gives me great pleasure to acknowledge them here and to express my deepest and heartfelt appreciation.

The four people who made the most meaningful contributions to this book are (in alphabetical order) Janet Fletcher, Jean-Marc Fullsack, Diane Reverand, and Helen Roe. Janet Fletcher acted as the managing editor, overseeing the project. Jean-Marc Fullsack created and tested many of the recipes, drawing on six years of experience collaborating with me along with his classical training as a French chef. The book was coordinated by Helen Roe, M.S., R.D., who is the senior dietitian and director of nutrition services at the Preventive Medicine Research Institute. Before that Helen spent fourteen years in Houston working with Antonio M. Gotto, Jr., M.D., Michael DeBakey, M.D., and other leading heart specialists. Together, Janet, Jean-Marc, and Helen developed and tested recipes and created menus that are both delicious and nutritionally sound.

Diane Reverand is vice president, editor-in-chief, and associate publisher at HarperCollins Publishers. She personally and expertly edited the manuscript, with assistance from Meaghan Dowling (assistant editor), David Flora (administrative assistant), Susan Kosko (assistant director of production), Lorie Young (managing editor), Estelle Laurence (copy editor), Nancy Singer (design supervisor), Jessica Shatan (designer), Jane Batt and Rose-Ann Mitchell (proofreaders), and Sydney Wolfe Cohen (indexer). I am especially indebted to Jack McKeown, group vice president and publisher of HarperCollins, for his vision and intelligence.

Sincere thanks to John Phillip Carroll, Peggy Fallon, Tina Salter, and Christine Swett for their help with developing and testing recipes, and to Gloria Parker for her assistance.

I appreciate so much everyone who contributed recipes to this book: Daniel Allen, Jessie and Maynard Amelon, Shari Wilgard Behar, Edith Bernstein, Heidi C. Bisbee, Kathy Bonanno, Bonita Boughman, Landis and Norma Butcher, Robert M. Butler, Jr., Patricia Byrne, Lin Carlson, Genevieve Case, Mark and Delila Chandler, Susan L. Collins, Elaine Conner, John Cardozo, Guy and Joan Coutanche, Katherine Chepenuk, C. W. Crawford, M.D., Betty and Frank Crisafi, Clair Crumpler, Roberta A. Dayton, Laura L. Dickinson, Roy and Norma Disney, Jo S. Dotson, LeRoy and Lucille Eastwood, Marianna Edgerton, William H. Fern, Gary Fingert, Judy and George Fried, Hannah and Sue Fuhrman, Lois and Frederick Gelbman, Christine Aubale Gerschel, Hank and Phyllis Ginsberg, Joan Goldberg, Vivian Gregory, Bev Gross, Franklin J. Gunsberg, George and Martha Hackney, Hugh and Helen Hackney, Sharon Hayden, Eva Hebenstreit, Judy Heyman, Barbara Hines, Frank D. Hoble, Win Hooper, Evelyne Johnson, Susan Jukubowicz, Lydia Karpenko, Elizabeth Kapstein, Cindy Kelley, Esther Kreike, Sallie Lampkin, Lola Langdon, Leon and Diane LeBeau, Miriam Leefe, Acy Lehman, Mrs. John H. Martin, Carolyn McDonald, Robert R. Minarik, Evelyn Mintzer, Martin C. J. Mongiello, Paula Moriarty, Natalie Ornish, Susan Parent, June Patinkin, Barbara C. Peterson, Barbara and Ralph Pisani, Isolde Pohl, David Popkin, Donald and Ruth Renier, David M. Rice, Art Richards, Marvin B. Riibner, Walter H. Robinson, Mr. and Mrs. Richard E. Romaine, Ruth Sartisky, Frank and Judy Sebron, Audrey and Bobby Sells, Leona and Khem Shahani, Valerie Shannon, James A. Shirk, Jeanne R. Stanis, Nell Steenburgen, Debra Steinberg, Frank Swihel, J. W. Szallies, Don W. TeRonde, Michael and Beth Thomas, Marilyn and David Thomasson, Joan I. Thompson, Shelby Toussaint, Robyn Webb, Anthony Wilson, and Linda Zacher. Unfortunately, space limitations precluded using all of these recipes.

When I first began conducting research almost twenty years ago, the idea that the progression of heart disease could be reversed was thought impossible by most physicians and scientists. Equally unlikely was the idea that people could make and sustain comprehensive changes in diet and lifestyle in the real world.

Over time, in a series of clinical trials, my colleagues and I at the nonprofit Preventive Medicine Research Institute demonstrated that most of the participants in our studies *were* able to change their lifestyles and that the progression of coronary heart disease often can begin to reverse. Because of our research and the studies of others, most physicians now believe that the progression of heart disease is often reversible.

Now my colleagues and I are training physicians and other health professionals at eight hospitals throughout the country in a Multicenter Lifestyle Heart Trial to demonstrate the practicality, medical effectiveness, and cost effectiveness of our program in diverse populations. This book evolved out of what my colleagues and I have learned from adapting and simplifying our program at these hospitals.

These eight sites include the Beth Israel Hospital at Harvard Medical School in Boston; Broward General Hospital in Ft. Lauderdale; Richland Memorial Hospital in Columbia, South Carolina; the Scripps Clinic and Hospitals in La Jolla, California; Mt. Diablo Medical Center/Heart Health Center in Concord (near San Francisco); the Beth Israel Medical Center in New York City; Mercy Hospital Medical Center/Iowa Heart Center in Des Moines; and Immanuel Medical Center/The Heart Institute in Omaha.

The staff from these hospital sites include Geoffrey Ginsburg, M.D., Peter Oettgen, M.D., Jacki Hart, M.D., Priscilla Robinson, Donna Folan, Kristina Nordensten, M.S., R.D., Mollie Diesroth-Kim, M.S., Irene Cross, LCSW, Cyndi Bullis-Long, R.N., Caitlin Hosmer, M.S., R.D., and Carline Wallace from Beth Israel Hospital, Boston; Caroll Moody, M.D., Brenda Sanzobrino, M.D., Michael Chizner, M.D., Miriam Chuang, R.N., M.S.N., Terry Ray, R.N., M.S.N., C.P.D., Bob Thompson, Sue Gauthier, Anita Meade, M.S., C.E.S., Leslie Feldman, M.S., C.E.S., Eston Dunn, Tami England, M.S., Marianne Donnan, R.N., M.A., C.E.S., Kevin Hall, R.N., C.E.S., Renee Kotchek, R.N.,

Sue Pickel, R.N., C.E.S., Lubelle D'Luna-O'Grady, R.N., Barbara Serko, Ph.D., and Katie Sparks, R.D., from Broward General Medical Center, Ft. Lauderdale; Donald Saunders, M.D., Joseph Hollins, M.D., Thomas A. Kleinhanzl, Donna Greenwold, R.N., B.S.N., R.V.T., Colleen Wracker, R.D., Susan Beverung, R.N., B.S.N., Julie Jenkins, M.S., Bruce Schell, Ph.D., Yvonne Russell, R.N., Jean Humphreys, Ph.D., Denise Hallemeyer, M.S.N., Bren Schell, Diane Barnes, Christine Leadbitter, M.S., Loretta Prescott, Mark Culp, and Michael Kester from Richland Memorial Hospital, Columbia; Mimi Guaneri, M.D., Mark Kalina, M.D., Paul Tierstin, M.D., Doug Triffen, M.D., Glenn W. Chong, Betty Christiansen, Steve Alper, L.C.S.W. and Caroline Murphy, R.N., M.S.N., from Scripps Clinic and Hospitals, La Jolla; Peter Kunkel, M.D., F.A.C.C., Barbara Kroll, B.S.N., R.N., Melissa Marcil, Lynn Olison, Ph.D., Mary Hyer, R.D., C.N.S.D., Louise Barrier, R.N., Conrad Knudsen, M.A., Kazuko Onodera, Dan Morrow, Al Gutierrez, Barbara Ackerman, Sharon Jenkins, and Teddi Grant-Adel from Mt. Diablo Medical Center/Heart Health Center, Concord; Steve Horowitz, M.D., Dahlia Garza, M.D., Roberto Roberti, M.D., Prateek Dalal, M.D., Bill Sasso, Laurie Jones, R.D., Deborah Matza, R.N., Shari Behar, M.S., Jane Kustin, M.S., Elizabeth Kapstein, Charles Leighton, C.S.W., Louis Shankman, C.S.W., Susan Jakubowitz, Ph.D., Daya Levy, Louis Sierra, Gayle Reichler, M.S., R.D., and Millie Carreras from Beth Israel Medical Center, New York City; William Wickemeyer, M.D., Phillip Bear, M.D., Shakun Advani, M.D., Dan Aten, Diane Sorensen, R.D., L.D., Mandy Corliss, R.D., L.D., Carol Throckmorton, R.D., L.D., C.D.E., Tom Lowe, M.S., Victoria Polich, R.N., Michele Martz, R.N., Donald Gilbert, M.S., Terrisue Johnson, Angie Thurm, Marianne Samorey, M.S., Debra Pietzsch, Beverly Gidden, Lois Owen-Kramer, R.D., L.D., George Volger, and Paul Smith from Mercy Hospital Medical Center/Iowa Heart Center, Des Moines; Rick Collins, M.D., Jim Morgan, M.D., Steve Fish, Sheila McGuire, Diane Schuette, M.S., Susan Wright, R.D., L.D., Shelly Oestmann, R.D., L.D., Pauli Nejezchleb, M.S., Ellen Wilson, R.N., B.S.N., Ann Nichols, R.N., B.S.N., Sherrel Fry, R.N., B.S.N., Mary Heimann, R.N., B.S.N., Christine Beardmore, M.S., Liz Easley, R.N., M.S., C.N.P., Rich Fetrow, M.A., Susan Gillespie, Robyn Tait, Jeri Morgan, R.N., M.S., Donna Schultz, R.N., and Mary Hansen and Tim Gaines from Immanuel Medical Center/The Heart Institute, Omaha.

Mutual of Omaha was the first major insurance company to reimburse the cost of our program at these hospital sites. Because of their vision and leadership, many other insurance companies are now covering our program. I want to express my gratitude to Jack Weekly, Ernie Johnston, Steve Booma, Mary McNulty, Randy Horn, Dr. Kenneth L. McDonough, Scott Stangl, PA-C, Dr. Marcus Wilson, Faruque Ahmad, and others.

Alexander Leaf, M.D., has been an inspiring mentor and friend for over fifteen years, for which I am deeply grateful. Dr. Leaf is chairing our central data management and statistical analysis center for the Multicenter Lifestyle Heart Trial, along with his colleagues, David Schoenfeld, Ph.D., and Judith Scheer, M.P.H., at Massachusetts General Hospital and Harvard Medical School.

I never intended to start a research institute. At first, almost all of our grant support was from private individuals, and it made more sense to establish an institute to administer the funds so that all of it could be used for research rather than for another institution's indirect costs. When we started, the institute was one room in my house; now it has evolved to include enough full-time staff that we occupy an entire building. While directing an institute can be challenging, the joyful part is being able to work with people who are extremely competent, caring, and compassionate.

Full-time staff members at the Preventive Medicine Research Institute include: James H. Billings, Ph.D., M.P.H. (senior vice president and director of clinical services), Lee Lipsenthal, M.D. (vice president and medical director), Ana Regalia, C.P.A. (vice president and chief financial officer), Heather Amador (retreat manager), Nischala Devi (stress management director, hospital programs), Melanie Elliott, R.N., M.S.N. (hospital liaison and supervisor), Amy Gage (stress management director, retreats), David Liff (director of network development), Ruth Marlin, M.D. (hospital liaison), Patty McCormac, R.N. (hospital liaison), Laurel Mellin, M.A., R.D., Myrna Melling (retreat coordinator), Terri Merritt, M.S. (hospital liaison), Helen Roe, M.S., R.D. (nutrition director), Stephen Sparler, M.A. (research coordinator), Larry W. Scherwitz, Ph.D. (research director), and Pamela Tuite (receptionist). I am especially indebted to Marjorie McClain, who coordinates and brings order to my otherwise chaotic schedule and life.

Others who have worked with PMRI recently or at our week-long residential retreats include: Barbara Ackerman, Margo Anand, Robert Avenson, Ph.D., Kimberly Baltzell, R.N., Judy Barr, Louise Barrier,

R.N., Phillip Bear, M.D., Suzanne Black, Ph.D., Joan Blady-Helfman, R.N., Betty Bozeman, R.N., M.S.W., C.C.R.N, Kathleen Brandley, R.N., M.S.N., Dan Broderick, M.S., Cathy Brooks-Fox, R.N., Ben Brown, M.D., Art Brownstein, M.D., M.P.H., Nutan Brownstein, Katherine Burleson, M.D., Patti Cappretta, R.N., Liz Carlson, R.N., M.S., C.C.R.N., Charles "Cy" Carpenter, Jnani Chapman, R.N., B.S.N., C.M.T., David Chernof, M.D., Margot Chmel, Ltjg. Deborah Cole, R.D., Richard Collins, M.D., Barbara Conway, R.N., M.S.N., Michael Conway, M.Ed., Chrystina Cook, Mandy Corliss, R.D., L.D., Maryann Cornell, M.S., Bruno Cortis, M.D., F.A.C.C., Sara Craig, Lila Crutchfield, R.N., N.P., Renie Del Ponte, M.S., Bhaskar Deva, Swami Divyananda, Honey Doublebower, Adam Duhan, M.D., Eston Dunn, M.S., Amy Dietrich, Carola Ekelund, P.T., Lara Ekelund, M.D., Ph.D., Gina Eldred, Mike Emerson, Tami England, M.S., Joanne Finkel, M.S.W., Robert Finkel, M.S., D.P.E., Lakshmi Fjord, William Forrest, Lillias Folan, Sue Fuhrman, R.N., M.S., Pat Gans, M.D., Lea German, R.N., M.A., Kathy Gillmore, R.N., M.P.A., Susan Godfried, M.D., Chef Joyce Goldstein, Kathryn Grado, R.N., M.S.N., Steve Halbert, M.D., Denise Hallemeyer, R.N., M.S.N., Steven Halpern, Ph.D., Larry Hancock, Joan Hansen, Susan Hanson, R.D., Jacqueline Hart, M.D., Douglas Hawley, Nirmala Heriza, Kathy Hesketh, Katherine Hirsch, R.N., M.S., Marla Hodes, M.A., Joe Hollins, M.D., Steven Horowitz, M.D., Jo Lil Howard, Mary Hyer, R.D, C.N.S.D., Yseult Imbuelten, R.N., C.R.N.A., Jan Lei Iwata, Pharm.D., Robert Jarski, Ph.D., P.A.-C., Jodie Jonas, P.T., Jon Kabat-Zinn, Ph.D., Sean Kaer, Anna Keck, R.N., F.N.P., Chef Hubert Keller, Deborah Kesten, M.P.H., Jamie Lee Kistler, R.N., Nick Kittredge, Peter Knoepfler, M.D., Conrad Knudsen, M.A., Elizabeth Kraatz, P.T., Jane Kustin, M.S., Cristine Leadbitter, M.S., M.P.H., Cristy Lee, Dane Lee, M.D., Miriam Leefe, Lenore Lefer, M.S., M.F.C.C., Mel Lefer, Charles Leighton, C.S.W., George and Annie Leonard, Joseph LePage, Dennis Malone, M.S.W., Pat McKenna, M.D., Sandra McLanahan, M.D., Kristen McLenahan, M.S., R.D., K. C. McQuillan, R.N., Leigh Miller, R.N., B.S.N., Radhika Miller, Nancy Minges, Meridith Murphy, M.F.C.C., Michael Murphy, Pauli Nejezchleb, M.A., Alice Nicolai, M.P.H., R.D., Deborah Novak, M.S., R.D., Lynn Olison, Ph.D., Jean O'Neil, M.S., June Kazuko Onodera, John Patterson, M.D., Glenn Perelson, Dr. Bradley Personius, Maj, USAF, M.C., Nancy Pinner, R.N., Victoria Polich, R.N., Gloria Powell, R.N., Swami Prakashananda, Kashi Rai, Jennifer Raymond,

---

M.S., R.D., Lauren Reel, M.S., Timothy Regoli, Gayle Reichler, M.S., R.D., Rachel Naomi Remen, M.D., Beth Shankari Rise, P.T., Martin Rossman, M.D., Shirley Sandler, A.S.C.T., Rob Saper, M.D., Gary Scales, Mary Dale Scheller, M.S.W., M.A., Franklin Schneider, M.D., Diane Schuette, M.S., C.M.S.W., F.C.O.C., Jessica Schulman, Kristin Shaeffer, Ellery Smith, Diane Sorensen, R.D., L.D., Rick Sullivan, M.S., M.F.C.C., Renie Tharp, R.D., Sharon Thompson, Mindy Utzinger, Wendy Valentine, Anthony Varriano, M.D., Laura Wallace, Mathilde "Teal" Weems, Marilyn Weinberg, Moriah Wells, P.A., John Welwood, Ph.D., Janet Wilson, R.N., B.S.N., Mike Wilson, Morgan Urquhart, M.A., Ginny Wojciechowicz, R.N., and Larry Yabroff, Ph.D.

Larry Scherwitz, Ph.D., and Shirley Brown, M.D., were co–principal investigators of the Lifestyle Heart Trial, and Richard J. Brand, Ph.D., was the senior biostatistician. Principal research collaborators included: William T. Armstrong, M.D., James H. Billings, Ph.D., M.P.H., Leonard Bolomey, Frank Dobbs, Ph.D., Amy Gage, K. Lance Gould, M.D., Mary Jane Hess, R.N., Richard Kirkeeide, Ph.D., LaVeta Luce, R.N., Marjorie McClain, Pat McKenna, M.D., Sandra McLanahan, M.D., Myrna Melling, Terri Merritt, M.S., Nizar Mullani, Carol Naber, Thomas Ports, M.D., Mary Dale Scheller, M.S.W., and Stephen Sparler, M.A.

Other collaborators included: Celeste Burwell, Pamela Lea Byrne, Ph.D., R.N., M.S., M.F.C.C., Mary Carroll, Carol Connell, Jean-Marc Fullsack, Richard Goldstein, M.D., Mark Hall, Mary Haynie, R.N., Mary Jane Hess, R.N., Georgie Hesse, R.N., Dale Jones, R.T., Yvonne Stuart, R.T., and Mary Tiberi, R.N.

Referring physicians and angiographers included: William T. Armstrong, M.D., Damian Augustin, M.D., G. James Avery, M.D., Richard Axelrod, M.D., Wayne Bayless, M.D., Robert Bernstein, M.D., Robert Blau, M.D., Craig Brandman, M.D., Bruce Brent, M.D., Roger Budge, M.D., Michael Bunim, M.D., Michael Chase, M.D., James A. Clever, M.D., Keith E. Cohn, M.D., James Cullen, M.D., Daniel Elliott, M.D., Richard Francoz, M.D., Gordon Fung, M.D., Kent Gershengorn, M.D., Gabriel Gregoratos, M.D., Lloyd W. Gross, M.D., Robert Hulworth, M.D., Timothy Hurley, M.D., Gerson Jacobs, M.D., Herbert Jacobs, M.D., Lester Jacobson, M.D., Thomas J. Kaiser, M.D., William Kapla, M.D., Hilliard Katz, M.D., John Kelly, Jr., M.D., Jonathan Keroes, M.D., Edward Kersh, M.D., Frederick London, M.D., Randall Low, M.D., Myron Marx, M.D., Roy Meyer, M.D., Felix Millhouse,

M.D., Frederick Mintz, M.D., Gene Nakamoto, M.D., Gerald Needleman, M.D., Morris Noble, M.D., Philip O'Keefe, M.D., Paul Ogden, M.D., Thomas Olwin, M.D., James Reid, M.D., J. Patrick Robertson, M.D., John Sarconi, M.D., H. C. Segars, M.D., Arthur Selzer, M.D., Gene Shafton, M.D., Richard Strauss, M.D., Brian Strunk, M.D., Martin Terplan, M.D., William Thomas, M.D., Anne Thorson, M.D., Michael Volen, M.D., Jon Wack, M.D., and Mark Wexman, M.D.

None of this work would have been possible without the dedicated and pioneering efforts of our experimental group research participants in the Lifestyle Heart Trial. They include: Ronald and Jeanne Becnel, Dwayne and Kathy Butler, Roger Camm, John and Phyllis Cardozo, Joseph and Anita Cecena, Robert Finnell and Marianne Pallotti, Elise Gendar, Victor Gilbert, Hank and Phyllis Ginsberg, Marsha Harrison, Joseph Hayden, Werner and Eva Hebenstreit, Don Henry, Foster Hibbard, Donald and Audrey Jones, Victor and Lydia Karpenko, Jim and Margaret Keith, Conrad Knudsen, M.A., Mel and Lenore Lefer, Leo and Rae Lembi, Demetreos and Norma Leonardos, Drs. Robert McAleese and Karen Sexton, Barbara Musser, Paul and Novella Paulsen, Leslie Peller, Bill Ranney, Robert Royall, Tom and Riya Ryan, Peggy Smyth, Donald and Mary Van Iderstine, Don Vaupel, James and Irene White. I am also deeply grateful to research participants in the comparison group.

Our research was conducted under the auspices of the Preventive Medicine Research Institute (PMRI), a nonprofit independent research institute associated with the University of California, San Francisco. Current board members include: Gerald D. Hines (chairman), Henry Groppe (secretary/treasurer), Martin Bucksbaum (recently deceased), Jenard Gross, Stuart Moldaw, and Fenton R. Talbott. They provided encouragement, guidance, and financial support at a time when this project was only a dream, and they have provided ongoing vision and leadership, for which my colleagues and I remain deeply grateful. I am also grateful to Barbara Hines, Carol Groppe, Melva Bucksbaum, Gail Gross, Phyllis Moldaw, and Judy Talbott for their friendship and support.

The major hospitals collaborating on our study have been Presbyterian Hospital of California Pacific Medical Center; Moffitt Hospital of the University of California, San Francisco; University of California, Berkeley; and the University of Texas Medical School, Houston.

Recent major supporters of our research include: Mutual of Omaha, the Smart Family Foundation, Inc., General Growth Properties, Inc., the Bucksbaum Foundation, F. G. Arnold, Norman Arnold, Ben Arnold Memorial Foundation, William L. Davis Family Foundation, Odyssey Partners, the Harold Grinspoon Charitable Foundation, the Wornick Family Foundation, Inc., and John P. and Anne Welsh McNulty Foundation.

Other recent support was provided by: Ken Hubbard and Tori Dauphinot, Robert Graham, American Express, the First Church of Danvers, Melvin Simon, G. R. Herberger's, Inc., Goldman, Sachs & Co., Bonnie Blades, Citibank Delaware, Lita and Morton Heller Foundation, Kandi Amelon, Carolyn and Preston Butcher, John O'Donnell, Randall Rowe, Aldrich Eastman Waltch, Ross Stores, Inc., Beth Rudin DeWoody, John Millar, Jean Schlermmer, Gymboree Corporation, Palace Clothiers, Inc., RDR Associates, Bissell Consulting, Phillip and Shirley Frank, Louis Somoza, Steven Busch, Neil Bluhm, James and Patricia McCarty, UBS Asset Management (New York), Inc., Robert Meisel, Burton M. Field Family, Inc., Robert Light, Pitlyke and Isso Baiz, George and Mary Stammer, Scott Greene, M. Leanne Lachman, D/E Hawaii Joint Venture, Lyle Gilbertson, Steven Keifer, Heather Hollister, Alan Winner, Stanley and Nancy Saddoris, Donald McLaughlin, Fujiyama, Duffy & Fujiyama, Clinton Gaulke, Errol Payne, William Pierce, and H. William and Margaret Rogers.

Earlier generous support was also provided by: the John E. Fetzer Institute (with special appreciation to the late John Fetzer, Robert Lehman, Judith Skutch Whitson, Bruce Fetzer, and others), the National Heart, Lung, and Blood Institute of the National Institutes of Health (RO1 HL42554, with appreciation to Stephen Weiss, Ph.D., Peter Kaufmann, Ph.D., Fred Heydrick, Ph.D., Antonio M. Gotto, Jr., M.D., and Claude Lenfant, M.D.), the Department of Health Services of the State of California (# 1256SC-01, with special appreciation to Assemblyman John Vasconcellos, Senators Art Torres and Nicholas Petris, Kenneth Kizer, M.D., Neal Kohatsu, M.D., the late Senator Bill Filante, and former Governor Deukmejian), Houston Endowment Inc. (J. Howard Creekmore and Jack Blanton), the Henry J. Kaiser Family Foundation (Alvin R. Tarlov, M.D.), the Enron Corporation Foundation (Kenneth Lay), Continental Airlines/Texas Air Corporation (Frank Lorenzo), ConAgra, Inc. (Charles M. Harper and others), the First

Boston Corporation (Fenton Talbott and others), Texas Commerce Bank (Ben Love), the Quaker Oats Company, the Emde Company, Corrine and David R. Gould, Dick and Kathy Dawson, General Growth Companies (Martin and Melva Bucksbaum), the Phyllis & Stuart Moldaw Philanthropic Fund, Gross Investments (Jenard and Gail Gross), Pritzker & Pritzker (Jay and Cindy Pritzker), Henry and Carol Groppe, Transco Energy Co., Pacific Presbyterian Medical Center Foundation (Dr. Bruce Spivey and Aubrey Serfling), Arthur Andersen & Co., Marvin and Marie Bomer, the Ziegler Corporation (Jack and Vyola Ziegler), Corporate Property Investors (Hans Mautner), the Ray C. Fish Foundation (James L. Daniel, Jr., Robert J. Cruikshank, CPA, and others), the Weatherhead Foundation (Albert and Celia Weatherhead), and the Nathan Cummings Foundation (Charles Halpern, Andrea Kydd, and others).

Additional support was provided by the Glenn Foundation (Paul Glenn and Mark Collins), Johnson & Johnson (Frank Barker), the M. B. Seretean Foundation, the Jewish Community Endowment Fund, United Savings Association of Texas, the Margoes Foundation (John Blum), Drexel Burnham Lambert (Michael Milken and Harry Horowitz), Hugh R. Goodrich, Edward O. Gaylord, Fayez Sarofim & Co., Eileen Rockefeller Growald, Lucy Rockefeller Waletzky, M.D., Biopsychosocial Research Fund of the Medical Illness Counseling Center, United Energy Resources, the Duncan Foundation (John Duncan), Mesa Petroleum (T. Boone Pickens), the Communities Foundation of Texas, Brown & Root, Inc. (T. Louis Austin), the Sackman Foundation, Physis Health Center (John Bagshaw, M.D.), Fenton and Judith Talbott, Leo Fields Family Philanthropic Fund, Bill and Uta Bone, Richard and Rhoda Goldman, Dr. and Mrs. James Langdon, Charles & Louise Gartner Philanthropic Fund, Frank A. Liddell, William and Lucero Meyer, Marianne Pallotti, Robert Finnell, T. B. Hudson, the Bob Hope International Heart Research Institute, Jeffrey Rhodes, Arnold and Carol Ablon, the William & Flora Hewlett Foundation, the Institute of Noetic Sciences (the late Brendan O'Regan), Pat McKenna, M.D., Werner and Eva Hebenstreit, Mel and Lenore Lefer, Amos and Dorian Krausz, Robert McAleese, Thomas Russell Potts, Victor and Lydia Karpenko, Edwin and Natalie Ornish, Simon and Paula Young, Doug Hawley, Van Gordon Sauter, PPG Industries, Burton Kaufman, James and Margaret Keith, Howard B. Wolf & Co., Joseph Frelinghuysen, Edward F. Kunin, David Harrison,

Dr. Kit Peterson, Joseph Forgione, the Institute for the Advancement of Health, and others.

For the past ten years we have held our week-long residential retreats at the Claremont Resort and Spa in Oakland, California. A major reason for this is our appreciation for Henry Feldman, the hotel's general manager.

Also for the past ten years I have been consulting with ConAgra, makers of Healthy Choice foods, to develop the *Life Choice* line of frozen low-fat dinners in order to make it easy, convenient, and inexpensive to follow the program described in this book. Those at ConAgra who are currently making this possible include: Philip B. Fletcher, Michael Trautschold, Lynn Phares, Jim Smith, Nancy Matthews, Sherri Coffelt, Sherry Polevoy, Bill Crosson, Rita Storey, M.S., R.D., Jack Goehausen, Tammy Vela, and others.

Thanks also to E. Connie Mariano, M.D., the Senior White House Physician, and her colleagues in the White House Medical Unit for her dedication in providing such excellent care of President Clinton and his family and for the privilege of consulting with her.

Each year since 1984 Arthur Andersen & Co. has provided a complete financial audit of the Preventive Medicine Research Institute on a pro bono basis, for which we remain deeply grateful. My appreciation and respect for Esther Newberg and for Michael Rudell and his associates only increases over time. Stafford Keegin, Bob Lieber, and Tom Silk have provided valuable advice and support to PMRI.

I feel especially blessed by my close friendships and family, the most meaningful part of my life. I remain deeply grateful to Sri Swami Satchidananda, the renowned spiritual teacher, from whom I have learned more of value in my life than from perhaps anyone else.

I hope you find this book to be useful. Thank you for this opportunity to be of service.

## AUTHOR'S NOTE

If you have coronary heart disease, obesity, or other health problems, please consult your physician before beginning this program. Each person is different, and decisions affecting your health are personal, ones that you should make only after consulting with your physician and other health professionals. If you are taking medications, your physician may wish to decrease or discontinue some or all of these if your clinical status improves. Do *not* make any changes in your medications without first consulting your doctor; it can be very dangerous to suddenly stop taking some drugs.

No treatment program, including drugs, surgery, or lifestyle changes, is effective for everyone. Some people may not lose weight or may become worse despite any treatments or lifestyle changes.

This book is based on the latest scientific information. Since science is always evolving, further understanding of human nutrition may lead to changes in the recommendations contained here.

As in my previous books, one of my goals in writing this book is to help increase your understanding of how powerful lifestyle choices can be in affecting your health and well-being. Another goal is to strengthen the communication between you and your physician and other health professionals. In this context, you may wish to share this book with him or her. Discuss it with your doctor so that the two of you can work together more effectively to help you achieve greater health and happiness.

# Everyday Cooking
# with Dr. Dean Ornish

# Choices Made Easy

## WHY I WROTE THIS BOOK

I enjoy reading my mail. I receive thousands of letters every year from people whose lives have improved, often dramatically, when they make the comprehensive dietary and lifestyle changes that my colleagues and I recommend. Since the publication of *Eat More, Weigh Less*, many have asked for simple, easy-to-prepare recipes with familiar, easy-to-find ingredients.

## DELICIOUS AND NUTRITIOUS

When I first began doing research demonstrating that the progression of even severe coronary artery disease could begin to reverse by making comprehensive changes in diet and lifestyle, there was a lot of misinformation about food. A common misconception was that you had to choose between gourmet high-fat foods that were delicious and beautifully presented and unhealthful, or low-fat foods that were boring and bland and might make you live longer—or just make it *seem* longer.

A few years ago, Molly O'Neill of the *New York Times*, one of the country's leading food writers, invited me to dinner at her home for an article she was planning, "The Nutritionist and the Gourmet." Dr. Marion Nestle, professor and director of nutrition at New York University, and I were the experts on nutrition. Jim Villas and Lydia Shire were the two well-known gourmet chefs. But you don't have to choose between good food and good health. Gourmet chefs can make low-fat foods that are delicious *and* nutritious.

In my first three books, I wanted to make the recipes as tasty and as beautifully presented as possible, at the same time meeting the nutritional guidelines of my program. Many people tend to associate high-fat foods as being tastier because the great chefs traditionally have worked in the high-fat arena. But it's not the amount of fat; it's how the food is prepared. High-fat foods can taste bad if they're prepared poorly, and low-fat foods can taste great if they're well prepared.

I realized that the best way to make low-fat food taste good was to work with great chefs, even if they weren't known for low-fat cooking. Great chefs know how to make great food.

So, I commissioned some of the country's most celebrated chefs— Hubert Keller, Wolfgang Puck, Joyce Goldstein, Deborah Madison, Michael Lomonaco, Jean-Marc Fullsack—and several others. I told them, "Work within these guidelines and see what you can create." (The only chef who ever turned me down was Julia Child, who said in her Julia Child voice, "This is not compatible with my philosophy of food!")

I didn't put any limitations on the chefs, in terms of making recipes practical or easy. As a result, the recipes were gourmet, but many were complex and time-consuming to prepare, using unfamiliar or expensive ingredients not available everywhere. One woman wrote me, "Where the hell am I going to get chanterelles? And what *are* chanterelles?"

## LOW FAT, HIGH FLAVOR

Now, in *Everyday Cooking with Dr. Dean Ornish*, I've presented 150 simple, yet extraordinary, recipes that use inexpensive, commonly found ingredients and follow easy, time-saving steps for making fresh, delicious, everyday meals. These recipes are organized into 45 seasonal menus to take advantage of the freshest ingredients. I hope that you find this to be an intensely pleasurable way of cooking and eating based on enhancing the joy of living, not out of fear of dying. These are very sensual foods, because I believe that life is to be enjoyed fully.

This book draws on what my colleagues and I have learned from training others to adapt this program to their own tastes, preferences, and cultures—from training health professionals and patients at hospitals throughout the country ranging from Harvard Medical School in Boston to Richland Memorial Hospital in Columbia, South Carolina (where cardiologist Joe Hollins, M.D., once told me, "Here in South Carolina, gravy is a beverage . . . ") to our work training the chefs at the White House, Camp David, the Navy Mess, and on *Air Force One* who cook for President and Mrs. Clinton. We've learned what works.

## BEYOND HEART DISEASE

The implications and the applications of what we are doing go far beyond just reversing heart disease. Clearly, if you can reverse the progression of heart disease, then you can help prevent it. Even though heart and blood vessel diseases still kill more Americans each year than just about every other illness *combined*, heart disease could be virtually eliminated if we simply put into practice what we already know. That is, if people followed this program.

The most motivating reason for changing your diet and lifestyle, however, is not just to live longer or to reduce the risk of something bad happening years later—it's to improve the quality of life *right now*. I began making these changes in my own life when I was nineteen. To me, there's no point in giving up something that I enjoy unless I get something back that's even better—and *quickly*. My cholesterol and blood pressure have always been very low, and I don't have any illnesses.

The reason I changed my diet and lifestyle is that I feel so much better than I did. I have more energy. I think more clearly. I have an overall improved feeling of well-being. I can eat whenever I'm hungry until I'm full, I can eat delicious food—and I don't have to worry about my weight.

Many men report that their sexual potency improves. (Your heart is not the only organ that gets more blood flow when you change your diet.) Others find that their bodies start to smell and taste better—even their breath improves. This makes sense when you remember that your body excretes toxic wastes not only in your bowel and bladder but also in your perspiration and breath. Many find that they have a greater sense of equanimity, their asthma gets better, their arthritis hurts less, their endurance and stamina improve, and so on.

By adopting and adapting this program, you will probably live longer than if you don't make any changes in your diet and lifestyle—but you never know, you might get hit by a truck (I hope not!). Most people tell me that even if they knew that they wouldn't live a moment longer, they would still adhere to this program—because the *quality* of life is so greatly enhanced. This program is not just about "risk factor modification," it's about living life to the fullest, with health, joy, and well-being.

Sometimes life gets so busy that I don't have time to make even simple recipes. The same may be true for you. For the past seven years, I've worked with ConAgra Frozen Foods to create a new line of meals called *Life Choice*, from the makers of Healthy Choice. It's part of my overall goal of making this program as simple and practical as possible. If you're interested, please call 1-800-328-3738 and they will send you meals on dry ice direct to your home via overnight delivery, as well as a variety of other resources and information. If you eat only these foods for a week or two, supplemented with recipes from this book, you may feel so much better that you become more inspired to continue eating this way.

In my research, I have found that most people want everyday food to be familiar and inviting. I remember what happened in my first study, back in 1977. Ten patients with severe heart disease spent a month on my program at the Plaza Hotel in Houston. The staff was just the cook, Marcia Acciardo, who loved to make Indian food, and me. After a few days of this cuisine, the patients rebelled and said, "No more curry!" And so she learned to do it differently.

In 1980, I directed a second study. This time, Martha Rose Shulman, a very gifted chef and author of many wonderful cookbooks, prepared all the meals for a month. Martha had lived in France for many years, and she loved to make French vegetable pâtés and other foods that she ran through her Cuisinart. After about three days, the patients said, "We won't eat food that we can't recognize!" They began to prefer corn on the cob, baked potatoes, black-eyed peas, okra, salads, and other foods that they were used to eating. Now we're relearning the same lesson. As Yogi Berra once said, "It was déjà vu all over again."

Many people are intimidated by food and even by spending time in supermarkets. I used to be one of them. I could go into the Oval Office and be very comfortable talking with the President of the United States, but put me in a supermarket and I'd get a panic attack.

Because I'd have no idea what to do with all of this stuff, I felt over-whelmed by all the choices, especially when I was on the outer aisles where the healthful foods tend to be. I mean, if it was a prepackaged food I could just follow the directions—but what did I do with a bag of beans? How much did I buy? What did I do with it when I got home? It just all seemed so intimidating and daunting. It was easier just to go out to eat or to buy something prepackaged.

*Everyday Cooking with Dr. Dean Ornish* is for people like me who can read this book and realize, "Hey, I can do this. It's not that hard. I don't have to worry about it. I don't need any fancy equipment. It's not com-plicated. It doesn't take any more time to prepare food that's low-fat as high-fat. It costs less. And the food tastes great."

## GOOD NUTRITION IS EASY

Nutrition can seem so complex and overwhelming, but the basic prin-ciples of good nutrition are easy. In my experience, I've learned to keep it simple. Otherwise, the more complex anything is, the less likely you are to do it.

The scientific rationale for the Life Choice program is described in great detail in my previous three books, *Stress, Diet & Your Heart;* *Dr. Dean Ornish's Program for Reversing Heart Disease;* and *Eat More, Weigh Less.* In this book, *Everyday Cooking with Dr. Dean Ornish,* I want to make it easy for you. I have included more in-depth nutrition information in the "Your Everyday Choices" section (page 297) and in my previous books.

I wrote my first book, *Stress, Diet & Your Heart,* in 1981, more than fifteen years ago. The recommendations I made in that book have stood the test of time. Since then, scientists have discovered even more scientific evidence and mechanisms to explain why a low-fat veg-etarian diet is the most healthful way to eat for most people.

The diet I recommended then is still what I recommend now: fruits, vegetables, grains, and legumes (beans), with the option of supple-menting your diet with moderate amounts of nonfat dairy and egg whites.

All oils are excluded because they are liquid fat. Even olive oil is 14 percent saturated fat and 100 percent total fat. The more olive oil you eat, the higher your cholesterol level will rise and the more weight you will gain. If you did nothing more than exclude all oils from your diet, you would likely find that both your cholesterol and your weight decrease.

If you drink alcohol, limit it to one drink per day (e.g., one glass of wine, one can of beer, one shot of whiskey). More than that, and the toxicities of alcohol outweigh any potential benefits. It would be unwise to begin drinking if you're not already doing so, especially if alcoholism runs in your family.

Reducing salt is a good idea for everyone, but it's most important if you have high blood pressure, kidney disease, or heart failure. Your body maintains a constant concentration of sodium. If you eat excessive amounts of salt, your body retains water to dilute the sodium back to the right concentration. When you retain water in a closed system (that is, your body), your blood pressure may rise. Your kidneys will try to excrete the excessive sodium, but some people do this more efficiently than others. To make matters worse, long-standing high blood pressure may damage your kidneys, making it more difficult to excrete the excessive sodium. As you reduce the amount of sodium in your diet, you will find that after a few weeks, your palate adapts and you need much less salt to provide the same flavor.

Wean yourself from caffeine. Caffeine is not strongly linked with heart disease, but it potentiates stress—in other words, it makes your fuse shorter. Besides coffee, caffeine comes in other forms, including black tea, chocolate, and many medications such as Excedrin, Anacin, and others. If you stop consuming caffeine abruptly, your body will likely go into withdrawal and you may experience a headache or feel lethargic or short-tempered for a few days.

Reduce your intake of simple carbohydrates, like sugar, for reasons I will detail later.

## THE LIFE CHOICE PROGRAM

This diet is part of the Life Choice program, which also includes moderate exercise, stress management training (stretching, breathing, meditation, visualization, and relaxation techniques), smoking cessation, and psychosocial support. I call this the Life Choice program to emphasize that this is a diet and lifestyle program based on (1) the joy of life, not the fear of death, and (2) *choice*, not coercion.

I have written this book to give you information that you can use to help make informed and intelligent choices. Whether or not you choose to change your diet and lifestyle, and to what degree, is entirely up to you. No shame, no guilt, no pressure.

## WHY A PLANT-BASED DIET?

Why do I recommend a plant-based (vegetarian) diet? Cholesterol is found only in animal products, which also tend to be high in saturated fat. Your body converts saturated fat to cholesterol. There is *no* cholesterol in a plant-based diet, and with few exceptions (avocados, seeds, nuts, and oils) a plant-based diet is low in both total fat and in saturated fat.

A meat-based diet is high in iron, which is an *oxidant*—that is, it oxidizes cholesterol to a form that makes it more likely to clog up your arteries. Iron also may cause the formation of free radicals that promote cancer and aging. In addition, a meat-based diet is low in the antioxidants that help prevent this from happening.

In contrast, a plant-based diet is low in oxidants like iron (it has enough iron without having too much) and high in antioxidants like beta-carotene and vitamins A, C, and E. Also, there is virtually no dietary fiber in meat, but there is a high concentration in a plant-based diet.

I also recommend taking a good multivitamin with $B_{12}$ and without iron (unless your physician tells you to take iron). You may want to take a supplement that includes 10,000 to 20,000 units per day of beta-carotene, 100 to 400 units per day of vitamin E, and 1,000 to 3,000 milligrams per day of vitamin C. Some recent studies indicate that 400 to 800 micrograms of folate per day may help to reduce the levels of a substance in your blood called homocysteine, which, in turn, may help prevent coronary heart disease.

In the past few years, scientists have discovered and documented new classes of chemicals that help prevent illness and slow the aging process. These include bioflavenoids, carotenoids, phytochemicals, and other substances that are high in a plant-based diet and low in a meat-based diet. Beta-carotene is only one of more than six hundred carotenoids in plants, including about forty that are prominent in common fruits and vegetables. In other words, there are more and more reasons to eat a plant-based diet.

A plant-based diet is linked not only with lower rates of heart disease and stroke, but also with significantly lower rates of the most common cancers, including breast, prostate, colon, lung, and ovarian cancers.

Low-fat vegetarian diets also may reduce the incidence of osteoporosis, adult-onset diabetes, hypertension, obesity, and many other illnesses.

## EAT MORE COMPLEX CARBOHYDRATES, WEIGH LESS

You can eat more and weigh less, but not if you eat a lot of simple carbohydrates. Simple carbohydrates—like sugar and other concentrated sweeteners, honey, white flour, and alcohol—are absorbed rapidly, causing your blood sugar to increase rapidly. In response, your body secretes insulin to lower blood sugar levels to normal. When your body produces more insulin, besides lowering your blood sugar, insulin causes you to be more likely to convert dietary calories into body fat. Also, after many years of overproducing insulin, some people become insulin-resistant, causing them to secrete even more insulin to compensate, which only makes matters worse in a vicious cycle.

On the other hand, complex carbohydrates—fruits, vegetables, grains, and legumes in their natural forms—are absorbed slowly, thus causing your blood sugar to remain more stable. Because of stable blood sugar, your body does not produce excessive amounts of insulin.

For example, the bran and fiber in whole wheat flour and brown rice cause them to be absorbed slowly. When whole wheat flour is "refined" into white flour, the bran and fiber are removed, so the flour is absorbed more quickly and converted to sugar, thereby provoking an insulin response. Thus, you don't have to give up pasta, bread, or rice; just change to whole wheat pasta, whole wheat bread, and brown rice. Even white-flour pasta is fine in moderation, especially when consumed with vegetables and other complex carbohydrates that will slow their absorption.

The major reason people who eat pasta gain weight is not the pasta, it's the oil they add to the sauce on the pasta. One tablespoon of *any* oil, including olive oil, has 14 grams of fat, about the same amount as in a scoop of ice cream. It is not unusual to have two or three tablespoons of oil on a serving of pasta. No one would eat two or three scoops of ice cream on a plate of pasta and expect to lose weight, yet that is about the same amount of total fat contained in two or three tablespoons of any oil. While the ice cream may have a higher percentage of heart-damaging saturated fat, it has the same amount of total fat. And from a weight standpoint, fat is fat; the type doesn't matter.

If you eat a very low-fat diet consisting primarily of fruits, vegetables, grains, and legumes—that is, complex carbohydrates—supplemented with moderate amounts of nonfat dairy and egg whites, then you will get full before you get too many calories. You can eat whenever you're hungry, you can eat until you're full (but not stuffed), and you will likely lose excess weight, without counting calories, without portion control, and without deprivation.

## WHY 10 PERCENT FAT?

The diet I recommend for most people comprises approximately 10 percent of calories from fat. The average American eats a diet that's about 40 percent fat. Why 10 percent?

Your body only needs about 4 to 6 percent of calories as fat to synthesize what are known as essential fatty acids. The Life Choice diet, also called the Reversal Diet, is about 10 percent fat, because it provides more than enough fat without giving you more than you need. It's the excessive amounts of fat and cholesterol in your diet—that is, more than 10 percent of calories as fat—that lead to obesity, heart disease, and other illnesses.

You don't need a computer to calculate a 10 percent fat diet. When you eat primarily fruits, vegetables, grains, and beans, nonfat dairy, and egg whites and no added oils, that's what you end up with. And that's what your body has evolved to handle.

For most people, a 10 percent fat diet allows approximately 20 to 25 grams of fat per day. This "fat quota" will increase or decrease to some degree based on your frame size, gender, and exercise levels, but it's a good place to begin. In my previous books, I showed how you can use insurance tables of "ideal body weights" to calculate this number more precisely, but in practical terms it is not usually necessary to do so.

If you eat primarily fruits, vegetables, whole grains, beans, nonfat dairy, and egg whites in their natural forms, then you don't need to calculate your fat intake. Your fat intake will be approximately 10 percent. If you eat some commercially prepared products, then read the nutritional label on the package. Since you want to keep your total fat consumption per day around 20 to 25 grams, try to choose foods that have no more than 3 grams of fat per serving. Even less is better.

## WHY SO LITTLE CHOLESTEROL?

Your dietary requirement for cholesterol is *zero*. In other words, your body will make all the cholesterol it needs. When you eat more fat and cholesterol than your body can metabolize (get rid of), it has to go somewhere—like in your arteries. If the arteries to your heart become clogged, then you may have a heart attack. If the arteries to your brain get clogged, then you may suffer a stroke.

Your body knows how to begin healing itself if you give it a chance to. If three times a day you eat more fat and cholesterol than your body can get rid of, then it tends to build up in your arteries. If you stop doing that, then instead of trying to get rid of the fat and cholesterol that were in the last meal you ate, your body may go to work to begin removing the fat and cholesterol that have been building up in your arteries for so many years.

There is a genetic variability in how efficiently or inefficiently your body can remove excess fat and cholesterol. The Nobel Prize in medicine was given to two scientists, Michael Brown and Joseph Goldstein, who discovered the cholesterol receptor. These receptors bind and remove excess cholesterol from your blood. The more receptors you have, the more efficiently you can remove cholesterol from your body. The number of receptors is, in part, genetically determined.

Some people are genetically lucky; they have lots of cholesterol receptors. As a result, they can eat almost anything and they'll never get heart disease. Those are the people who live to be ninety-nine and talk about the twelve eggs they have for breakfast and the cheeseburgers for lunch and you wonder, "Gee, maybe diet doesn't have much to do with heart disease. Look at what they're eating!"

When you think about it, you realize that's who you're left with at age ninety-nine—everyone else who wasn't as genetically efficient at getting rid of fat and cholesterol died of heart disease or other illnesses before they reached that age.

On the other end of the spectrum are people who have coronary heart disease. In general, they have fewer cholesterol receptors, so they tend to be much less efficient at getting rid of dietary fat and cholesterol. That's one of the major reasons they have heart disease: They are eating more fat and cholesterol than their bodies can eliminate. For this reason, the moderate reductions in fat and cholesterol recommended by most government agencies—30 percent fat, 200 to 300 milligrams of dietary cholesterol—are still too rich.

In virtually every study that has come out, including ours, the majority of people who have coronary heart disease who follow the conventional dietary recommendations—less red meat, more fish and chicken, take the skin off the chicken, four eggs per week, et cetera—get *worse*. Their arteries become more clogged over time. They may get clogged more slowly than if they made no changes, but they still worsen.

The good news is that even if you are not very efficient at getting rid of fat and cholesterol due to genetic factors, if you reduce your intake of fat and cholesterol sufficiently to the levels I recommend here, then you are no longer saturating your cholesterol receptors. You may then begin removing the cholesterol that's been building up in your arteries. As a result, your body begins to heal.

## WHAT IS THE CAUSE?

A fundamental theme of all of my work is that it is better to address the underlying *cause* of a problem—any problem—than to literally or figuratively bypass it. I've discussed this at length in my other books, using the examples of bypass surgery and angioplasty. If you undergo bypass surgery or angioplasty without also making the comprehensive changes in lifestyle that I recommend, then you are likely to need another one in a few months or a few years—like mopping up the floor around an overflowing sink without also turning off the faucet.

I just keep finding more and more examples of this. A recent study in the *New England Journal of Medicine* found that women who took estrogen lowered their incidence of heart disease and osteoporosis but showed a substantial increase in the incidence of breast cancer by about the same amount. Since the incidence of heart disease is ten times more common than breast cancer, the researchers said that estrogen is worth taking. What a choice—a Faustian bargain.

A better choice would be to address the underlying cause of all three illnesses. Women who change to a low-fat vegetarian diet may reduce the incidence of heart disease, osteoporosis—*and* breast cancer. Adding the other aspects of my program (stress management techniques, psychosocial support, smoking cessation, and exercise) described in my earlier books helps even more.

## BIG CHANGES ARE EASIER THAN SMALL ONES

As I described in *Eat More, Weigh Less*, it's actually easier to make big changes in diet and lifestyle—all at once—than to make small, gradual changes. First, you feel so much better, so quickly, that the choices become clearer and, for many people, worth making. Second, your palate adjusts quickly when you make comprehensive changes in your diet so that you begin to *prefer* low-fat foods.

Fat is an acquired taste. It's not one of your four basic tastes—sweet, sour, salty, and bitter—so your palate adapts even more quickly to low fat than to low salt. For example, have you ever switched from drinking whole milk to skim milk? At first, most people find that the skim milk tastes like water, not very good. After a week or two, it tastes fine. If you then go out to dinner and are served whole milk, it doesn't even taste very good—too greasy, too rich, like cream.

Of course, the cow didn't change; your palate adapted. If you always drank some whole milk and some skim milk, the skim milk would never taste very good. It's easier if you just make a comprehensive shift and stop drinking whole milk altogether.

Similarly, while eating less meat is a step in the right direction, you may find it easier to give it up completely and to consume foods that are more healthful. Otherwise, you get the worst of both worlds: you're eating enough meat to still have a taste for it, but you're not really getting all you want—and you don't feel much better.

Once your palate has adapted, you may find that the natural flavors of the food come through much better when you reduce the fat in your diet. Fat often masks flavor. Although people often think fat tastes good, it really doesn't. Nobody raids the Crisco jar in the middle of the night. Crisco is pure fat; lard is mostly fat; Wesson Oil is pure fat. Any kind of cooking oil is pure fat.

We're always making choices. Sometimes when I lecture, I'll ask, "How many of you have children?" Of course, many people raise their hands. "Was that a big change in your lifestyle?" Monumental.

"Now, imagine that you're in bed with your beloved and you're about to conceive your first child. Suddenly, a movie screen appears behind you and shows you in great detail just how hard it's going to be to raise that child. How many sacrifices you'll have to make. How many sleepless nights. How much money it's going to cost you. How your life will never be the same. Because most people don't *really* know how hard it is to be a parent beforehand. How many of you would *still* choose to have a child knowing in advance how hard it's really going to be?" Even knowing the difficulties, the vast majority of people still raise their hands.

The point, of course, is that most of us are not afraid to make big

*Everyday Cooking with Dr. Dean Ornish*

changes in our lives—we do it every day. Even monumental ones like having a child. Or going to work every day. Or changing to a plant-based diet. When we think it's worth it.

While this program *does* involve making big changes in your diet and lifestyle, many people find it to be worth it. In our studies, my colleagues and I found that the primary determinant of improvement was how much people changed their diet and lifestyle, not how old they were or how sick they were. When I began the study, I thought the younger patients with milder disease would be more likely to show reversal, but I was wrong. We measured the most reversal in the oldest patient, Werner Hebenstreit, who is now eighty-one—and who followed the program more closely than anyone.

In short, the more people changed, the better they got. That's a very hopeful message. If you're willing to do the work, if you're willing to make the changes, then you also are likely to benefit to that degree.

Whether or not you want to make these changes is up to you. I don't tell people—even my own patients—what to do or not do because I believe these are very personal decisions. And once I tell somebody to do something, I have an investment in whether or not he or she does it. Then we're engaged in a manipulative relationship. If they don't change, then I'm going to feel like a failure. They may feel as if they have let me down or let themselves down by not changing. They're less likely to tell me the truth, because they don't want to disappoint me, or if they do, they may feel guilty or ashamed.

When that happens, then they're more likely to overeat, or smoke, or eat a lot of fat, or abuse alcohol or other drugs, or work too hard, or make other self-destructive choices in lifestyle. Then I get stressed, they get stressed, and it only contributes to more illness and more suffering.

Instead, my role as a scientist is to try to study, to learn, and to document as clearly as I can what works, to what degree, under what circumstances, for whom, and by what mechanisms—and then to share this information. My goal is to convey information to physicians and other health professionals by lecturing at hospitals and scientific meetings and publishing our research findings in medical journals, and to the general public by writing books and being interviewed in the general media.

To say, in effect, "Here's what we've done and here's what we've found. If you want to do it, here's how. Here are the risks, the benefits, the costs, and the side effects of these choices and of other alternatives, including drugs and surgery if indicated. Whatever you want to do is fine, because you're the one who has to take the consequences—for better or for worse—not I." If you decide that these lifestyle changes are worth making, this book is designed to make the changes in diet easier.

Many of the recipes are by Jean-Marc Fullsack, who has been working with me for the past six years. Jean-Marc looks and sounds like central casting's idea of a French chef. He was classically trained in Strasbourg, France, in Alsace, and later was a chef at some of the greatest restaurants in the United States, including Lutèce in New York and L'Ermitage in Los Angeles. When I met him, he was one of the chief instructors at the California Culinary Academy in San Francisco.

Jean-Marc has traveled with me to the White House on several occasions to consult with many of the chefs who cook for the First Family on how to cook more healthful foods for them.

Whatever one's politics, I admire President and Mrs. Clinton, who are setting a wonderful example for all Americans by making a personal commitment to regular exercise and to more healthful eating. If they can do it, anyone can.

Jean-Marc also travels regularly to each of the hospitals in our demonstration network. I remember his look of dismay when he first entered the kitchen of one of these hospitals. There was only one burner in the entire hospital kitchen. Instead of being cooked for the hospital patients, almost all the food was frozen and defrosted. A big challenge for Jean-Marc.

Over time, though, he learned to teach these hospital chefs to modify our cuisine to meet the preferences of the people in that region of the country, using the limited equipment available. Much of what he learned is included in this book.

I would welcome any comments and suggestions. Please send them to me at:

Dean Ornish, M.D.
Preventive Medicine Research Institute
900 Bridgeway, Suite One
Sausalito, CA 94965

Because of the volume of my correspondence, I will not be able to reply to you personally but I will read your comments with great interest and appreciation.

For more information about my program, including the Life Choice frozen meals, please call 1-800-328-3738. For information about our retreats, our hospital programs, or other related information, please call 1-800-775-7674.

Having seen what a powerful difference this program can make in so many people's lives, I am grateful for the opportunity to share this information with you. I hope you find this book to be useful, easy, and fun.

DEAN ORNISH, M.D.
September 1995

# New Everyday Cooking

## JEAN-MARC'S TOP 17 TECHNIQUES FOR COOKING WITH NO ADDED FAT

"A lot of my job is working with the chefs and food service people at the hospital sites in our demonstration network. I also do a lot of demonstrations for the press and dinners for referring physicians.

"Food in hospitals is a low priority. It's the last thing they worry about. In some of these sites, they never see fresh eggplant or asparagus or peppers. So I take the chef and we go to markets together and try to find where he or she can buy the products for the Ornish program. And we contact bakeries and find one that can bake bread without fat. We line up sources, then we open a small 'Ornish kitchen' within the kitchen of the hospital. It's like opening a little restaurant within the hospital.

"But sometimes you go into these hospitals, and there's no stove, nothing to cook on, not even a griddle. There's just a big kettle and a steamer and an oven. So you have to find recipes that work for this.

"You know, until I met Dean, my goal in life was to make food as complicated and as rich in calories as it could be. Now, it's to make food as low in fat and tasty as it can be. A lot of people just don't believe it's possible. That's why, when you show them something simple and delicious, they're so happy."

It's not difficult to make delicious food without adding fat, but a few simple tricks and techniques make it easier. Here are some of the methods Jean-Marc favors:

•Sauté vegetables in a small amount of vegetable broth, wine, or water instead of oil. You can control the speed of the evaporation by cooking with the lid on or off, and by raising or lowering the heat. At the end of the cooking time, the liquid should be evaporated so the vegetables' natural sugar caramelizes slightly. In this book, you will see this method often, especially with onions and garlic at the start of a recipe. Sautéing brings out the onion's sweetness and mellows the garlic. Take care not to use too much liquid or you will be boiling, not sautéing, and you won't achieve the caramelization of sugars that you want.

•When a recipe calls for vegetable broth or water, use broth whenever possible. It adds a lot of flavor. There are some good powdered and canned broths available now (page 324), and it takes only 20 minutes to make your own. If you want an even more intense flavor, reduce the vegetable broth by half over high heat.

## VEGETABLE BROTH

You will use this tasty broth so often in nonfat cooking that it makes sense to have it on hand all the time. It takes less than half an hour to make, whether you make a little or a lot, so it's smart to double or triple this recipe and freeze the extra in small containers for up to 3 months.

Don't hesitate to experiment with this recipe. You can substitute one vegetable for another, or one herb for another. Some nice additions: chopped tomatoes, summer or winter squash, corn cobs (with or without the corn), fennel, parsley, or basil. Avoid strong-flavored members of the cabbage family, such as cabbage, broccoli, and cauliflower. And stay away from potatoes; they absorb the other flavors.

MAKES 4 CUPS

2 large carrots, peeled, ends removed, diced

2 onions, diced

2 cups sliced mushrooms

4 ribs celery, diced

1 leek, white and pale green parts only, diced

2 large garlic cloves, minced

1 teaspoon dried thyme

1 bay leaf

6 whole cloves

2 teaspoons whole coriander seed

Combine all ingredients in a large pot. Add water to cover, about 6 cups. Bring to a simmer over moderate heat. Simmer, uncovered, 20 minutes. Strain through a sieve.

> **TIP**
>
> If you cut the vegetables into small pieces—½ inch or smaller—they will release their flavor to the water in 20 minutes. If you cut them larger, you will need to cook the broth longer to extract all their flavor.

*Contributes no significant nutrients*

•Expand the range of herbs and spices you cook with. They can help make dishes lively and varied. Seek out a source for fresh herbs, or try growing some yourself. Their intense flavor can compensate for the lack of fat. Add them to a dish at the last minute for maximum impact and save a sprig or two for a pretty garnish. Dried herbs need to simmer in a soup or stew for a few minutes before they impart their character. Whole spices can be toasted first to intensify their flavor. Try toasting whole cumin, coriander, or fennel seed in a dry skillet until the spice colors slightly, then grind it to a powder in a coffee mill or mortar. A little ground toasted cumin does wonders for steamed carrots.

•Experiment with salad dressings made with soft tofu or nonfat yogurt. Or mix the two together. They're both good substitutes for high-fat mayonnaise or sour cream. Add whole grain mustard for texture and vinegar for tang. Add fresh herbs such as dill, basil, cilantro, mint, or parsley. Sweeten with a touch of honey, if desired, or puree with cucumbers to make a creamy dressing.

•Vinegars and citrus juice can add a spark to dishes. Choose the milder vinegars—rice vinegar, balsamic vinegar, sherry vinegar—for dressing salads or steamed vegetables. If you want to use wine vinegar or cider vinegar, balance their sharpness with a touch of sugar or other sweet component. A squirt of lemon or lime juice added at the end of cooking can invigorate a stew or bean soup. Or stir grated citrus zest into stews or fruit salads. It adds fragrance and flavor without adding acidity.

•When baking with nonfat dairy products, take care not to overcook. Fat keeps baked goods moist, and without the fat, it is easy for them to taste dry. Better to undercook slightly than to overcook. Also, be careful not to overmix muffin or cake batters. Without the tenderizing effects of fat, muffins and cakes can be tough. By mixing lightly, you don't overdevelop the gluten that can make baked goods tough.

•Take advantage of nonfat dairy products, but be aware of their limitations. Yogurt is terrific for uncooked sauces and dressings, but it will curdle if boiled. If you are adding it to a hot sauce, do so at the end, off the heat. You can boil nonfat sour cream and nonfat milk but not in the presence of acid; lemon juice, tomato, or vinegar will make them curdle. Nonfat cheeses are getting better and better. In the past, they wouldn't even brown when heated, but now they melt and brown nicely. For sauces and other cooked dishes, nonfat ricotta is a better choice than nonfat cottage cheese, which is grainier.

•Canned tomato products are a great medium for braising. You can simmer mushrooms, zucchini, and herbs in store-bought tomato sauce to make a quick vegetable stew. Or you can reheat leftover cooked beans or steamed vegetables with canned diced tomatoes and basil. Supermarket shelves offer a variety of tomato products, so be sure you choose the right one for the job. Choose a thick tomato puree, for example, if the dish won't cook for very long; diced tomatoes in puree will give the same dish more texture. Use diced tomatoes in juice if you don't want a thick texture—in a minestrone, for example. Peeled whole tomatoes can be diced and simmered with herbs and garlic until they thicken into a sauce for pasta or for braising vegetables. Also check the prepared tomato-based pasta sauces at your market for brands with no added fat. These can be big time-savers. Simmer them with greens or chopped broccoli or canned beans to make a quick pasta sauce. Or simmer with a variety of beans and vegetables to make a hearty stew.

•Make meatless dishes hearty by adding beans and grains. On this eating program, vegetables aren't side dishes anymore; they are usually the main event. Make them into substantial meals by adding pinto beans, chickpeas, brown rice, lentils, or wheat berries. Here's an example: You could roast a sweet potato and steam some spinach for dinner. Or you could easily make the meal more robust and satisfying by topping the sweet potato with corn kernels or tossing the spinach with canned chickpeas and instant brown rice.

•Use fruit juice concentrates in place of refined sugar when a fruity taste would be appealing. Apple juice, orange juice, and white grape juice concentrates contribute a more complex sweetness to baked goods, sauces, salad dressings, and fruit desserts. Other sweeteners, such as maple syrup and honey, can also give a dish a dimension that refined sugar won't. Of course any sweetener should be used sparingly, within these dietary guidelines.

•Use cornstarch to give body to poaching liquids for fruit. In traditional cooking, sugar adds the body, turning a poaching liquid into a syrup. To compensate for the sugar, dilute a little cornstarch in cold water (never add it directly to a hot liquid) and stir it into the poaching medium. It will thicken the juices and give them a more syruplike texture. See Sliced Oranges in Spiced Syrup (page 252) for an example.

•Keep roasted onions on hand. They take 5 minutes to make in a microwave oven, and their caramelized flavor enhances so many dishes. Many conventional recipes start with an onion sautéed in fat to develop its sweetness. Roasted onions will give your dishes that same pleasing taste. You can also roast other vegetables to intensify their flavor, such as garlic (page 93), bell peppers (see Tip, page 90), eggplant (page 136), beets (page 116), and tomatoes.

# ROASTED ONIONS

Conventional oven: Preheat oven to 400 degrees F. Place whole unpeeled onions on a baking sheet and bake until they are soft to the touch and lightly browned on the outside, about 30 minutes. Cool, then cut off root end and squeeze out the soft interior. One onion yields 1 to 1½ cups diced roasted onion, depending on size.

Microwave oven: Microwave whole unpeeled onions on full power until very soft, 4 to 5 minutes. Cool, then cut off root end and squeeze out the soft interior. One onion yields 1 to 1½ cups diced roasted onion, depending on size.

•Invest in a pepper mill if you don't have one. Freshly ground pepper has far more punch than store-bought ground pepper. And when you are cooking without fat, every flavor advantage counts.

•Look to pungent or intensely flavored ingredients to give your dishes heightened taste. Mustard, horseradish, soy sauce, Japanese miso, hot pepper sauces, capers, and other piquant ingredients can add excitement or dimension to dishes. Foods with concentrated flavor, such as sun-dried tomatoes and shiitake mushrooms, can boost the appeal of dishes that might otherwise seem bland.

•Strive for variety. A very low-fat vegetarian diet can become boring if you eat only a limited range of fruits, vegetables, grains, and beans. But if you keep an adventuresome attitude, you will never grow tired of this way of eating. Today's supermarkets offer so many more produce, bean, and grain varieties than they used to. The rice selection alone may surprise you, offering many types and rice blends you've never tried before.

•Invest a few moments in thinking about food presentation so your meals will please the eye. Put a salad in a pretty bowl to enhance its appetite appeal. Sprinkle some chopped fresh herbs or green onions atop a bowl of cooked beans or a potato salad. Aim for contrasting colors when you plan your meals: how will foods look together on the plate? Just placing a dark soup in a light bowl or a light food on a dark plate can make it look more inviting.

•Start with high-quality fruits and vegetables, properly grown and ripe. Select other products critically for quality. Respect cooking techniques. Avoid overcooking. And finally, add tender loving care.

## HELP FOR HIGH-FAT RECIPES

You don't have to throw out all your old recipes when you adopt a low-fat vegetarian diet. Just toss out the fat. You'll find that you can modify many of your favorite recipes successfully by replacing high-fat ingredients with some of the nonfat products now on supermarket shelves. Just for starters:

- •Replace sour cream with nonfat sour cream or nonfat yogurt in dressings and sauces. Don't let a sauce boil after adding nonfat yogurt, or it may separate.
- •Replace whole eggs with liquid egg substitute or egg whites in baked goods. Read the egg substitute label carefully; some have added fat.
- •Replace oil for sautéing onions and garlic with a few tablespoons of fat-free vegetable broth, wine, or water. Simmer vegetables until tender.
- •Replace oil-and-vinegar dressing with bottled fat-free Italian dressing on salads and chilled vegetables, or drizzle salads and vegetables with flavorful balsamic vinegar, raspberry vinegar, or tarragon vinegar.
- •Replace mayonnaise on sandwiches and in potato salad with nonfat mayonnaise or yogurt. Add a little whole grain mustard for a flavor boost, or use mustard alone.
- •Replace the fat in baked goods with prune puree or unsweetened applesauce. Make the puree yourself by whipping together 4 ounces of pitted prunes and 5 tablespoons of water. You can also buy prepared prune puree or use baby food. Read labels before buying prepared prune products marketed as fat replacers. They may have added fat and sugar. Use prune puree in the ratio of ½:1. For instance, if the recipe calls for ½ cup butter, use ¼ cup prune puree.
- •Replace the cream in pasta sauces with nonfat sour cream or with skim milk thickened with cornstarch. Dissolve cornstarch in a little cold water first. A tablespoon of cornstarch will thicken 1 cup of liquid.

## CUTTING-EDGE NUTRITION

Helen Roe, M.S., R.D., is the senior dietitian and director of nutrition services at the Preventive Medicine Research Institute. Before that, Helen spent fifteen years in Houston working with some of the world's leading heart surgeons.

I grew up in rural Arkansas knowing the pleasures of fresh-picked food. We kept a vegetable garden, and Mom and Dad valued the dinner table. We kids learned to appreciate fresh foods and to freeze and can foods for use throughout the year. We grew potatoes, corn, purple-hull peas, lady peas, all kinds of beans, tomatoes, onions, squash, cucumbers, peppers of all kinds, eggplant, lettuce, broccoli, cabbage, collards, and turnip greens. What we didn't grow we would swap or buy from other local farmers. We had plenty of fresh peaches, strawberries, and watermelon, of course. And we would gather wild fruits for jam and jelly. Once a week, on Sunday, we had meat—usually chicken. I didn't realize we were practically vegetarians, but we were.

My interest in food as related to disease led to a master's degree in nutrition and dietetics. I worked for twelve years at The Methodist Hospital in Houston with Doctors Antonio Gotto and Michael DeBakey teaching preventive medicine programs, nutrition, and weight control. I also managed a heart-healthy restaurant at the hospital called Chez Eddy.

I believe that all this training and experience prepared me for where I am now: teaching Ornish program participants and coordinating the nutrition component of the program. I teach the diet to the nutritionists at the hospitals that have Ornish programs, and then I become the troubleshooter, dealing with any questions or problems that arise. I also work with chef Jean-Marc Fullsack in training the hospital chefs. He teaches them the cooking, while I teach the nutritional requirements of the program.

Before I came to PMRI, I was on "the other side of the fence," with the group that raised the eyebrows about Dean's program. At that time, I was teaching the American Heart Association's 30-percent-fat diet and knew what its limitations were, that it probably wasn't the way to go. I knew it was too liberal. I didn't know then what Dean's program really was. Now I know the program is not for everybody, but those who choose to do it are usually successful, and that's so rewarding. I'd never before experienced people turning their lives around.

A lot of the people who come into this program have an almost hopeless look about them. They've often been through surgery and are living in fear that they're going to have another heart attack or have to have surgery again. But as they start doing the program, they start feeling better, and soon they are glowing and positive. Particularly if they do it with their spouses, they develop a whole new perspective and they radiate hope. It's immediate positive feedback, and not very many of us get to experience that in our work.

I think we are on the cutting edge of nutritional science. One of my goals is to educate more nutritionists across the country who can work with people who don't have a hospital with an Ornish program. The nutritionists are key, because a lot of physicians don't know much about nutrition. I am confident Dean's program will continue to make significant contributions to nutritional science. And it's exciting to be a part of that.

## Keep a Plentiful Pantry

Colleen Wracker, R.D., teaches the nutrition classes for Dr. Ornish's program at Richland Memorial Hospital in Columbia, South Carolina: "I ask participants to go home, gather some boxes, and begin going through the pantry label by label. Every product that does not fit our guidelines should go into the boxes. They know if the food is on hand they will eventually eat it. Since most people don't want to throw food away, I encourage them to call their local food bank and donate. Then they can go to the grocery store feeling good about beginning their new way of eating."

One common obstacle is not having the right kinds of foods on hand when you're ready to eat. When you're hungry, you don't want to spend 45 minutes assembling a casserole, or even 20 minutes making a salad. Nor is it a good time to go shopping. Have nutritious, ready-to-eat foods on hand all the time. By filling your pantry with wholesome low-fat options, you can increase the variety in your meals and prepare healthful meals or snacks in minutes.

The following list is meant to give you ideas and to show how varied your pantry can be. It is not a must-have list, and it's certainly not comprehensive. Food companies introduce thousands of new items a year, and many of them now are fat-free. Read the labels carefully (page 307) and compare brands to find the ones you like. The brands mentioned below meet the guidelines. Even for foods on this list, it's a good idea to read the label because formulations change. Make sure the food you're considering meets the following guidelines for fat:

- no more than 3 grams of fat per serving
- no added fat

If you have trouble locating some of the products on this list, check a natural foods store. You can also contact the manufacturer (see pages 320–328 for product information) to see if there's a way to get the product in your area. Or just ask the manager at the grocery store where you shop. They will usually be happy to get it for you.

A pantry can also include foods to prepare when you don't feel so pressed for time, like dried beans and whole grains. These complex carbohydrates are the backbone of a sensible low-fat diet. You may be surprised, when you first begin looking, to find so many different bean and grain types, each with its own distinctive flavor. It's fun sometimes to expand your horizons and buy some you don't know; you'll find that their unique flavors, colors, and textures keep your meals varied and satisfying.

You might want to photocopy this list and take it with you when you shop. Note that not all the items in this list will be available in all areas. For more guidance about how to shop smart, see "Shop Smart: Supermarket Tips and Traps" (page 35).

BEANS

### Canned Beans
Choose beans with no added fat such as meat or oil:

Eden Organic Pinto Beans, Kidney Beans, Garbanzo Beans
Home and Garden Dry-Cooked Black-eyed Peas, Pinto Beans, Kidney
    Beans, Butter Beans
Progresso Fava Beans, Black Beans, Cannellini Beans (white kidney
    beans)
S&W Kidney Beans, Garbanzo Beans, Black Beans, Pinquito Beans,
    Small White Beans

## Other Canned Bean Products
  Bearitos Fat-Free Refried Beans, Refried Black Beans, Baked Beans,
    Vegetarian Chili
  Bush's Vegetarian Beans
  Dennison's Chili Beans
  Hain Fat-Free Vegetarian Refried Beans
  Health Valley Spicy Vegetarian Chili
  Heinz Vegetarian Beans
  Las Palmas No Fat Refried Beans
  Rosarita No-Fat Refried Beans
  S&W Maple Sugar Beans, Chili Beans with Chipotle Peppers

## Dried Beans, Lentils, Peas
Look for your favorite dried beans, lentils, and peas in bulk bins and in
packages:

  black beans
  black-eyed peas
  cannellini beans
  garbanzo beans (chickpeas)
  Great Northern white beans
  lentils
  lima beans
  navy beans
  pinto beans
  red beans
  split peas

## Specialty Bean Products
  Bean Cuisine: a large variety of dried beans and bean mixes
  Buckeye Beans and Herbs, Black Bean Chili
  Country Pea Patchwork Soup
  Fantastic Foods Instant Black Beans, Instant Refried Beans, Vegetarian
    Chili
  Lundberg Family Farms: specialty bean and rice mixes

## Breads

When selecting bread, check the label or ask the bakery for an ingredient list to make sure the bread does not contain whole milk, low-fat milk, nuts, seeds, or added fats and oils. Choose whole grain breads when possible. Whole grain breads will contain naturally occurring fat, but check the ingredient list to make sure no oils or fats have been added. For more information on shopping for breads, see page 37.

> corn tortillas
> flour tortillas (fat-free only)
> French baguettes
> Middle Eastern lahvosh
> whole grain breads
> whole wheat bagels
> whole wheat pita bread

## Cereals

### Cold Breakfast Cereals

Select high-fiber cereals with no added fat, nuts, seeds, sugar, or salt. Read the label and avoid brown sugar, corn syrup, honey, high-fructose corn syrup, concentrated fruit juices, or partially hydrogenated oils. Most cereals are sweetened, but there are still plenty of great choices in one of the most heavily stocked sections in the supermarket.

> Arrowhead Mills Puffed Wheat, Puffed Corn, Puffed Millet,
>    Nature O's
> Barbara's Shredded Wheat
> Erewhon Crispy Brown Rice, Whole Grain Raisin Bran
> General Mills Fiber One
> Kellogg's All-Bran
> Nabisco 100% Bran, Shredded Wheat, Shredded Wheat Spoon Size,
>    Shredded Wheat 'n Bran

### Hot Breakfast Cereals

> American Prairie Porridge Oats, Quick Oats, 5-Grain Cereal
> Arrowhead Mills Rice and Shine, Bear Mush, Raw Wheat Germ

---

Aunt Jemima White Hominy Grits
Erewhon Oat Bran with Toasted Wheat Germ
Kretschmer Toasted Wheat Bran, Wheat Germ
Krusteaz Zoom 100% Whole Wheat Cereal
Malt-O-Meal
McCann's Quick Cooking Irish Oatmeal
Old Fashioned Quaker Oats, Quick Oats, Multi-grain Oatmeal,
    Unprocessed Wheat Bran
Quaker Oat Bran


*Other Breakfast Products*
Aunt Jemima Original Pancake Mix (other flavors may contain oil)
Kellogg's Special K fat-free frozen waffles

## Grains

Many supermarkets have greatly expanded their selection of grains and grain blends. For convenience, keep a variety of quick-cooking grains and specialty grain mixes on hand. If the directions call for adding fat, just skip this step. You may want to avoid those that contain MSG. Take time to browse in the grains aisle—don't forget the bulk bins—and take home some grains you've never tried before.

barley
bulgur
cornmeal
couscous
cracked wheat
Fantastic Foods Whole Wheat Couscous
kasha (buckwheat groats)
millet
polenta
rice:
    brown rice
    long-grain rice
    quick-cooking brown rice
    short-grain rice
    wild rice
    rice blends and specialty mixes:

Della Rice

Fantastic Foods: Basmati Rice, Jasmine Rice, Brown Basmati Rice,
    Brown Jasmine Rice

Great Valley Long Grain and Brown Rice, Brown and Wild Rice

Hinode Seasoned Rice Blends

Lundberg Family Farms Bean and Rice Mixes: Curry, Chili, Basil

Lundberg Family Rice Blends: Gourmet Wild and Brown Rice,
    7 Brown Rices, Black Japonica

Mahatma Black Beans and Rice

Po River Valley Risotto (microwavable)

R. M. Quiggs' Red Beans and Rice Mix

## Flours

Arrowhead Mills Brown Rice Flour, Stone-ground Whole Wheat
    Flour, Whole Grain Oat Flour, Whole Grain Rye Flour

Arrowhead Mills Mixes for Bread Machines and Conventional
    Methods: Kamut, MultiGrain, Whole Wheat

Gold Medal Whole Wheat Flour

Krusteaz Whole Wheat Flour for Bread Machines and Conventional
    Methods

Stone-Buhr Whole Wheat, Unbleached White Flour

## CRACKERS, CHIPS, DIPS, AND OTHER SNACKS

## Chips

Fat-free Gourmet Tortilla Chips

Guiltless Gourmet Fat-free Tortilla Chips

Kettle Creek Baked Tortilla Chips

Vera Cruz Baked Tortilla Rounds

## Crackers

Auburn Farms' Multigrain Crackers

Finn Crisp Crispbread

Health Valley Foods Fat-Free Crackers

Kavli Crispbread

Nabisco Fat-Free Premium Crackers

Ry-Krisp

Ryvita

Stella d'Oro Fat-Free Bread Sticks

Tree of Life Fat-Free Crackers
Wasa Crispbread

## Dips

Bearitos Bean Dip
Garden of Eatin' Baja Black Bean Dip
Guiltless Gourmet Black Bean Dip
La Victoria Salsa
Old El Paso Salsa
Pace Picante Sauce

## Other Snacks

Hain Rice Cakes
Laura Scudder's Fat Free Pretzels
Quaker Rice Cakes
Rold Gold Fat Free Pretzels
Trader Joe's Popcorn Cakes

### DRIED PASTA AND PASTA SAUCES

You will find it useful to stock your pantry with a wide array of dried pasta shapes for quick meals. If you can boil water, you can cook pasta. It's a good idea to have on hand some long pasta (such as spaghetti and linguine), short pasta (such as penne, rigatoni, farfalle, and fusilli), and small shapes for soup (such as stelline, tubetti, or orzo). Buy whole wheat versions whenever you can, and check the label to avoid noodles made with whole eggs.

## Pasta

De Cecco Whole Wheat Spaghetti
Westbrae Natural Whole Wheat Lasagna
Westbrae Natural Whole Wheat Spaghetti

## Sauces

Read labels carefully. Some manufacturers produce both fat-free and regular pasta sauces.

Ci'Bella Fat Free Pasta Sauce
Healthy Choice Fat Free Pasta Sauces
Millina's Finest Fat Free Pasta Sauces

Muir Glen Fat Free Pasta Sauce
Tree of Life Fat Free Pasta Sauces
Weight Watchers Smart Options Pasta Sauce

## SEASONINGS, CONDIMENTS, AND DRESSINGS

### Seasonings and Condiments

capers
catsup, low-sodium
chiles, canned
dill pickles
jams, jellies, and fruit spreads, no sugar added
mayonnaise, nonfat:
    Smart Beat Mayonnaise
    Weight Watchers Fat-Free Mayonnaise
mustard, Dijon-style
mustard, whole grain
soy sauce, low-sodium:
    Kikkoman Milder Soy Sauce
Talk of Texas Crisp Okra Pickles
vinegar, balsamic
vinegar, cider
vinegar, raspberry
vinegar, rice
vinegar, sherry
vinegar, tarragon
vinegar, wine
Worcestershire sauce

### Salad Dressings

Cook's Fat-Free Dressings
Good Seasons Fat-Free Dressing Mix (Italian, Creamy Italian)
Hidden Valley Ranch Fat-Free Honey Dijon Ranch
Kraft Free Salad Dressings (1000 Island, Catalina)
Lady Lee Fat-Free Zesty Italian Dressing
Pritikin Salad Dressing
S&W Vintage Lites Oil-Free Dressings
Trader Joe's Fat-Free Salad Dressing

Weight Watchers Italian Salad Dressing
Weight Watchers Salad Celebrations Ranch Dressing

SOUPS AND BROTHS

Soups containing grains or beans may have naturally occurring fat, so they may not be fat-free. That's okay. Just read the ingredients list and don't buy any that have fat *added*. Also, some instant soups may be high in sodium and contain cheese, butter, or nuts. Check the label carefully.

**Vegetable Broth**
Morga Fat Free Instant Vegetable Broth Mix
Swanson Clear Vegetable Broth

**Instant Vegetarian Dried Soups**
Fantastic Foods Soup Cups
Health Valley Dried Soups
Nile Spice Soup Cups
Soken Ramen
Spice Hunter Soup Cups
Taste Adventure Dried Soups
Westbrae Ramen

**Canned Soups**
Andersen's All Natural Split Pea Soup
Bearitos Homestyle Fat Free Soups
Health Valley Fat Free Soups
Healthy Choice Garden Vegetable

STAPLES
baking powder, nonaluminum
baking soda
evaporated skimmed milk
extracts: vanilla, almond, lemon
herbs
nonfat dry milk
nonstick spray made with canola oil
soy milk (in aseptic packages)

spices

sweeteners: sugar, honey, molasses

tomato products, canned: whole peeled tomatoes, tomato paste,
    tomato sauce, diced tomatoes

FRUIT

### Canned Fruit

Choose varieties packed in water or fruit juice without added sugar.

applesauce, unsweetened

### Dried Fruit

Consider dried apples, apricots, mixed fruit, pineapple, prunes, raisins,
or papaya. Some dried fruits have been sprayed with oil, so read the
labels. When fruit is dried, the naturally occurring sugars become concentrated, so you may want to eat these sparingly.

JUICE

low-sodium V-8 Juice

tomato juice

## FILL UP THE FREEZER

Supplement your plentiful pantry with a well-stocked freezer. Most
supermarket freezer sections contain a wide variety of fruits, vegetables, and other convenience foods that you can use to make meals on
the double.

frozen apple juice concentrate

frozen fruits: berries (no sugar added), bananas

frozen orange juice concentrate

frozen vegetables: corn, peas, spinach, lima beans, broccoli, mixed
    vegetables

phyllo dough: Athens Fillo Dough

vegetable stock, frozen

vegetarian burgers, nonfat: Boca Burger "No Fat Original," Chef Paul
    Wenner's Garden Vegan

The colorful, crowded shelves and aisles at your neighborhood super-market offer plenty of wholesome, low-fat foods that can add variety to your daily diet. Think of yourself as a food detective for the products that meet your needs.

This quick guide to the supermarket points you to the most promising areas and flags those where you need to be on your guard. Allow extra time on your first shopping trip to read labels and familiarize yourself with acceptable products.

You may find it helpful to avoid shopping when you're hungry. Having a snack before you go or shopping after a meal will help you cut down on impulse buys, which are usually snack items.

**Produce:** Start your shopping here and fill your cart high. Almost everything in this aisle is fair game, although watch out for cross-merchandised foods, like the shortcake displayed next to the strawberries or the high-fat dressings with the lettuces. If you're usually pressed for time when you cook, look for pre-cut vegetables and prewashed salad mixes. Prewashed spinach is a big time-saver.

Most of the time you'll probably buy what's most familiar, which is fine. Sometimes it's fun to buy some produce you've never tried before: an exotic fruit, an unusual vegetable, a fresh herb. Try a mango for breakfast, or perhaps some jicama for a salad or some fresh tarragon for a soup. Over time, you may expand your tastes and have a lot more to cook with than you used to. You might want to check out your market's mushroom section and take home some shiitake mushrooms for a pasta sauce or some meaty portobello mushrooms to throw on the grill. What else have you never tried? Spaghetti squash? Parsnips? Napa cabbage? Fennel? Mustard greens?

Scout the produce section for fruits and vegetables you can use for snacks. Bags of peeled baby carrots make great drive-time or desktop snacks. So do broccoli and cauliflower florets that you can blanch at home, then take to work, or sweet potatoes that you can microwave at the office.

Tofu is sometimes in the produce section, sometimes in the dairy case. If you have the choice, take it from the dairy case. The colder temperature keeps tofu fresher.

Think of the produce section as the foundation for your meals. Shop here first to see what's freshest, what's on special, or what simply piques your fancy. Even if you plan menus before you shop, be open to serendipity: if the market has just received a shipment of sweet local corn, you will surely want to make room in your menus for it.

The menus in this book can help you stay in tune with the seasons, so that you are buying produce when the price is low and the quality high. Check the produce list at the start of each chapter for guidance on the fruits and vegetables at their peak that season. It just makes sense to buy produce in season: you don't have to do much to a vine-ripened tomato or juicy spring strawberries to make them taste good.

**Snacks:** Some great snacks are hidden in the supermarket's interior aisles. Look for popcorn for the microwave or hot-air popper; rice cakes; pretzels; fat-free crackers and chips; dried ramen soups with steamed (not fried) ramen, and other instant fat-free soups. Read the list of ingredients, not just the nutrition label. For example, even "fat-free" products can have some fat (up to a half-gram per serving), which usually takes the form of oil or shortening. And be aware that many fat-free cakes, cookies, and frozen desserts are quite high in sugar and calories, which means you will need to limit your serving size if you want to avoid gaining weight.

**Grains:** The packaged grain mixes and pilafs are a great boon to grain novices because the packages include cooking directions. Don't worry if the directions call for adding fat; just leave it out. You can even make tabbouleh (cracked wheat salad) from a package mix if you leave out the oil. Once you have become more familiar with grains like couscous, polenta, and bulgur, you may want to buy them in bulk to save money.

**Pasta:** Take home lots of different shapes to add variety to your meals. If your market doesn't stock whole wheat pasta, ask the buyer to order it. Also, look for spinach pasta, beet pasta, mushroom pasta; the flavors don't add much nutrition, but they do make a change of pace. Check the label to make sure the noodles don't contain egg yolk. Dried pasta rarely has egg (except for egg noodles, of course); fresh pasta often does.

**Beans, Dried and Canned:** Canned beans save time. Take home beans of every kind: kidney beans, cannellini beans, pinto and pinquito beans, navy beans, lima beans, black beans, chili beans, fat-free baked beans. A can of beans adds instant nutrition, flavor, and fiber to soups and stews or, on its own, makes a filling snack. Dried beans take time to cook, but it is unattended time; what's more, some of the tastiest bean varieties don't come in canned versions. For days when you want dinner fast, stock up on lentils and split peas; they cook in only 30 minutes and don't need soaking.

**Breakfast Cereals:** Look high and look low. The unhealthful cereals are usually right in the middle, where kids can grab them. But amid the junk food there are lots of great choices, from Shredded Wheat to Irish oatmeal. Check the label for fat and sugar; in particular, note how many times sugar in all its guises (sugar, malt, corn syrup, dextrose . . . ) appears in the ingredient list. Look for cereals made from whole grains and be skeptical about claims. "Contains oat bran" sounds good, but what else is in it? Despite granola's healthful image, most brands are high in fat and sugar. See pages 28–29 for more guidance in choosing breakfast cereal.

**Breads:** You can find nutritious fat-free choices in this aisle, but you may have to search for them. Many supermarket breads contain fat, sugars, nuts, seeds, and refined wheat. Read labels carefully. Even healthful-sounding multigrain breads may not be delivering as much fiber as a simple whole wheat bread. Avoid breads with sweeteners. Bread doesn't need sweetener to taste good, so why not "reserve" your sugar for foods where it counts? See "Choosing Better Bread" (page 51) for more guidance in making optimum selections in the bread aisle.

**Juices:** Fruit juice meets the Life Choice dietary guidelines, but it's hardly an ideal breakfast food or thirst-quencher. It has no fiber, unlike the fruit it comes from, so it delivers calories and simple sugars without filling you up. And some fruit juices are hardly more than sugared water, with little real fruit juice in them. Your best choice in this aisle is fruit juice with no sugar added. (Even better is to have whole fruit, not juice.) On the other hand, vegetable juice is great for you. Some stores sell freshly squeezed vegetable juices, such as carrot juice. Tomato juice and low-sodium V-8 juice are also good choices for a mealtime beverage or a between-meal snack.

*Freezer Case:* Keep your freezer filled with berries and peaches that you can thaw and puree for dessert sauces, yogurt toppings, and smoothies. Choose brands with no sugar added. Frozen vegetables are a time-saving convenience. Keep a wide variety on hand for days when you don't have time to shop for fresh produce. Frozen peas, corn, or lima beans can make a quick soup; just thaw or cook, then puree with vegetable broth or nonfat milk; season to taste with herbs or spices; add body with pasta or rice. If you hate chopping onions, check your supermarket's freezer case for frozen chopped onions.

Frozen orange, apple, and white grape juice concentrates are also useful for sweetening vegetable dishes and desserts. Many fat-free frozen desserts, such as sorbets and yogurt, meet our guidelines but are high in sugar. Check the sugar content and enjoy these desserts in moderation. An even better idea is to make your own, so you can keep the sugar level in check. Use the Strawberry Sorbet on page 134 as a model for making sorbets with fresh seasonal fruit.

The freezer case is also the place to look for frozen meat substitutes, such as soy burgers. These products can add a satisfying "meaty" taste to soups, pasta sauces, and pizza. Read the label to avoid brands with added fat.

*Sauces:* Chances are your market stocks a tomato sauce (which may be labeled marinara sauce or pasta sauce) with no fat added. If not, ask the buyer to order one. Many of the recipes in this book call for a store-bought tomato sauce for topping pasta, making vegetable and bean stews, or flavoring chili. Keep several jars on hand for quick pasta dinners. Check the salsa selection, too. Many salsas have no added fat and make great toppings for bean dishes and salads, as well as a tasty dip for raw vegetables.

*Soups:* In the soup aisle, you can probably find a canned fat-free vegetable broth or bouillon cubes or powder for making it. You may find that you use vegetable broth constantly in cooking, so keep a constant supply around. Also look for other canned soups with no fat added and for the dry soup mixes that you can take to work or take with you when you fly. Some manufacturers make delicious dried vegetarian bean soups with no fat added. Dried ramen soups are great, but make sure the ramen have been steamed, not fried.

**Condiments:** On the condiment aisle, you will find many of the "free foods" that add flavor without adding fat—such as capers, mustard, pickles, chutneys, and flavored vinegars. They add zest and spice to your dishes. Experiment with products you haven't tried before. Balsamic vinegar is delicious drizzled on sliced beets or braised red cabbage. Tarragon vinegar is lovely on steamed asparagus or broccoli. Rice vinegar has such a mild flavor that it can be used alone on salads; seasoned rice vinegar—which has sugar added—can season a salad or steamed carrots. Add capers and tarragon mustard to nonfat yogurt to make a dressing for steamed cauliflower or sliced tomatoes. On this aisle, you should also find fat-free mayonnaise and fat-free salad dressings. Fortunately, fat-free salad dressings—and fat-free products in general—are a rapidly expanding category and we can look forward to more and better products every year.

**Miscellaneous Packaged Products:** Check the herbal tea selection and take home several varieties to try for hot or iced tea. A cup of hot tea spiced with cinnamon or peppermint can help assuage a sweet tooth. Evaporated skimmed milk is also handy to have on hand; use it to add a creamy quality to pureed vegetable soups. Soy milk in aseptic containers has a long shelf life before it's opened. Use it as a cholesterol-free alternative to nonfat cow's milk.

## EQUIPPING YOUR LOW-FAT KITCHEN

You don't need any fancy or expensive equipment to prepare the recipes in this book. If you have kitchen basics—knives, pots, pans, bowls, measuring spoons and cups—you can make low-fat food. However, a few pieces of special equipment can make meal preparation faster and easier, and thus more enjoyable.

With nonstick skillets, you can sauté easily without fat. Many manufacturers now make these skillets in a range of sizes; unless your family is large, a 10-inch skillet is probably the most useful. A nonstick pot, roasting pan, and baking sheet are also nice to have (see page 108).

If you don't have one, consider buying a blender to puree soups and sauces and to make fruit shakes. A food processor is even more useful. It not only purees soups and sauces, but also can chop onions, slice potatoes, and grate cheese with great speed. Food processors come in a range of sizes. If you cook for a large family, look for a model with a large work bowl. The small ones are ideal for a single person, or for chopping small quantities of garlic or parsley.

A collapsible metal steamer that fits inside your pots is good for steaming vegetables over water or broth. Even better are the tiered bamboo steamers available in many kitchenware stores, especially stores with Chinese or Japanese customers. They hold more than the collapsible steamers, and you can put different foods in each tier. Make sure the bamboo steamer you buy fits comfortably over one of your pots, without a lot of overhang. With such a setup, you can do two things at once: for example, you could steam corn tortillas over a simmering vegetable soup, or reheat some leftover rice over a pot of bean stew.

A cutting board, plastic or wood, makes an easy-to-clean, all-purpose work surface. You don't need a thick one, but a large one allows you to chop and dice several things at once.

A microwave oven is excellent for reheating nonfat foods, which can't rely on fat to protect them against dehydration. You can reheat cooked rice or pasta without adding water; low-fat bean dishes won't stick to the pot when reheated in the microwave, as they can when warmed on the stove top. And it does a great job of steaming vegetables quickly, with minimal loss of nutrients, texture, and color. The microwave also cuts some cooking times drastically. You can have a baked potato in 6 to 8 minutes (versus an hour in a conventional oven) and roasted onions in 5 minutes (versus 45 minutes).

If you don't use beans or grains because you think they take too long to cook, a pressure cooker may change your ways. You can make beans, brown rice, chili, whole grain breakfast cereals, or hearty soups in half the time in a pressure cooker. And because the flavor is trapped inside, dishes made in a pressure cooker seem to taste better. A good cookbook on pressure cooking can teach you the basics, which you can then apply to some of the recipes in this book.

## How to Cook Legumes (Beans and Peas)

From deep maroon kidney beans to pale green limas, from speckled pinto beans to dark-as-night black beans, legumes can add tremendous diversity and pleasure to your diet. Take advantage of the many different bean and pea varieties available at supermarkets, natural food stores, and through mail-order sources (page 321) to expand your palate.

There's nothing wrong with supermarket navy beans, but imagine a soup or a salad made with Tongues of Fire, Scarlet Emperor, or Wren's Egg beans. Don't those just sound better? Beans are so inexpensive that you can afford to experiment and fill your pantry with dozens of different ones to suit your whim.

Beans play a significant role in the Life Choice diet. They supply protein, complex carbohydrate, fiber, and essential vitamins and minerals. They have no cholesterol and are low in total fat, saturated fat, and sodium.

Your body digests the starch in beans slowly, so you have a constant energy supply and are hungry less often. Soluble fiber in beans helps lower blood cholesterol levels. Studies have shown that a bean-rich diet can help people with diabetes control their blood glucose levels, appetite, and weight.

Soybeans have about twice the protein of most other beans. Furthermore, they contain complete protein and are a good plant source of the omega-3 fatty acids. Soybeans may even lower your cholesterol level. For smart ways to incorporate more soy foods into your eating plan, see page 313. Two servings a day (½ cup each) from the legume group are optimal.

### Preparing Dried Beans for Cooking

Most dried beans need to soak in cold water for about 8 hours before you cook them. This extended soaking time ensures that the beans will cook evenly. Lentils and split peas do not need soaking and may be cooked directly.

Before soaking, rinse the dried beans in a sieve or colander. Inspect them for any bits of stone or foreign matter.

Overnight soak: Put the beans in a bowl with 3 cups cold water to each 1 cup beans. Refrigerate if the weather is warm; in cool weather, leave at room temperature. Let stand 8 hours or overnight, then drain. Now the beans are ready to cook.

Quick soak: Put the beans in a pot with 4 cups cold water to each cup of beans. Bring to a simmer over moderate heat, simmer 3 minutes, then cover and remove from heat. Let stand 1 hour, then drain. Now the beans are ready to cook.

Beans soaked overnight generally cook more evenly and keep their shape better than quick-soaked beans, but the quick-soak method is a good option when you're in a hurry.

## Cooking Dried Beans

Place the soaked beans in a pot with 3 cups fresh cold water for each 1 cup beans. Bring to a simmer over moderate heat, skimming any foam that rises to the surface. Add seasonings such as sliced onion, peeled and smashed garlic cloves, chunks of carrot and celery, bay or sage leaves, thyme or rosemary sprigs, or sliced ginger. Return to a simmer, cover partially, adjust heat to maintain a bare simmer and cook until beans are tender but not mushy. Let cool in cooking liquid. Remove bay leaves and herb sprigs before serving.

Dried beans generally take 1 to 2 hours to soften, depending on the variety and their age. Lentils and split peas are exceptions; they take only 25 to 30 minutes. Black-eyed peas also cook more quickly than most dried beans, usually in less than an hour.

## COMPARING LEGUMES
### FOR 3½ OUNCES (½ CUP COOKED)

| | CALORIES | FAT (G) | PROTEIN(G) | CALCIUM (MG) | IRON |
|---|---|---|---|---|---|
| Adzuki beans | 128 | <1 | 8 | 28 | 2 |
| Black beans | 132 | <1 | 9 | 27 | 2 |
| Black-eyed peas | 76 | <1 | 5 | 17 | 1 |
| Chick-peas | 164 | 3 | 9 | 49 | 3 |
| Cranberry beans | 136 | <1 | 9 | 50 | 2 |
| Fava beans | 118 | <1 | 8 | 36 | 2 |

| | CALORIES | FAT (G) | PROTEIN(G) | CALCIUM (MG) | IRON |
|---|---|---|---|---|---|
| Great Northern beans | 118 | <1 | 8 | 68 | 2 |
| Kidney beans | 127 | <1 | 9 | 28 | 3 |
| Lentils | 116 | <1 | 9 | 19 | 3 |
| Lima beans | 126 | <1 | 8 | 29 | 2 |
| Mung beans | 105 | <1 | 7 | 27 | 1 |
| Navy beans | 142 | 1 | 9 | 70 | 3 |
| Pinto beans | 137 | <1 | 8 | 48 | 3 |
| Soybeans | 173 | 9 | 17 | 102 | 5 |
| Split peas | 118 | <1 | 1 | 14 | 1 |

*(Source: Reprinted with permission from* The Wellness Encyclopedia of Food Nutrition, © *Health Letter Associates, 1992.)*

---

## ABOUT INTESTINAL GAS

Many people say that beans give them intestinal gas. The problem arises particularly in people who have been eating a low-fiber diet and then switch to a diet rich in beans and other high-fiber foods. Their digestive tract doesn't have enough of the enzymes needed to digest bean sugars, so the sugars pass undigested into the lower intestine where bacteria metabolize them and generate gas.

Although the gas may produce discomfort, rest assured that it is not harmful. And as your body adjusts to your new bean-rich diet, it will produce the enzymes it needs and the problem will lessen. In other words, it will pass. . . .

Many people find some relief with Beano, a product containing an enzyme that will break down the troublesome bean sugars into digestible sugars. The manufacturer recommends sprinkling about five drops of liquid Beano on top of cooked beans or other gas-producing foods just before you take the first bite, or chewing Beano tablets before eating. (See product information on page 321 for more information on Beano, and be sure to follow package directions. Beano is contraindicated for a very few people who are allergic to some molds.)

Eating slowly and chewing food thoroughly should also help; at least some portion of intestinal gas comes from swallowed air taken in as we eat and drink. Another approach is to introduce problem foods gradually to give your body time to adjust.

---

## How to Cook Grains

Those who think that a low-fat vegetarian diet is bound to be bland and boring probably haven't explored the huge realm of grains. Thanks to renewed interest in vegetarian eating and in high-fiber diets, any good natural food store today will have row after row of bins filled with grains grown and appreciated around the world: couscous, quinoa, barley, cracked wheat, millet, and more. Even supermarkets have a larger selection than they used to; most carry packaged couscous, brown rice, wild rice, barley, and cornmeal. These grains have full, nutty flavors and a rich nutritional profile that make them far more satisfying than the familiar mound of steamed white rice.

Rice is a good example of how little most of us know about grains. There are more than 2,000 different rice varieties, yet the typical American pantry holds only one kind: converted (or instant) long-grain white rice.

If you want to add interest and variety to your meals, try fragrant basmati rice from India, jasmine rice or black rice from Thailand, popcorn rice from Louisiana, Italian short-grain Arborio rice, Chinese sticky rice, or Texmati rice, a Texas-grown relative of aromatic basmati. And that's just rice. Stock your pantry with whole oats, wheat berries, polenta, hominy grits, bulgur, and other grains and you will have the foundation of some delicious meals.

Grains are easy to cook. They require no special equipment and no sophisticated techniques. All you need to know is how much water (or broth) to add and how long to cook them. Some need stirring, but most don't. Although the highly nutritious whole grains take longer than cracked or processed grains, it's unattended time: you can be reading, studying, sewing, or whatever you enjoy doing. If you're in a hurry, a pressure cooker can cut the cooking time dramatically. Or check out the rice cooker/vegetable steamers on the market (page 143).

Cooked grains keep reasonably well. If you cook a large batch of brown rice on Sunday, you can add it to soups, stews, burritos, stir-fries, and salads throughout the week. Refrigerate the cooked grains in a tightly covered container and use within four or five days.

Whole grains still contain the oil-rich germ, which goes rancid over time, a process accelerated by warmth and light. For that reason, it's best to store whole grains in the refrigerator, where they will keep for about six months. Replace them whenever they begin to lose their fresh nutty taste. Processed grains that have had the germ removed, such as white rice, can be kept in a cool, dry place for at least a year. Be sure to keep them in tightly closed containers to keep insects out.

The following chart gives basic cooking guidelines for readily available grains. The timing and liquid suggestions are not hard-and-fast rules. You may like your grains a little chewier, or a little softer. If the grains are done to your liking and there is still liquid in the pot, either drain the grains immediately, or uncover the pot and keep cooking until excess liquid evaporates. Check the product information (page 321) for mail-order sources for grains you can't find in your area.

## BASIC GRAIN COOKERY

All directions are for 1 cup of raw grain. Liquid can be salted water or nonfat vegetable broth. For salted water, figure about ¼ teaspoon salt per cup of raw grain.

| GRAIN | LIQUID | METHOD | YIELD |
|---|---|---|---|
| Barley, pearl | 3 cups | Bring liquid to a boil. Add barley, stir and cover. Cook over low heat until water is absorbed and grain is tender, about 45 minutes. | 3 cups |
| Buckwheat groats, roasted (kasha) | 1½ cups | Bring liquid to a boil. Add groats, stir and cover. Cook over low heat 8 minutes. Remove from heat and let stand 5 minutes. | 3 cups |
| Bulgur Bulgur is cracked wheat made from berries that are steamed, then dried before cracking. | 1½ cups | (for pilaf): Bring liquid to a boil. Add bulgur, stir and cover. Cook over low heat 10 minutes. Remove from heat and let stand 10 minutes. | 2½ cups |
| | | (for salad): Bring liquid to a boil. Pour over bulgur. Let stand 5 minutes.Drain. Wrap in several thicknesses of cheesecloth and squeeze dry. Fluff with a fork. | 1¾ cups |
| Couscous | 1 cup | Bring liquid to a boil. Add couscous, stir and cover. Remove from heat and let stand 10 minutes. Fluff with a fork. | 2¾ cups |

*Note: Couscous can vary in texture and cooking requirements from one manufacturer to another. The first time, follow the package directions or follow the guidelines above for couscous purchased in bulk. You may need to adjust the amount of liquid or the cooking time slightly. For best results, cook couscous in a wide pan so the couscous is not too deep.*

| GRAIN | LIQUID | METHOD | YIELD |
|---|---|---|---|
| Hominy grits, quick-cooking | 4 cups | Bring liquid to a boil. Add grits gradually, whisking constantly. Simmer 5 minutes, stirring. | 3½ cups |
| Millet | 2 cups | Bring liquid to a boil. Add millet, stir and cover. Cook over low heat 10 minutes. Remove from heat and let stand 10 minutes. | 3½ cups |
| Oats, rolled | 2½ cups | Bring liquid to a boil. Add oats while stirring. Simmer uncovered for 10 minutes. | 2 cups |
| Polenta (coarse cornmeal) | 4 cups | Bring liquid to a boil. Add polenta gradually, whisking constantly. Cook over low heat, stirring often, until thick and creamy, about 20 minutes. | 3½ cups |
| Quinoa Although not technically a grain, it looks and cooks like one. It is a valued protein source in the mountainous Andes, because it will grow where other grains won't. Quinoa should be rinsed before cooking to remove a bitter residue that sometimes clings to the seeds. | 1½ cups | Rinse quinoa well. Bring liquid to a boil. Add quinoa, stir and cover. Cook over low heat 15 minutes. Remove from heat and let stand 5 minutes. | 2½ cups |
| Rice, brown Brown rice has been hulled but the bran and germ are still intact. It can be short-grain or long-grain. The cooking method is the same. | 2 cups | Bring liquid to a boil. Add rice, stir and cover. Cook over low heat 45 minutes. Remove from heat and let stand 5 minutes. | 3 cups (long grain); 2½ cups (short-grain) |
| Rice, long-grain white (basmati type; not converted rice) | 1½ cups | Bring liquid to a boil. Add rice, stir and cover. Cook over low heat 18 minutes. Remove from heat and let stand 5 minutes. | 3 cups |
| Rice, short-grain white | 1½ cups | Rinse rice in a sieve until water runs clear. Drain. Bring liquid to a boil. Add rice, stir and cover. Cook over low heat 25 minutes. Remove from heat and let stand 5 minutes. | 2¾ cups |
| Rice, wild | 2½ cups | Bring liquid to a boil. Add rice, stir and cover. Cook over low heat 1 hour. | 3 cups |

| GRAIN | LIQUID | METHOD | YIELD |
|---|---|---|---|
| Wheat, cracked | 1½ cups | (for pilaf): Bring liquid to a boil. Add wheat, stir and cover. Cook over low heat for 15 minutes, then remove from heat and let stand 10 minutes. Fluff with a fork. | 2 cups |
| | | (for salad): Bring liquid to a boil. Pour over cracked wheat and let stand 15 minutes. Drain. Wrap in several thicknesses of cheesecloth and squeeze dry. Fluff with a fork. | 1¾ cups |
| Wheat berries Whole, unprocessed wheat kernels are sometimes called wheat berries. | 3 cups | Bring liquid to a boil. Add wheat berries, stir and cover. Cook over low heat until tender, about 1½ hours. | 2¾ cups |

## Cooking Grains in a Slow Cooker

How would you like to wake up to hot whole grain cereal for breakfast, or to come home from work to find a pot of ready-to-eat steamed grains? If you rarely have the time or patience to give whole grains the cooking time they need, consider buying a slow cooker. A slow cooker can do the work while you're sleeping or at the office. Just put your chosen grain and appropriate liquid in the slow cooker (using slightly less liquid than you would for stove-top cooking), set on low, and come back in 8 hours.

## TIME FOR LUNCH

Chances are, you don't have your midday meal at home very often. Perhaps you typically have your lunch at your desk or in an employee cafeteria; in a restaurant; or even in your car (not the optimal place for a relaxed lunch). Whatever your routine, you don't have to be at the mercy of others at midday. You can be in control of what you eat. If you do have to eat in restaurants for business, read the "Guidelines for Dining Out" on page 303. If you don't, you might want to pack your own lunch. The possibilities for your brown bag are much broader than you might think.

## Pack a Smarter Lunch Box

It's helpful to move away from the idea that you have to build your lunch around a sandwich. If you have access to boiling water at work, consider these three ideas:

•Keep an assortment of dried soups at work. Taste Adventure, Nile Spice, Fantastic Foods, and others make several kinds of satisfying soups—such as split pea, minestrone, lentil chili, and black bean—with no added fat. Just add boiling water and let stand a few minutes. Enjoy with whole wheat bread or crackers. Bring fresh greens and fruit from home to complete your nutritious low-fat lunch.

•Pack some fat-free bean dip or spread. Several companies—among them, Guiltless Gourmet and Fantastic Foods—make these tasty dips. Some are ready-to-eat; others must be reconstituted with water. Take along some broccoli, cauliflower, carrots, zucchini, and celery sticks for dipping. Add whole wheat bread or crackers and fresh fruit to make a meal.

•Take ramen to work. These instant Japanese-style noodles are quickly reconstituted with water. Westbrae Natural makes several varieties. You will need to bring your own soup mug to work, as these noodles come in packages, not cups. Round out your lunch with some raw or blanched vegetables, or leftover steamed vegetables from last night's dinner; and some fresh fruit.

Dinner leftovers can make great lunches. Why not plan to have leftovers by making extra at dinnertime? If you have a microwave at work, you can reheat last night's soup, chili, or bean stew. Or pack leftover roast potatoes, potato salad, coleslaw, steamed vegetables, or poached fruit. Add bottled nonfat Italian dressing to leftover rice, beans, or steamed vegetables to make a portable salad. Reheat leftover stir-fried vegetables in a microwave and tuck into pita bread or a nonfat flour tortilla. For safety's sake, refrigerate foods from home as soon as you arrive at work. If you don't have access to a refrigerator, it may be worthwhile to invest in a small one for your office to expand the range of foods you can enjoy for lunch.

If you do have a refrigerator at work, stock it with nonfat milk, nonfat soy milk, or nonfat yogurt. Keep whole grain cereals on hand and have cereal and milk with fruit for lunch. Cereal isn't just for breakfast anymore!

If you have a freezer and a microwave at work, the Life Choice frozen meals make lunch quick and easy.

---

Other lunch box additions:

    baby carrots
    cucumber spears
    fat-free crackers
    fat-free pretzels
    fat-free salsa with fat-free baked chips
    flavored rice cakes in place of cookies
    grapes
    herbal tea or grain coffee (see page 327)
    low-sodium vegetable juice
    radishes

## Sandwiches As You Like Them

If you do like a sandwich at midday, consider moving beyond the tried-and-true. Variety in your lunch box will keep you feeling well fed and make it easy to resist foods that don't meet the Reversal Diet guidelines.

You can make a great vegetarian sandwich just by omitting the meat and keeping the "extras": tomatoes, onions, pickles, sprouts, cucumbers, and lettuce. Enjoy it on whole wheat bread with nonfat dressing or mayonnaise. If you aren't ready to move away from the idea of meat, you may want to consider meat analogs. Both Yves and White Wave make fat-free deli slices, such as turkey and bologna, from gluten. Lightlife makes fat-free Smart Dogs, which can satisfy a hot dog craving, especially if you add "trimmings" such as sauerkraut and mustard. The soy-based Boca Burgers—a favorite at the White House Navy Mess—are tremendously popular at our retreats; Chef Paul Wenner's Garden Vegan (page 34) is a good alternative. For all these meat analogs, check the label for added fat.

The chart below may give you some fresh ideas for lunch box or at-home sandwiches. Select a bread, add a spread and/or filling, enhance it with a garnish. As you can see, the possibilities are almost beyond counting.

To keep your sandwich from getting soggy, it's a good idea to pack wet ingredients—like lettuce and tomato—separately and add them at the last minute. Be sure to keep your sandwich or sandwich components refrigerated at work.

---

| BREADS | SPREADS | FILLINGS | GARNISHES |
|---|---|---|---|
| bagel | balsamic vinegar | Boca Burgers or | arugula |
| baguette | bean purees | Gardenburgers | baby lettuces |
| country French or | bottled nonfat salad | gluten ham, turkey, or | Creamy Coleslaw |
| Italian loaf | dressing | pastrami | (page 164) |
| lahvosh | Buttermilk Dressing | grilled or sautéed | fresh parsley, basil, or |
| nine-grain bread | (page 258) | mushrooms | cilantro |
| rye bread | Caesar Dressing | nonfat cheese | fresh spinach |
| sourdough bread | (page 186) | (mozzarella, | lettuce |
| sprouted-wheat buns | catsup | Monterey Jack, | peperoncini (mild |
| tortillas, corn or | Creamy Tofu | Swiss, Cheddar) | pickled peppers) |
| nonfat flour | Dressing | roasted bell peppers | pickled jalapeño rings |
| whole wheat bread | (page 164) | (see Tip, page 90) | pickle relish |
| whole wheat pita | Green Pea | roasted eggplant | pickles |
| bread | Guacamole | (page 136) | radishes |
| | (page 191) | sliced seitan | Roasted Onions |
| | Hummus (page 152) | Smart Dogs | (page 21) |
| | mustard | smoked or grilled tofu | romaine lettuce |
| | nonfat barbecue | steamed vegetables | sauerkraut |
| | sauce | Tabbouleh (page 153) | shredded carrots, |
| | nonfat cream cheese | | zucchini, cabbage, |
| | nonfat mayonnaise | | daikon, or jicama |
| | nonfat sour cream | | sliced cucumber |
| | nonfat vegetarian | | sliced radishes |
| | refried beans | | sliced red onions |
| | nonfat yogurt | | sliced tomatoes |
| | Ranch Dressing | | sprouts |
| | (page 195) | | watercress |
| | roasted garlic | | |
| | (page 93) | | |
| | salsa | | |
| | Spinach and | | |
| | Cucumber Raita | | |
| | (page 241) | | |

## SAMPLE SANDWICHES

**1.** bagel
nonfat cream cheese
sliced cucumber
sliced red onion
sliced tomato
sprouts

**2.** whole wheat pita
Hummus (page 152)
romaine lettuce
sliced tomato
Tabbouleh (page 153)

**3.** sprouted-wheat bun
mustard
nonfat soy hot dog
sauerkraut or pickle relish

**4.** rye bread
fresh spinach
gluten ham
nonfat mayonnaise
nonfat Swiss cheese
sliced tomato

**5.** baguette
arugula or butter lettuce
balsamic vinegar
fresh basil leaves
nonfat mayonnaise
nonfat mozzarella cheese
sliced tomato

**6.** whole wheat bread
Caesar Dressing (page 186)
lettuce
nonfat mozzarella cheese
roasted eggplant
(page 138)
roasted bell peppers
(see Tip, page 90)
sliced tomato

**7.** lahvosh
Creamy Tofu Dressing
(page 164)
sliced radishes
sliced steamed potato
sliced tomato
watercress or fresh spinach
Spread surface of bread
with dressing. Top with
potato, tomato, radishes,
and greens. Roll into a log.
Wrap in plastic or
aluminum foil. Let stand
20 minutes to set the
shape, then unwrap and
slice.

**8.** nonfat flour tortilla
cilantro
Green Pea Guacamole
(page 191)
shredded lettuce
tomato salsa
whole black beans or
refried beans

## Choosing Better Bread

"When I was teaching weight control classes in Houston, one of the participants believed that bread was her downfall to losing weight," recalls Helen Roe, M.S., R.D., senior dietitian and director of nutrition services for the Preventive Medicine Research Institute. "To avoid temptation, every morning Barbara would take all the bread products from her pantry and put them into the trunk of her husband's car. When he returned from work, so would the bread for the evening meal."

Barbara's misconception is common. Whole wheat breads and other complex carbohydrates are not the deterrent to weight loss. The problem is the company they usually keep—the spreads and high-fat sauces. Check out the Reversal Diet Pyramid (page 298) and you'll see a foundation of whole grain breads and cereals.

Good bread enhances every meal. Whether it's a whole wheat bagel at breakfast or whole wheat pita bread soaking up the last drops of soup at dinner, bread in its many forms makes meals more filling and satisfying. But from a nutritional perspective, some loaves are definitely better than others.

Supermarket shelves today offer breads in almost endless variety, which makes it important to know which choices offer the best nutritional value. Think "whole grain," and think "no added fat." Read the ingredient label. Many so-called multigrain breads and wheat breads are not made entirely, or even mostly, of whole grains. Refined white flour may be the first ingredient on the label, with whole grains present in only trivial amounts. Look for breads that say "whole wheat"—not just "wheat" or "wheat flour"— on the label; they must be made from 100 percent whole wheat flour. Even after enrichment, white flour lacks many of the nutrients and most of the fiber of whole wheat flour.

Also, check the label for fat and sugar content. Many breads contain fat to make them softer and increase their shelf life. Sugar is also not essential to good bread. Avoid breads made with seeds, such as sesame and poppy seeds, since these are sources of added fat.

**What to Buy? Here Are Some Ideas to Keep Your Bread Box Full and Varied:** Many of the traditional French baguettes and Italian loaves contain only flour, water, yeast, and salt and are satisfyingly chewy and crusty. They are a good nonfat choice; even better, because of their higher fiber and nutrient content, are the hearty French- and Italian-style breads that contain some whole wheat flour.

Almost everybody likes bagels for breakfast, but they also make great sandwiches and snacks. Spread them with nonfat cream cheese or Hummus (page 152), or fill two halves with nonfat mayonnaise, lettuce, sliced red onion, sprouts, and juicy sliced tomatoes. Toasted whole wheat bagels can accompany a dinner soup or salad or a hearty lentil stew. Keep a supply of bagels at work to nibble on when hunger strikes; cinnamon-raisin bagels can appease a sweet tooth. Avoid egg bagels and bagels with seeds. And be aware that some bagel manufacturers do add fat. Read the package label or ask for an ingredient list at the bakery.

Pita bread, also known as pocket bread, opens to hold bulky sandwich fillings. Put a salad in a pita—Caesar Salad (page 186), Creamy Coleslaw (page 164), or Tabbouleh (page 153)—or fill pitas with a vegetable and tofu stir-fry (page 74). Cut pita into wedges and toast to make crisp "chips" for bean dip or salsa. Many markets carry whole wheat pita bread.

Crumpets typically contain no fat and are delicious toasted. Add fresh fruit and a dollop of nonfat yogurt for a tasty dessert. Well-stocked supermarkets carry them; or check a specialty bakery.

Rye bread is also usually fat-free (check the label) and pleasantly full-flavored, excellent with soups and egg-white omelets or for sandwiches. But it is rarely nutritionally superior to white bread. Most rye breads contain more refined white flour than rye flour, and even the rye flour is not whole grain. Pumpernickel is typically a rye bread with molasses or caramel added. A better choice would be a rye bread with some whole wheat flour.

Matzo, the cracker-like unleavened bread eaten by Jews at Passover, is available in many markets year-round, sometimes in whole wheat versions. Its crisp texture and wheat flavor are as pleasing as any cracker, and it has no added fat.

Do you like tortillas? Inspect the ingredient label carefully. Corn tortillas typically have no added fat (the natural fat from the corn is okay), but flour tortillas often contain added fat. Look for nonfat flour tortillas, or stick with the corn version. Avoid taco shells, which have been fried.

Tortillas are great to have on hand for chili and soups; or spread them with nonfat refried black beans, shredded lettuce, chopped tomato, and salsa to make a quick nonfat taco. After dinner, warm a nonfat flour tortilla, fill it with sliced strawberries, roll it and top it with nonfat sour cream or yogurt to make a delicious dessert "crepe." Tortillas do get stale quickly. Keep leftovers in a plastic bag in the refrigerator. To reheat, wrap them in damp paper towels and microwave, or wrap them in a damp dishtowel and steam in a bamboo steamer, or wrap with damp paper towels and aluminum foil and reheat in a moderate oven.

## NUTRITIONAL CONTENT OF BREADS

| BREAD | CALORIES | PROTEIN | FAT |
|---|---|---|---|
| Whole Wheat 1 oz. slice | 70 | 3 grams | 1 gram |

*Comments: Must be made from 100 percent whole-wheat flour. Good source of vitamins, minerals, and fiber. May contain sugar, honey, and molasses, which add calories. Bread labeled "wheat bread," "cracked wheat," or "sprouted wheat" usually contains white flour.*

| BREAD | CALORIES | PROTEIN | FAT |
|-------|----------|---------|-----|
| White, enriched 1 oz. slice | 75 | 3 grams | 1 gram |

Comments: Made from white flour, which lacks the bran and germ of the wheat grain. Most of the lost nutrients are not replaced, even in "enriched flour," which has only niacin, thiamin, riboflavin, and iron added. Fiber is reduced. Avoid bleached flour.

| | | | |
|-------|----------|---------|-----|
| Rye 1 oz. slice | 70 | 3 grams | Trace |

Comments: Most rye breads contain mostly white flour. Look for rye flour, especially whole-rye flour, as a primary ingredient.

| | | | |
|-------|----------|---------|-----|
| Pumpernickel 1 oz. slice | 70 | 3 grams | Trace |

Comments: Most American loaves are made from white and rye flour colored with caramel, so they have no advantage over white or rye bread.

| | | | |
|-------|----------|---------|-----|
| Italian/French | 80 | 3 grams | Trace |

Comments: Loaves made at local bakeries are usually free of preservatives and may contain little or no sugar or fat. Look for whole-grain varieties.

| | | | |
|-------|----------|---------|-----|
| Bagel, plain 2½ oz. | 200 | 7 grams | 2 grams |

Comments: Usually made of high protein flour and little or no fat, making it dense. Egg bagels contain added fat and cholesterol.

| | | | |
|-------|----------|---------|-----|
| Pita 2 oz. | 165 | 6 grams | 1 gram |

Comments: Often made of just flour, salt and water. May have sweeteners and additives.

| | | | |
|-------|----------|---------|-----|
| Croissant 2 oz. | 235 | 5 grams | 12 grams |

Comments: Contains butter and sugar. High in saturated fat, cholesterol and calories.

| | | | |
|-------|----------|---------|-----|
| English Muffin, white 2½ oz. | 140 | 5 grams | 1 gram |

Comments: Has no nutritional advantage over white bread.

(Source: Reprinted with permission from The Wellness Encyclopedia, © Health Letter Associates, 1991.)

## GLOSSARY OF INGREDIENTS

Most of the ingredients used in this book should be familiar to you and are easy to find at a supermarket or natural food store. The ingredients in this section are those few for which you may need some guidance in purchasing or using.

**Arborio rice:** This stubby, short-grain Italian rice is the classic choice for risotto (see pages 81 and 140). The rice is high in amylopectin, a type of starch that helps produce the creamy consistency a risotto should have. Many supermarkets now carry Arborio rice, and some natural food stores offer it in bulk. Arborio rice also makes a lovely rice pudding: cook it in nonfat milk with a strip of lemon peel and thicken with cornstarch, if desired.

**Balsamic vinegar:** This aged vinegar from Italy has a pleasing sweet-tart taste and is more mellow than other wine vinegars. Use it to add depth of flavor to sauces and stews or to perk up cooked vegetables such as red cabbage, beets, spinach, and roasted peppers. Or sprinkle it over salad greens, mushrooms, or sliced tomatoes. Some Italians think a few drops enhance strawberries.

**Basmati rice:** This long-grain Indian rice perfumes the kitchen with a nutty, toasty aroma as it cooks. The slender grains cook up fluffy and separate, and their flavor far surpasses that of the standard American long-grain or converted rice. It costs a little more, but you will proba-bly find that you are happy to pay extra for the superior taste. Look for basmati rice in bulk in natural food stores or Indian markets. Texmati, a Texas-grown hybrid of basmati and long-grain Texas rice, has less fra-grance but is an economical alternative. In California, Lundberg Family Farms grows a brown basmati hybrid called Wehani; another brown basmati type from Arkansas is also entering the market. Louisiana popcorn rice and pecan rice—so named because of their aroma when cooked—are among the other fragrant rices you can sub-stitute for basmati. (See page 321 for sources.)

**Carob powder:** Valued as a caffeine-free substitute for cocoa, carob is derived from the pods of an evergreen tree that grows in Mediterranean regions. The pods contain several large seeds and pulp. It's the pulp—sun-dried and ground—that makes carob powder. It's naturally sweet, so when you substitute it for cocoa in a recipe, you can use less sugar. Look for carob powder in natural food stores. Store it in an airtight container in a cool place. If you love chocolate, you may find that carob is not really a satisfying substitute; as a food in its own right, however, carob is quite good.

**Dashi kombu:** *Dashi* is the word for Japan's all-purpose broth. *Kombu* (sometimes written *konbu*) is giant kelp. *Dashi kombu*, it follows, is the type of kelp used to make Japanese broth. The dark greenish-brown kelp leaves are dried in the sun, then folded and packaged. Kombu sometimes has a powdery surface, but don't try to wash the powder off; a lot of the flavor is on the surface. Simmering kombu briefly in water with other aromatic vegetables yields a flavorful broth that you can use to make miso soup (page 74).

**Lahvosh:** This Armenian flat bread comes in large rounds that are as pliable as a flour tortilla. You can spread them with softened nonfat cream cheese, Green Pea Guacamole (page 191), or other dressings; top with sliced tomato, soft lettuce, sprouts, and nonfat cheese; and roll like a jelly roll. If you then wrap the roll tightly in plastic wrap for 20 minutes, it will keep its shape when unwrapped and you can slice it into pinwheel rounds. See page 51 for one lahvosh filling suggestion, but use your imagination to make a wide variety of lahvosh sandwiches. You should be able to find it in a supermarket; if not, check a natural food store or Middle Eastern market.

**Liquid egg substitute:** Most cholesterol-free liquid egg substitutes are made of egg whites with some yellow coloring added. Some contain gums to increase viscosity, but the gums do not contribute fat. A few brands do contain vegetable oil, so check the label carefully and choose one without added fat. You can scramble egg substitute, make an omelet (page 107) or frittata (page 288) with it, or use it in baking. In most of the recipes in this book, you can replace egg whites with liquid egg substitute, cup for cup. However, liquid egg substitutes will not whip, so you must use egg whites in recipes that call for beating the whites to peaks, such as Corn Pancakes (page 157). Most supermarkets keep liquid egg substitute in the freezer case and/or the dairy case. The popular Fleischmann's Egg Beaters comes in both frozen and refrigerated formulations. The ingredients are identical, but the products are made differently, and you shouldn't freeze the refrigerated version or it may separate when thawed.

**Meat substitutes:** Made from soy protein, wheat gluten, rice, tofu, oats, or other ingredients, these simulated meat products can satisfy a taste for the flavor and texture of meat. Since they are from plant sources, they are a good source of protein without the cholesterol, but they can be high in fat.

One of the most popular meat substitutes is Textured Vegetable Protein, or TVP. It is made from compressed soy flour and is available in granules that resemble ground beef or in chunks that resemble beef stew meat.

The Boca Burger "No Fat Original" used in some of the recipes in this book is made from defatted soy protein and can be used in recipes in place of meat. It has the texture and smoky taste of a char-broiled burger. Other soy-based meat substitutes are flavored to taste like pork, chicken, even tuna. These products and others, such as imitation hot dogs and deli meats, are becoming more available in all parts of the country.

**Miso:** A fermented paste made from soybeans and, for some types, rice or barley, miso adds a nutty flavor to soups, stews, and dressings. Japanese markets and natural food stores typically carry several kinds, ranging from white to yellow to red to brown. As a generalization, the white and yellow misos are more delicate and sweet; the darker ones are saltier and more pungent. A spoonful of miso whisked into a soup or stew will give it depth and richness. Add it at the end of the cooking time to preserve its flavor, and use it sparingly as it is high in sodium and does contain fat. Miso keeps in the refrigerator for several months after opening.

**Rice vinegar, plain and seasoned:** Considerably milder than wine vinegar, cider vinegar, or distilled white vinegar, rice vinegar can be used as a condiment on its own. Sprinkle it on salad greens or on steamed or grilled vegetables to heighten their flavor. Seasoned rice vinegar has salt and sugar added, so avoid it if you are on a salt-restricted diet. You should have no trouble finding rice vinegar in supermarkets.

**Shiitake mushrooms:** Available fresh and dried, the fleshy, full-flavored shiitake mushroom is much-used in Chinese and Japanese cooking. It is growing in popularity in this country now because it delivers so much more flavor than the standard supermarket button mushroom. Its firm, chewy texture and woodsy taste make it particularly satisfying in meatless cooking. Add it to vegetable stews, soups, and stir-fries, to pasta sauces or omelet fillings. When buying fresh ones, look for firm, thick, dry caps with a pleasing aroma. Refrigerate them in a single layer on a tray, covered with a dampened towel. They will keep that way for a few days. Dried shiitakes come in several sizes and grades, from crumbled bits to premium whole caps. For a sauce, the bits may be good enough, whereas you will probably want pretty caps for stir-fries and soups. Dried shiitakes must be softened first in water—either in hot water for about half an hour, or in cold water for several hours. Always try to use the soaking water, too; it will have a lot of flavor.

If you can't find fresh shiitake mushrooms, substitute standard button mushrooms. Look for dried shiitake mushrooms in Chinese or Japanese markets.

**Tofu:** To make tofu, dried soybeans are soaked in water to soften, then crushed and boiled. The pulp is then separated from the soybean "milk," and a coagulant is added to the milk. Just as in the cheese-making process, the milk separates into curds and whey, and the curds are poured into molds. Within hours, the tofu is ready and is transferred to water. When you buy tofu, it should still be covered with or packed in water. If it's in an open container of water, sniff it to make sure it doesn't smell sour. Tofu is extremely perishable. Try to buy it from a store that has a rapid turnover and refrigerate it when you get it home. If you buy packaged tofu and don't plan to use it immediately, it's a good idea to transfer the tofu to a new container and cover it with fresh water and then refrigerate. Changing the water daily will prolong the tofu's life, but you should use it within a week.

You will probably find at least two kinds of tofu at your supermarket: soft and firm. The soft tofu, which contains more whey, is best for dressings and sauces. The firm tofu is sliceable and thus better for stir-fries, stews, and soups. Tofu is high-quality protein, but 4 ounces of tofu contain 6 grams of fat. For that reason, it's prudent to limit yourself to no more than 4 ounces a day (see page 313).

Tofu tends to take on the flavor of whatever else is in the dish. Only the most ardent tofu lovers enjoy it straight from the package.

# New Everyday Meals

How do you assemble a well-balanced, low-fat vegetarian meal? What goes together, nutritionally and aesthetically? How can a meatless meal be filling and satisfying?

The forty-five menus that follow are appetizing examples of meals that are balanced in every respect. They meet the Reversal Diet guidelines. In many cases, these menus incorporate fruits, vegetables, beans, *and* grains. They offer well-balanced colors, textures, and flavors. And they demonstrate again and again that low-fat vegetarian meals can leave you wanting for nothing.

What's more, these easy menus won't keep you in the kitchen for hours or have you running all over town for exotic ingredients. With few exceptions, you should be able to put any of these meals on the table in less than an hour—sometimes much less. The exceptions are 8 special-occasion menus—2 per season—for celebrating holidays or entertaining friends. Even these menus, although they ask for a little more effort, are not particularly time-consuming.

For the most part, these are recipes for everyday meals—just good, home-style cooking. You'll find slimmed-down versions of familiar foods like Old-Fashioned Potato Salad (page 165), Creamy Coleslaw (page 164), enchiladas, and lasagne. And you'll find recipes for quick dishes that you may not have in your repertoire, such as Creamy Mushroom Stroganoff (page 177), Chickpea Stew with Couscous (page 207), creamy corn soup (page 128), and Pizza with Roasted Eggplant and Peppers (page 136). These are the kinds of dishes you'll want to make again and again, comfort foods that make it much more pleasurable to eat at home than to dine out.

The tips sprinkled throughout the following pages suggest new techniques, share nutrition information, advise you on using leftovers, and suggest alternative ways to season or serve a dish. You may find other useful guidance in the recipe headnotes and in suggestions for timing that accompany each menu. These latter guidelines are meant to help you use your time in the kitchen efficiently by making the dishes that have to cook longest first.

Of course, you don't have to follow these menus recipe for recipe and word for word. They are intended as models and teaching tools. If you don't like black bean soup, substitute another bean soup, another bean dish, or another dish entirely. Nutritionally, of course, it makes most sense to substitute one green vegetable for another or one grain dish for another, but you shouldn't feel tied to that. And if you want to serve a spring menu in summer, and summer dishes in fall, go for it.

These menus are organized by season for a reason, and not just because it's romantic or tidy. Most fruits and vegetables are seasonal. (Most grains and beans are available year-round.) To keep yourself satisfied with the new regime, treat yourself to the best produce you can find. When you eat fruits and vegetables at the peak of their local season—when they don't have to be picked underripe and shipped to you from another continent—you get more nutrients and much more flavor. And you save time, because these naturally delicious fruits and vegetables need little done to them to make them taste good.

At the start of each seasonal chapter, you will find a list of the fruits and vegetables that are likely to be at their peak during that time. The seasonal menus incorporate these produce items, as well as others that straddle the seasons or that are available in good quality year-round. Use these seasonal produce lists for your own shopping, to guide you to the fruits and vegetables that most likely taste the best. Another reason to cook with the seasons: when quality peaks, price is usually at its lowest.

Following the seasonal chapters is a brief collection of breakfast foods, ten favorite low-fat recipes for dishes to help you start the day. But who's to say you can't have pancakes for dinner?

## How to Use the Nutrient Analysis

The nutrient analysis at the end of each recipe was designed to give you a useful nutritional profile of the food. The serving size listed is not a recommended serving but a tool for computing the nutritional values. If some of the portion sizes seem a little generous for you, simply reduce the amount you eat. On the other hand, if you want to eat more, or have smaller, more frequent portions, that is your choice as well. The recipes are all very low in fat and cholesterol and can fit into your individual nutrition plan.

The recipes were analyzed by computer, using information from USDA handbooks of food composition supplemented by product information. The analyses are based on a single serving. If a recipe includes an ingredient that can be used either fresh or canned, the analysis specifies the type used in the calculation. For example, if a recipe calls for "2 cups sliced cooked beets, fresh or canned," the analysis shows whether the calculation was done with fresh or canned beets.

In recipes calling for nonstick spray, the oil in the spray has not been included in the analysis. If you are spraying properly (see Tip, page 251), the amount of oil used should be insignificant. A couple of recipes use large amounts of salt—for wilting cucumbers, in one case, and for baking potatoes in a bed of salt. Although most of the salt is rinsed off or brushed off, the analyses incorporate an estimate of the amount of salt absorbed by the food.

When a recipe lists salt as an ingredient but in no specific amount (giving the cook the option to season to taste), salt is not included in the sodium calculation. In recipes calling for vegetable broth, the analysis is based on unsalted homemade broth. Using canned vegetable broth will increase the recipe's sodium content.

*Some of the recipes may be too high in sodium for salt-sensitive persons. To reduce the sodium in the recipes: use fresh or frozen products instead of canned; use homemade broth and sauces instead of store-bought; don't add salt to recipes; and omit or reduce the amount of high-sodium ingredients such as nonfat cheese. Compensate with herbs or other seasonings.*

*Some canned beans and canned bean products can have as much as*

---

*1,000 milligrams of sodium per cup. Canned vegetables can have 300 milligrams or more sodium per cup. Consider this example:*

| GREEN BEANS | SODIUM |
|---|---|
| ½ cup fresh | 2 mg |
| ½ cup frozen | 9 mg |
| ½ cup canned | 259 mg |

*Sodium content can vary from brand to brand. Check the label to find the brands with the lowest sodium content, or look for reduced-sodium or salt-free formulations.*

# Spring

Artichoke Halves with Rémoulade Sauce
Tuscan Vegetable Minestrone
Warm Whole Grain Bread
Strawberry-Rhubarb Parfait

Miso Soup with Leeks
Spring Vegetable Stir-Fry
Brown Rice and Shiitake Pilaf
Pineapple Compote with Candied Ginger

Spinach, Beet, Cucumber, and Red Onion Salad
Risotto with Peas, Zucchini, and Sun-Dried Tomatoes
Toasted Herb Bread
Quick Mango Sherbet and Sliced Kiwi Fruit

Quick Black Bean Soup
Mexican Green Rice with Spinach
Sliced Okra with Tomatoes and Onions
Whole Wheat Tortillas
Fresh Pineapple Spears

Creamy Split Pea Soup
Rye Crackers
Baked Potatoes with Herbed Cheese
Steamed Broccoli Spears
Fresh Cherries and Apricots

Hearts of Romaine with Marinated Artichokes
Whole Wheat Spaghetti Marinara with Spinach
Roasted Garlic Toast
Chilled Papaya Fans with Lemon

Hearts of Butter Lettuce with Julienned Beets
**Spring Vegetable Ragout**
**Steamed Bulgur with Lemon Zest**
Crusty French Bread
**Warm Whole Wheat Crepes with Strawberries and**
**Frozen Vanilla Yogurt**

☼

**Wild Rice and White Bean Salad**
**Carrot-Cauliflower Soup with Tarragon**
Warm Multigrain Bread
**Sour Cherry Pudding**

☼

**Julienned Spinach Salad with Jicama and Oranges**
**Southwest Pizza**
**Frosty Pineapple Shake**

☼

"EASTER BRUNCH"
**Fresh Asparagus Omelets with Herbs**
**New Potatoes Baked in Rock Salt**
**Pear-Ginger Muffins and Blueberry Muffins**
**Layered Spring Fruit Medley**

☼

"PASSOVER SEDER"
**Vegetable Broth with Matzo Balls**
**Savory Mushroom Pudding**
**Sweet and Sour Red Cabbage**
**Roasted Carrots, Parsnips, and Beets**
**Cucumber Salad with Horseradish and Dill**
**Baked Vanilla Custard**
Sliced Fresh Strawberries

These spring menus take full advantage of the first vegetables and fruits that appear in the market when the weather warms. You'll find steamed artichokes halved and topped with a French-style chopped egg dressing (page 67); a delicate stew of turnips, English peas, carrots, and sugar snap peas (page 94); a hearty minestrone stocked with fresh spring vegetables (page 69); and a creamy carrot-cauliflower soup with a hint of tarragon (page 100). Of course strawberries have their day, spooned into a warm crepe and served with a topping of frozen yogurt (page 96), or as part of an old-fashioned fruit parfait with rhubarb and yogurt (page 73). Celebrate the season's holidays with fresh asparagus-herb omelets (page 107) and blueberry muffins at Easter (page 110) or with matzo ball soup and an impressive Passover seder table (page 113).

In spring, look for:

apricots
artichokes
arugula
asparagus
beets
carrots
cauliflower
cherries
fava beans
leeks
mangoes
papayas
peas: English peas, sugar snap peas, snow peas

pineapple
red onions
rhubarb
spinach
strawberries

**Artichoke Halves with Rémoulade Sauce**
**Tuscan Vegetable Minestrone**
Warm Whole Grain Bread
**Strawberry-Rhubarb Parfait**

Make a hearty minestrone into a filling main course by serving it with a basket of whole grain bread. Precede the soup with artichokes "on the half shell," their cavity filled with a dipping sauce for the leaves. For dessert, a strawberry-rhubarb parfait unites two spring fruits that bring out the best in each other.

The timing: Start the parfait first. Cook the strawberry-rhubarb mixture so it has time to chill while you're having dinner, then assemble the parfait just before you're ready for dessert. Make the minestrone next, and while it's simmering, boil the artichokes. You can make the rémoulade sauce while the artichokes and soup are cooking.

## ARTICHOKE HALVES WITH RÉMOULADE SAUCE

*You'll surely find lots of uses for this nonfat version of French rémoulade, a piquant mayonnaise-based sauce with chopped egg, onion, and capers. Spoon it over steamed asparagus, broccoli, or cauliflower; or drizzle it over crisp romaine hearts or sliced tomatoes. In this recipe, it fills the cavity of a steamed and halved artichoke. If you prefer, you can buy smaller artichokes and serve them whole. Just scrape out the hairy choke in the middle after steaming and spoon the dressing inside.*

SERVES 4

2 large artichokes
1 lemon half

*Rémoulade Sauce:*
2 eggs
½ cup diced fresh tomato
¼ cup nonfat mayonnaise
1 tablespoon finely diced red onion
2 tablespoons chopped parsley
2 teaspoons whole grain mustard

2 teaspoons red wine vinegar

1 teaspoon capers

Trim artichokes: Cut off and discard the artichoke stem. Rub the cut end with lemon half to prevent browning. With a serrated knife, cut off about the top ¾ inch of the artichokes. Rub edges with lemon. With scissors, cut across each exterior leaf to remove the sharp, pointed tip. Bring a large pot of salted water to a boil over high heat. Add artichokes. Put a large, heatproof plate on top to keep the artichokes immersed in water. Simmer until you can slip a knife easily into the artichoke bottom or until a leaf pulls out easily, about 25 minutes, or less if the artichokes are small. Drain on towels. Halve artichokes. With a spoon, scrape out the hairy "choke" and prickly inner leaves.

Make rémoulade sauce: Place eggs in a saucepan. Cover with hot water. Bring to a boil over high heat, adjust heat to maintain a simmer, and cook 12 minutes. Drain and cool in cold water. Peel eggs, then cut in half lengthwise. Remove the yolks and discard. Gently wash the whites to remove traces of yolk. Pat dry. Chop the whites. Place chopped whites in a bowl and add all remaining dressing ingredients. Stir to blend. Taste and adjust seasoning.

Serve artichokes warm, at room temperature, or chilled if desired. To serve, put a halved artichoke on each plate. Spoon ¼ cup dressing into the cavity.

*Serving size: ½ artichoke, ¼ cup
    dressing*
*Calories: 45*
*Fat: 0.35 g*
*Cholesterol: 0 mg*
*Carbohydrate: 8.6 g*
*Protein: 4.3 g*
*Sodium: 270.0 mg*

**TIP**

Add herbs or spices to the cooking water to flavor the artichoke. Good choices: bay leaf, thyme, mint, clove, mustard seed, celery seed, whole peppercorns, or cardamom. Other dipping sauces suited to artichokes include Spinach and Cucumber Raita (page 241), Hummus (page 152), nonfat yogurt with minced garlic and herbs, bottled nonfat dressing, Fresh Tomato Salsa (page 192) or store-bought salsa, or homemade Ranch Dressing (page 195). Cook extra artichokes and refrigerate; they will keep for 2 or 3 days and make a satisfying lunch or snack.

# TUSCAN VEGETABLE MINESTRONE

*This easy, Italian-style vegetable soup can make appearances year-round in your kitchen. You can add other vegetables in season, such as fresh tomatoes (in place of canned), fennel, or butternut squash. You can replace the kidney beans with white beans, lentils, or even rice. And if you are lucky enough to have leftover soup, use it the next day as a sauce for pasta, or serve it Tuscan-style over thick slices of toasted bread.*

SERVES 4

2 cups diced green cabbage
½ cup diced onion
½ cup diced carrots
½ cup diced celery
½ cup diced peeled baking potato
1 cup canned ground tomatoes or diced tomatoes diced finer by hand
5 cups Vegetable Broth, homemade (page 18) or store-bought
½ cup diced zucchini
1 (15-ounce) can kidney beans or 2 cups home-cooked kidney beans
 with ¾ cup liquid
¼ cup dried elbow macaroni
1 tablespoon minced fresh oregano
Salt and pepper

In a large pot, combine cabbage, onion, carrots, celery, potato, tomatoes, and vegetable broth. Bring to a simmer over moderate heat. Cover, adjust heat to maintain a simmer, and cook until vegetables are half done, about 15 minutes. Add zucchini, beans with their juice, and macaroni. Cover and simmer until vegetables are tender and pasta is al dente, about 15 minutes. Add oregano. Season to taste with salt and pepper.

*Serving size: 1¾ cups*
*Calories: 184*
*Fat: 0.9 g*
*Cholesterol: 0 mg*
*Carbohydrate: 36.5 g*
*Protein: 9.6 g*
*Sodium: 581.0 mg*

| TIP |
| --- |
| In a hurry? The smaller you dice the vegetables, the faster the soup will cook. But if you're not handy with a knife, you may find it easier to cut the vegetables into largish pieces and allow more cooking time for them to soften. |

Researchers continue to find reasons to recommend a high-fiber diet. Even small increases in daily fiber intake can reduce cholesterol levels (most of it the harmful LDL cholesterol) and thereby reduce the risk of coronary heart disease.

Fiber is the nondigestible part of plants. Fruits, vegetables, beans, and grains all contain fiber in varying amounts. Fiber can be soluble in water or insoluble, and most plant foods have some of both types. Wheat bran is a good source of insoluble fiber, which passes quickly through the body, adding bulk to the stool and preventing constipation. By helping waste pass through the digestive tract quickly, a diet high in insoluble fiber may also help prevent colon cancer, but it has no effect on cholesterol.

Soluble fiber does, however. Oat bran, pinto beans, kidney beans, and carrots are all high in soluble fiber, which appears to sweep cholesterol from the blood. But beyond its cholesterol-lowering abilities, a diet high in soluble fiber can help control diabetes and battle obesity, both risk factors for heart disease.

You can get 5 grams of soluble fiber in just ¾ cup of pinto beans, 1½ cups of brussels sprouts, or a cup of Quaker Oat Bran cereal. Whole grains, dried beans, peas, sweet potatoes, apples, oranges, and dried prunes are all good low-fat soluble fiber sources.

Americans now eat about 11 grams of total fiber daily. The National Cancer Institute recommends doubling the amount to between 20 to 30 grams per day. Aim for the high end—28 to 30 grams of total dietary fiber from a wide variety of sources. If you follow the Reversal Diet, which is high in both soluble and insoluble fiber, you should have no trouble meeting that goal.

The following Sample Menu shows how easy it is to get adequate fiber on the Reversal Diet.

**SAMPLE MENU**

| BREAKFAST | FIBER (in grams) |
| --- | --- |
| ½ banana | 1.2 |
| Shredded Wheat, 1 biscuit | 2.2 |
| Whole wheat toast, 2 slices | 2.8 |
| Nonfat milk | 0 |

| SNACK | FIBER (in grams) |
|---|---|
| 1 apple | 3.5 |

**LUNCH**

| | |
|---|---|
| Spinach, fresh, 1 cup | 1.2 |
| Mushrooms, raw, ½ cup | 0.9 |
| Navy bean soup, 1 cup | 6.0 |
| Whole wheat bread, 2 slices | 2.8 |
| Strawberries, ½ cup | 1.5 |

**SNACK**

| | |
|---|---|
| 1 orange | 0.8 |

**DINNER**

| | |
|---|---|
| Whole wheat pasta, 1 cup | 3.9 |
| Tomato basil sauce with ½ cup cooked zucchini | 1.8 |
| Whole wheat bread, 2 slices | 2.8 |
| Fresh blueberries, ½ cup | 2.6 |
| Nonfat yogurt, ½ cup | 0 |
| *Total* | *34.0* |

## TOTAL FIBER CONTENT OF SELECTED FOODS

| | SERVING | CALORIES | GRAMS FIBER |
|---|---|---|---|
| ***Breads, Grains, and Cereals*** | | | |
| All-Bran-Extra Fiber | ½ cup | 60 | 13.0 |
| Fiber One | ½ cup | 60 | 12.0 |
| All-Bran | ⅓ cup | 70 | 8.5 |
| 100% Bran | ⅓ cup | 75 | 8.4 |
| Bran Buds | ⅓ cup | 75 | 7.9 |
| Bran Chex | ⅔ cup | 90 | 4.6 |
| Corn Bran | ⅔ cup | 100 | 5.4 |
| Bran Flakes | ¾ cup | 90 | 4.0 |
| Whole Wheat Spaghetti | 1 cup | 125 | 3.9 |
| Raisin Bran | ¾ cup | 90 | 3.6 |
| Ralston, cooked | ¾ cup | 100 | 3.2 |
| Wheat Germ | ¼ cup | 108 | 3.0 |
| Rye Crackers | 3 | 63 | 2.3 |
| Shredded Wheat | 1 biscuit | 83 | 2.2 |
| Oatmeal, cooked quick, regular | ¾ cup | 108 | 1.6 |
| Whole Wheat Bread | 1 slice | 60 | 1.4 |
| Grape-Nuts | ¼ cup | 100 | 1.4 |
| Air-popped Popcorn | 1 cup | 25 | 1.0 |
| Brown Rice, cooked | ½ cup | 97 | 1.0 |
| Bulgur, cooked | ½ cup | 113 | 0.9 |

|                         | SERVING   | CALORIES | GRAMS FIBER |
|-------------------------|-----------|----------|-------------|
| **Beans and Peas, cooked** |        |          |             |
| Kidney Beans            | ½ cup     | 110      | 7.3         |
| Navy Beans              | ½ cup     | 130      | 6.0         |
| Dried Peas              | ½ cup     | 115      | 4.7         |
| Lima Beans              | ½ cup     | 130      | 4.5         |
| Lentils                 | ½ cup     | 95       | 3.7         |
| **Vegetables, cooked**  |           |          |             |
| Green Peas              | ½ cup     | 55       | 3.6         |
| Corn                    | ½ cup     | 70       | 2.9         |
| Parsnip                 | ½ cup     | 50       | 2.7         |
| Potato, with skin       | 1 medium  | 95       | 2.5         |
| Brussels Sprouts        | ½ cup     | 30       | 2.3         |
| Carrots                 | ½ cup     | 25       | 2.3         |
| Broccoli                | ½ cup     | 20       | 2.2         |
| Spinach                 | ½ cup     | 20       | 2.1         |
| Zucchini                | ½ cup     | 10       | 1.8         |
| Beans, green            | ½ cup     | 15       | 1.6         |
| Cabbage                 | ½ cup     | 15       | 1.4         |
| Kale                    | ½ cup     | 20       | 1.4         |
| Cauliflower             | ½ cup     | 15       | 1.1         |
| Asparagus               | ½ cup     | 15       | 1.0         |
| **Vegetables, raw**     |           |          |             |
| Bean Sprouts            | ½ cup     | 15       | 1.5         |
| Spinach                 | 1 cup     | 10       | 1.2         |
| Celery                  | 1 stalk   | 15       | 1.1         |
| Mushrooms               | ½ cup     | 10       | 0.9         |
| Lettuce                 | 1 cup     | 10       | 0.1         |
| **Fruits**              |           |          |             |
| Apple, medium           | 1         | 80       | 3.5         |
| Grapefruit, large       | ½         | 60       | 3.1         |
| Raisins                 | ¼ cup     | 110      | 3.1         |
| Strawberries            | 1 cup     | 45       | 3.0         |
| Prunes                  | 3         | 60       | 3.0         |
| Orange, medium          | 1         | 60       | 2.6         |
| Banana, medium          | 1         | 105      | 2.4         |
| Blueberries             | ½ cup     | 40       | 2.0         |
| Dates, dried            | 3         | 70       | 1.9         |
| Peach, medium           | 1         | 35       | 1.9         |
| Apricot, fresh          | 3         | 50       | 1.8         |
| Pear, medium            | ½         | 35       | 1.6         |
| Apricot, dried, halves  | 5 halves  | 40       | 1.4         |
| Cherries                | 10        | 50       | 1.2         |
| Pineapple               | ½ cup     | 40       | 1.1         |
| Cantaloupe              | ¼ melon   | 50       | 1.0         |
| Grapes                  | 20        | 36       | 0.6         |

(*Source: Adapted from* "A Critical Review of Food Fiber Analysis and Data" *by Elaine Lanza,
Ph.D., and Ritva R. Butrum, Ph.D.,* Journal of the American Dietetic Association, *vol.
86:732, June 1986.*)

# STRAWBERRY-RHUBARB PARFAIT

*Cooking strawberries and rhubarb together yields a compote with a deep ruby color that looks stunning layered in a wineglass with yogurt. For the prettiest results, purchase rhubarb with a full red color. This elegant dessert is an adaptation of a recipe that appeared in Bon Appétit magazine, and it's a good reminder that you can adapt favorite high-fat recipes to suit your new way of eating.*

## SERVES 4

1 pint fresh strawberries, hulled and quartered (or halved if small)
½ pound fresh rhubarb, cut in ½-inch lengths
¼ cup sugar
3 tablespoons orange juice
1⅓ cups nonfat plain yogurt

In a medium saucepan, combine strawberries, rhubarb, sugar, and orange juice. Bring to a boil over moderate heat, stirring to dissolve sugar. Reduce heat, cover and simmer slowly until strawberries and rhubarb are very soft, about 10 minutes. Transfer to a small bowl and refrigerate until cold.

To serve, spoon alternate layers of yogurt and fruit into four balloon wineglasses or parfait glasses, ending with a spoonful of fruit. Allow a total of ⅓ cup fruit and ⅓ cup yogurt per serving. Refrigerate remaining fruit for another use. Serve parfaits immediately.

*Serving size: ⅔ cup*
*Calories: 125*
*Fat: 0.5 g*
*Cholesterol: 1.3 mg*
*Carbohydrate: 26.0 g*
*Protein: 5.0 g*
*Sodium: 58.0 mg*

> **TIP**
> You should have a little more than 1 cup of strawberry-rhubarb compote left over. Enjoy it in the next few days as a topping for waffles, pancakes, oatmeal, or yogurt.

**Miso Soup with Leeks**
**Spring Vegetable Stir-Fry**
**Brown Rice and Shiitake Pilaf**
**Pineapple Compote with Candied Ginger**

✿

This Asian dinner incorporates flavors, ingredients, and techniques from Japan and China. Set the table with chopsticks, if you have them, and serve herbal tea with the meal or afterward. Dinner starts with a warming bowl of nutty miso soup, followed by a quick stir-fry of fresh spring vegetables served with aromatic mushroom-rice pilaf. Chilled cooked pineapple flavored with spicy candied ginger makes a refreshing finale.

The timing: Make dessert several hours ahead or the night before, so the pineapple can chill. Begin soaking the shiitake mushrooms about 1½ hours before dinner. While the brown rice and shiitake pilaf is cooking, make the miso soup. Then you can have mugs of steaming soup in the kitchen while you slice and stir-fry tofu and vegetables.

## MISO SOUP WITH LEEKS

*Miso—a creamy, salty soybean paste—is what Japanese cooks use to give their delicate soups an intriguing nutty flavor. Here's a classic rendition of miso soup, similar to what you might have tasted in a Japanese restaurant or sushi bar. It's based on dashi, the all-purpose Japanese soup stock. You can vary dashi throughout the year with seasonal vegetables, replacing the leeks with green onions, peas, julienned snow peas, sliced asparagus, or mushrooms. Look for dried seaweed and white miso in natural food stores or Japanese markets. The seaweed will keep unrefrigerated for months if wrapped airtight. If it has a powdery white appearance, wipe it with a dampened cloth but don't rinse it. Much of the flavor is on the surface. Miso will also keep for months in the refrigerator.*

MAKES 4 CUPS • SERVES 4

1 cup diced carrots
1 cup diced onion
1 cup diced celery
One 4-inch square dried seaweed (dashi kombu)

1 cup thinly sliced leeks, white and pale green part only
3 tablespoons white miso

In a saucepan, combine carrots, onion, celery, seaweed, and 5 cups cold water. Bring to a simmer over moderate heat. Adjust heat to maintain a simmer and cook, uncovered, until broth is flavorful, about 20 minutes. Strain through a sieve and return to a clean saucepan. Add leeks and simmer over moderate heat until leeks are tender, about 5 minutes. Whisk in miso. Serve immediately.

*Serving size: 1 cup*
*Calories: 80*
*Fat: 1.0 g*
*Cholesterol: 0 mg*
*Carbohydrate: 15.0 g*
*Protein: 3.0 g*
*Sodium: 545.0 mg*

| TIP |
|---|
| Some cooks claim that cooking beans with a piece of kombu will make the beans more digestible. |

## SPRING VEGETABLE STIR-FRY

*Use this recipe as a model for other stir-fries made with whatever vegetables strike your fancy. You might want to try this combination first to get a feel for the technique and balance of flavors, then branch out on your own. Consider using broccoli, cauliflower, cabbage, sugar snap peas, bok choy, sweet peppers, or mushrooms. Just be sure to cut the vegetables in small pieces so they cook quickly. Stir-fried vegetables should be al dente—what some cookbooks call "crisp-tender."*

SERVES 4

¼ cup plus 6 tablespoons Vegetable Broth, homemade (page 18) or store-bought
2 teaspoons minced garlic
1 teaspoon minced fresh ginger
2 cups sliced asparagus, cut ¼ inch thick on the diagonal (peel first if large)
1 cup sliced carrots, cut ⅛ inch thick on the diagonal
1 cup snow peas, strings removed and halved widthwise

½ cup sliced red onion
1 (14-ounce) package firm tofu, cut in ¾-inch cubes
2 tablespoons soy sauce
1 tablespoon cornstarch
1 teaspoon sugar
2 cups bean sprouts
1 teaspoon red wine vinegar
Black pepper

Combine ¼ cup vegetable broth, garlic, and ginger in a large skillet or wok. Simmer over moderate heat for 2 minutes. Add asparagus, carrots, snow peas, and onion. Cook, stirring, over moderately high heat until vegetables soften slightly, about 5 minutes. Add tofu and soy sauce. In a small bowl, stir together remaining 6 tablespoons vegetable broth, cornstarch, and sugar. Add to skillet, bring to a simmer, and simmer until sauce thickens and vegetables are crisp-tender, about 5 minutes. Add sprouts and vinegar and toss. Season with black pepper. Serve immediately.

*Serving size: 1¼ cups*
*Calories: 210*
*Fat: 7.5 g*
*Cholesterol: 0 mg*
*Carbohydrate: 22.5 g*
*Protein: 19.0 g*
*Sodium: 30.1 mg*

> **TIP**
>
> You don't need a wok to stir-fry foods. You just need a large skillet, preferably with sloping sides, so that you can keep all the ingredients moving. By keeping them moving, you ensure that they will cook evenly.

## BROWN RICE AND SHIITAKE PILAF

*This hearty rice dish will perfume your kitchen as it cooks. The intensely aromatic shiitake mushrooms impart their fragrance to the rice and add a pleasantly chewy texture. On another occasion, when you want a simple supper, serve this pilaf with a leafy green salad.*

FROM WIN HOOPER OF FORT WORTH, TEXAS: *Win and Mary Jane Hooper have attended the Ornish residential lifestyle retreat in California.*

*Both are busy professionals who enjoy spending time together cooking. But given their schedule, they often make quick stir-fry dishes by tossing together fresh ingredients from Win's backyard organic vegetable garden.*

SERVES 4

1 ounce dried shiitake mushrooms
½ cup diced celery
2 teaspoons minced garlic
2 cups brown rice
½ cup thinly sliced green onion
Soy sauce, to taste
Black pepper

In a small bowl, soak mushrooms in 2 cups hot water until soft, 20 to 30 minutes. Lift mushrooms out with a slotted spoon. Cut off and discard stems and slice caps into thin strips. Add enough water to soaking liquid to make 2 cups and set aside.

In a medium saucepan, combine celery, garlic, and ¼ cup water. Bring to a simmer, covered, over moderate heat and simmer until vegetables are softened, about 5 minutes. Stir in rice, mushrooms, and 2 cups reserved liquid. Bring to a boil over high heat. Cover and reduce heat to lowest setting. Cook until rice is tender and all liquid has been absorbed, about 45 minutes. Remove from heat and stir in green onions with a fork. Season to taste with soy sauce and black pepper.

| TIP |
| --- |
| Dried mushrooms keep practically forever in an airtight glass jar. Keep them on hand to add depth of flavor to soups, pasta sauces, and grain dishes. They may seem expensive by weight, but a little goes a long way. When you don't need pretty slices, you can economize by buying the less-expensive packages of dried mushroom pieces instead of whole caps. |

*Serving size: 1½ cups*
*Calories: 362*
*Fat: 2.8 g*
*Cholesterol: 0 mg*
*Carbohydrate: 76.0 g*
*Protein: 8.0 g*
*Sodium: 127.8 mg*

# PINEAPPLE COMPOTE WITH CANDIED GINGER

*It's hard to believe that just three ingredients could produce something so delicious. Sautéing the pineapple softens it, caramelizes its sugar, and helps it absorb the complementary flavors of ginger and orange.*

SERVES 4

½ large pineapple
4 teaspoons finely minced candied ginger
1 cup orange juice

Cut the half-pineapple in quarters lengthwise. Cut off and discard the core on each quarter. Carefully slice the flesh away from the rind in one piece, then cut the flesh into ½-inch-thick slices.

In a nonstick skillet over moderate heat, cook the pineapple pieces until lightly caramelized on both sides, about 3 minutes per side. Transfer to a serving platter. When all the pineapple has been browned, add the ginger and the orange juice to the skillet. Raise heat to high and simmer briefly to release the ginger flavor, then pour the mixture over the pineapple. Cover and refrigerate overnight or until very cold. Serve chilled.

*Serving size: 1 cup*
*Calories: 89*
*Fat: 0.3 g*
*Cholesterol: 0 mg*
*Carbohydrate: 22.0 g*
*Protein: 1.4 g*
*Sodium: 3.3 mg*

> **TIP**
> Look for candied ginger in your supermarket's spice rack.

---

**Spinach, Beet, Cucumber, and Red Onion Salad**
**Risotto with Peas, Zucchini, and Sun-Dried Tomatoes**
Toasted Herb Bread
Quick Mango Sherbet and Sliced Kiwi Fruit

Spring fruits and vegetables take center stage in this Italian-accented menu, a dinner pretty enough for company but easy enough for weekday meals. A creamy risotto is the centerpiece, with a cool, crisp salad sprinkled with balsamic vinegar to start. (Or you can also serve the salad with the risotto.) To make the toasted herb bread, brush baguette halves with bottled nonfat Italian salad dressing and sprinkle with minced fresh oregano or parsley. Toast until golden. For the sherbet, follow the recipe for Quick Peach Sherbet (page 141), substituting diced mango for peaches, and serve on a dessert plate or in a compote with sliced kiwi fruit.

The timing: The mango sherbet should be whipped up just before you are ready to eat it, but you must freeze the fruit several hours ahead or overnight. Make the spinach salad up to the point of sprinkling it with balsamic vinegar; set it aside. A risotto won't wait. Expect to sit down to dinner 20 to 25 minutes after you start it. Just before the risotto is finished, prepare the toast and sprinkle balsamic vinegar on the salad.

## SPINACH, BEET, CUCUMBER, AND RED ONION SALAD

*This is a particularly pretty salad of contrasting textures and flavors. To save preparation time, buy bagged spinach leaves already washed and dried and use canned beets. However, the flavor of fresh baked beets is truly superior; do use them when you have the time. You can bake and peel them a day ahead. If you don't have balsamic vinegar, substitute rice vinegar or red wine vinegar.*
SERVES 4

2 bunches fresh beets (about 8 beets), or 2 (15-ounce) cans sliced beets, drained
4 cups fresh spinach leaves
1 small cucumber, peeled and thinly sliced
1 small red onion, thinly sliced and separated into rings
1 tablespoon chopped fresh tarragon, mint, chervil, or parsley
2 teaspoons balsamic vinegar

*If using fresh beets*, remove beet greens and save for another use. Preheat oven to 375 degrees F. Wash beets well and place in a covered baking dish or wrap loosely in heavy-duty aluminum foil. Bake until tender when pierced, about 55 minutes. When cool enough to handle, peel and cut into ⅛-inch-thick slices.

Arrange spinach leaves on a serving platter. Arrange alternating rows of beet and cucumber slices over the spinach. Scatter onion rings over all. Scatter tarragon over the top and sprinkle with balsamic vinegar.

*Serving size: 1 cup spinach, 2 beets,*
*¼ cucumber, ¼ onion*
*Calories: 50*
*Fat: 0.3 g*
*Cholesterol: 0 mg*
*Carbohydrate: 10.1 g*
*Protein: 2.9 g*
*Sodium: 21.7 mg (with fresh beets)*

### TIP

If you have no more than a small sunny spot on a patio, you can grow your own herbs in pots. Start a mini culinary herb garden with the ones you like best: consider rosemary, thyme, oregano, tarragon, sage, mint, dill, parsley, basil, and chives. Even if you can find these fresh herbs in your market, you will save time and money growing them yourself. Their lively aromas enhance soups, sauces, salads, and stews and make up for the missing fat.

You can preserve your homegrown herbs for winter cooking by drying or freezing them. Freezing is the better choice for delicate herbs such as parsley, basil, chives, and chervil. Remove the leaves from the stems and pack the leaves in small plastic bags, putting just enough for one meal in each bag and releasing as much air as possible from the bags. Label the bags and put them all in a larger plastic bag, then freeze. Do not thaw before using.

You can dry sturdy herbs such as rosemary, sage, thyme, and oregano in your microwave. Put four or five stems on a double layer of paper towels and top with a single paper towel. Microwave on high until leaves are dry and crumbly, 2 to 3 minutes. Remove leaves from stems and store in an airtight container.

# RISOTTO WITH PEAS, ZUCCHINI, AND SUN-DRIED TOMATOES

*A creamy risotto is a delicious foundation for showcasing seasonal vegetables—in this case, fresh spring peas and zucchini. Use this recipe as a blueprint for a basic risotto and vary it with whatever vegetables are best at the market: consider chopped cauliflower, asparagus, butternut squash, yellow summer squash, chard, or savoy cabbage. For other risotto ideas, see pages 140 and 270.*

## SERVES 4

6 cups Vegetable Broth, homemade (page 18) or store-bought
1½ cups Arborio rice (page 54)
½ cup diced Roasted Onions (page 22)
¼ cup sun-dried tomatoes (not oil-packed), quartered
1 garlic clove, minced
1½ cups diced zucchini
1 cup green peas, fresh or frozen
½ cup grated nonfat cheese
¼ cup minced parsley
Salt and pepper

Put broth in a saucepan and bring to a simmer; adjust heat to keep liquid barely simmering.

In a saucepan, combine rice, onions, sun-dried tomatoes, garlic, and 3 cups hot broth. Bring mixture to a simmer over moderately high heat, adjust heat to maintain a simmer, and cook, stirring occasionally, until most of the broth has been absorbed, about 10 minutes. Add more hot broth 1 cup at a time, stirring often and waiting until rice has absorbed most of the liquid before adding more. After 7 more minutes, the rice should still be a little firm to the bite, and it should have absorbed about 5 cups total liquid. Add zucchini and peas and cook until they are tender, about 3 minutes more, adding a little more liquid if rice seems underdone or mixture seems dry. Risotto should be creamy, but not soupy. Remove from heat and stir in cheese and parsley. Season with salt and pepper. Serve immediately.

*Serving size: 1¼ cups*
*Calories: 358*

Fat: 0.7 mg
Cholesterol: 0 mg
Carbohydrate: 75.0 g
Protein: 10.5 g
Sodium: 144.0 mg

**Quick Black Bean Soup**
**Mexican Green Rice with Spinach**
**Sliced Okra with Tomatoes and Onions**
Whole Wheat Tortillas
Fresh Pineapple Spears

Mexican food doesn't have to be high-calorie, high-fat, and heavy. This menu shows what it *can* be: zesty, fresh, healthful, and thoroughly satisfying. You can start the meal with a bowl of the black bean soup and then follow it with the rice, braised okra, and tortillas, or you can serve a cup of soup alongside the rice and vegetables. Check the supermarket for whole wheat tortillas with no fat added. They make great "wrappers": spoon a little of the rice and the okra inside and fold up like a burrito. For dessert, offer a platter of chilled pineapple spears.

The timing: Cut the pineapple spears and refrigerate, then start the soup. While the soup is simmering, prepare the rice. About 10 minutes before the rice is done, start the okra. Then wrap the tortillas in damp paper towels, overwrap with aluminum foil, and heat in a moderate oven.

## QUICK BLACK BEAN SOUP

*This thick and hearty soup tastes as if it has simmered for hours, yet it takes only a half-hour to make. Cumin and Tabasco give it a Mexican accent, but you could add some diced chiles, if you like, or omit the heat entirely. On another occasion, serve it with a dollop of salsa and a drizzle of nonfat yogurt.*

SERVES 4

1 cup diced onion
2 garlic cloves, minced
1¼ cups Vegetable Broth, or more to taste, homemade (page 18) or
   store-bought
2 (15-ounce) cans black beans
1 (15-ounce) can diced tomatoes
1 cup diced peeled russet-type baking potato
½ teaspoon dried thyme
½ teaspoon dried cumin
½ teaspoon Tabasco sauce, or to taste

*Garnishes:*
Diced red onion or green onion
Minced cilantro or parsley

Combine onion, garlic, and ¼ cup vegetable broth in a large pot. Bring to a simmer and simmer until onions are softened, about 5 minutes. Add 1 cup of broth, black beans with their juice, tomatoes, potatoes, thyme, and cumin. Bring to a simmer, cover, adjust heat to maintain a simmer, and cook until potatoes are tender, about 25 minutes. Thin soup if necessary with a little more vegetable broth. Add Tabasco. Taste and adjust seasoning. Serve hot, topping each portion with some of the onion and herbs, or pass the garnishes separately at the table.

*Serving size: 1½ cups*
*Calories: 164*
*Fat: 0.7 g*
*Cholesterol: 0 mg*
*Carbohydrate: 32.5 g*
*Protein: 8.6 g*
*Sodium: 578.0 mg*

> **TIP**
>
> Cilantro, the Spanish name for fresh coriander, is a pungent parsley-like herb widely used in Mexican, Indian, and Chinese cooking. Most supermarkets carry it now, a reflection of America's growing interest in ethnic cuisines. It is not universally loved, however. If you are not one of cilantro's fans, substitute parsley.

# Mexican Green Rice with Spinach

*A version of what Mexicans call* arroz verde *(green rice), this fragrant pilaf gets its color and nutrition from chopped spinach added in the final 5 minutes. If you've never cooked basmati rice, here's a good place to start. The long grains cook up fluffy and separate, and they are wonderfully aromatic.*

Serves 4

1 cup diced onion
2 tablespoons minced jalapeño chile (seeds removed)
2 large garlic cloves, minced
¼ cup Vegetable Broth, homemade (page 18) or store-bought
1 cup long-grain basmati rice
½ teaspoon ground cumin
½ teaspoon salt
½ teaspoon black pepper
2 cups chopped fresh spinach
¼ cup chopped cilantro

In a medium saucepan, combine onion, jalapeño, garlic, and vegetable broth. Bring to a simmer, covered, over moderate heat and simmer until vegetables are softened, about 5 minutes. Add rice, cumin, salt, pepper, and 1½ cups water. Bring to a boil over high heat. Cover and reduce heat to lowest setting. Cook 15 minutes. Add spinach and stir it in gently with a fork. Cover and cook until rice is tender and all liquid has been absorbed, about 5 more minutes. Remove from heat. Stir in cilantro gently with a fork.

*Serving size: 1 cup*
*Calories: 149*
*Fat: 0.3 g*
*Cholesterol: 0 mg*
*Carbohydrate: 30.7 mg*
*Protein: 7.1 mg*
*Sodium: 306.0 mg*

| TIP |
| --- |
| For a more elegant presentation, pack the cooked rice into a wet custard cup or individual soufflé cup and unmold onto a dinner plate. |

# SLICED OKRA WITH TOMATOES AND ONIONS

*Okra gets high marks on any nutritional scorecard. It's a good source of vita-min C, B vitamins, and calcium, and a great source of fiber. It also cooks in just a few minutes, a real selling point on some days. You may be able to find fresh okra in summer, but at other times of the year, keep a supply of frozen okra on hand to make quick dishes such as this one.*

## SERVES 4

1 cup Vegetable Broth, homemade (page 18) or store-bought
½ cup chopped onion
2 garlic cloves, minced
1 (28-ounce) can diced tomatoes
1 pound fresh or frozen okra, in ½-inch slices
2 tablespoons chopped fresh oregano or 2 teaspoons dried oregano
½ teaspoon balsamic vinegar
Salt and pepper

In a medium saucepan, combine broth, onion, and garlic. Bring to a simmer over moderately high heat and simmer 3 minutes. Stir in toma-toes, okra (still frozen is okay), oregano, balsamic vinegar, and salt and pepper to taste. Return to a simmer, cover, and reduce heat to low. Cook until okra is tender but not mushy, about 8 minutes.

*Serving size: 1 cup*
*Calories: 50*
*Fat: 0.3 g*
*Cholesterol: 0 mg*
*Carbohydrate: 10.5 g*
*Protein: 2.4 g*
*Sodium: 26.1 mg (with no salt added)*

---

**TIP**

Mellow balsamic vinegar helps to moderate the acidic character of canned tomatoes. If you don't have it, substitute ½ teaspoon sugar.

---

**Creamy Split Pea Soup**
Rye Crackers
**Baked Potatoes with Herbed Cheese**
Steamed Broccoli Spears
Fresh Cherries and Apricots

Sometimes nothing is more inviting for dinner than a comforting bowl of soup and a plump baked potato. Put some crisp rye crackers on the table to go with the soup and serve the potato with a creamy herbed topping and steamed fresh broccoli. Nature makes dessert: a bowl of sweet ripe cherries and apricots.

The timing: Start the potato first if you are baking it in a conventional oven, then make the soup. Prepare the herbed cheese while the soup simmers, and trim the broccoli. Remove the broccoli ends if they are tough or woody. Slit the stalks partway up so they cook as quickly as the florets. Place the stalks in a bamboo steamer or collapsible metal steamer but don't start cooking them until you have finished eating your soup. Then steam them over boiling salted water until crisp-tender.

## Creamy Split Pea Soup

*You'll want to make this hearty, homey soup often, especially on the rainy days that spring so often brings. For variety, make it with yellow split peas or even lentils. Leftovers? Add cooked pasta or rice the next day and a pinch of curry powder; reheat, then top each portion with a drizzle of nonfat yogurt. Note that the soup tends to separate as it stands; just whisk it and it will become thick and smooth again.*

FROM RUTH RENIER OF WEST DES MOINES, IOWA:
*Donald and Ruth Renier are participants in the Ornish program at Mercy Hospital Medical Center/Iowa Heart Center in Des Moines, Iowa. Ruth began cooking Ornish food after Don had his heart attack and before the program began in Iowa. Since then, Don has lost about 50 pounds. Ruth says she has noticed that food tastes fresher, that you can actually taste the food instead of everything added to it.*

*Everyday Cooking with Dr. Dean Ornish*

"Look at your old favorite recipes as a challenge," says Ruth. "You'll be surprised at how good they will turn out. With all the new products on the market now, fat-free cooking is a lot easier than it used to be."

"I gave a talk to one of the new groups joining the Ornish program in Iowa," adds Don. "They were shocked to hear me say, 'I am happy I had a heart attack.' I went on to explain that that made me join the Ornish program, and my life has changed so much for the better. I handle stress much better, I have lost 5½ inches in my waist, and at age sixty, I feel better than I did at twenty. I have more energy and have actually learned to breathe again."

SERVES 4

1 cup finely diced yellow onion
1 cup finely diced celery
2 garlic cloves, minced
8¼ cups Vegetable Broth, homemade (page 18) or store-bought
2 cups dried green split peas
1 cup diced carrots
2 teaspoons minced fresh thyme, or 1 teaspoon dried thyme
¼ cup minced parsley
Salt and pepper

In a large saucepan, combine onion, celery, garlic, and ¼ cup vegetable broth. Bring to a simmer, covered, over moderate heat and simmer until vegetables are softened, about 5 minutes. Add split peas and remaining 8 cups broth. Bring to a boil, cover, adjust heat to maintain a simmer and cook until peas begin to soften, about 30 minutes. Add carrots and thyme. Cover and simmer until carrots are tender and peas are very soft, about 20 minutes. Remove from heat and stir in parsley. Season to taste with salt and pepper.

> **TIP**
>
> Leftover split pea soup, which tends to thicken as it stands, can also be pureed or mashed to make a spread for toast or warm bread. Bean purees also make flavorful, low-fat spreads for bread. Use canned beans, cooked dried beans, or frozen lima beans. Blend in a food processor or blender with some of their cooking liquid until smooth. Season with salt, pepper, minced garlic, and herbs. Spread on fat-free crackers, matzo, pita crisps, or toasted baguette rounds and top with a dot of nonfat sour cream or salsa, if desired. Cannellini beans, chickpeas, black beans, lentils, split peas, and lima beans are good choices.

*Serving size: 2 cups*
*Calories: 376*
*Fat: 5.5 g*
*Cholesterol: 0 mg*
*Carbohydrate: 69.0 g*
*Protein: 26.0 g*
*Sodium: 95.3 mg (with no salt added)*

## BAKED POTATOES WITH HERBED CHEESE

*If you don't like cilantro, substitute basil, parsley, dill, or another fresh herb of your choice.*

### SERVES 4

4 large russet-type baking potatoes
1⅓ cups nonfat cottage cheese or nonfat ricotta cheese
¼ cup minced green onion
¼ cup chopped cilantro
1 tablespoon lemon juice
Salt and pepper

Preheat oven to 425 degrees F.

Prick potatoes in several places with a fork. Bake until tender when pierced with a knife, about 1 hour. Alternatively, prick potatoes and microwave on high for 6 to 8 minutes per potato, turning occasionally.

In a medium bowl, combine cottage cheese, green onion, cilantro, and lemon juice. Stir to blend. Season to taste with salt and pepper.

To serve, cut an "X" in the top of each potato, gently squeeze open and fluff the interior with a

### TIP

Some people have a harder time staying on a low-fat diet than others, but the reasons may not be what you think. In a Seattle survey of women on low-fat diets, many of the backsliders had two factors in common: they had erratic eating patterns and frequently missed meals; and they did not have full responsibility for choosing and preparing their meals. The lesson? Make mealtimes important, a highlight of your day, and keep a well-stocked pantry (page 25) so you can make quick low-fat meals if need be. The easy recipes in this book can help you take control of meal preparation, or they can help whoever does the shopping and cooking at your house to support your goals.

fork. Top each potato with ⅓ cup of the cheese mixture and serve immediately.

*Serving size: 1 potato with ⅓ cup topping*
*Calories: 218*
*Fat: 0.2 g*
*Cholesterol: 3.8 mg*
*Carbohydrate: 40.5 g*
*Protein: 14.7 g*
*Sodium: 59.2 mg (with no salt added)*

## Hearts of Romaine with Marinated Artichokes
## Whole Wheat Spaghetti Marinara with Spinach
## Roasted Garlic Toast
Chilled Papaya Fans with Lemon

You can have a dinner such as this one at a casual Italian restaurant, or you can make it yourself for a fraction of the cost, with little effort and no added fat. Start with a crisp salad using the pale, inner leaves of romaine, red pepper, and baby artichoke hearts. Follow it with whole wheat pasta tossed with a marinara sauce that gets a nutritional boost from spinach. Instead of traditional garlic toast, serve the California version—a basket of toast and, for each diner, a whole head of roasted garlic. The soft, mild cloves slip right out of their skins and can be spread on the toast like butter. To complete the meal, offer fresh papaya fans: halve, seed, and peel the papayas; then turn each half rounded side up and make several lengthwise slices, up to but not through the stem end. Press gently on the papaya to spread it out like a fan.

The timing: Put the garlic in the oven to roast about 2 hours before dinnertime; the heads take 1½ to 2 hours to cook. You can make them several hours ahead and serve at room temperature. Or see page 93 for an alternative cooking method. Marinate the artichoke hearts. Make the marinara sauce. Prepare the papaya fans and refrigerate. When the garlic comes out of the oven, raise the oven temperature and make the toasts. Assemble the salad just before serving. Cook the pasta and gently reheat the marinara sauce when you have finished the salad.

# HEARTS OF ROMAINE WITH MARINATED ARTICHOKES

*You've probably had those high-fat (and high-cost) marinated artichokes in jars. Here's an alternative: a nonfat version that you can keep on hand for snacks, salads, and sandwiches. These tender herbed artichokes will keep in the refrigerator for up to 3 days.*

SERVES 4

**Marinated Artichoke Hearts:**

24 fresh baby artichokes (about 1 to 1½ ounces each), or 2 (9-ounce) packages frozen artichoke hearts

2 lemons, halved

1 teaspoon salt

⅔ cup bottled nonfat Italian salad dressing

2 tablespoons chopped fresh parsley

2 heads romaine lettuce

1 roasted red bell pepper, peeled and sliced in thin strips (see Tip, below)

Make marinated artichoke hearts: *If using fresh artichokes*, fill a medium bowl with cold water and add the juice of ½ lemon. Peel back the outer leaves on each artichoke until they break off at the base. Keep removing leaves until you reach the pale green "heart." Cut about ⅓ inch off the top of the heart to remove the pointed tips. Cut away any stem. Trim the base to remove any dark green parts. Immediately rub each heart all over with lemon to prevent browning, using two of the remaining lemon halves. Drop the hearts into the bowl of water. In a medium saucepan, bring 4 cups water to a boil over high heat. Add salt and the juice of the remaining lemon half.

> **TIP**
>
> You can use bottled roasted bell peppers or pimientos for this dish, but here's how to make your own. Place peppers under a preheated broiler, over a charcoal fire, or directly on a gas stove-top burner and cook peppers on all sides until skin blackens and blisters. Transfer to a paper or plastic bag, close, and set aside until peppers are cool. Peel them with your fingers; the skin will slip right off. Try not to rinse them or you will wash away the flavor. Scrape off any stubborn black bits with a small knife. Halve and remove seeds, ribs, and stem. Slice thinly.

Drain artichokes and add to boiling water. Cook until tender when pierced with a knife, about 10 minutes. Drain and pat dry. When cool enough to handle, cut each artichoke in half lengthwise.

*If using frozen artichokes,* thaw them and pat them dry. Cut in half if whole.

In a small bowl, combine artichoke halves, dressing, and parsley. Toss gently. Let fresh artichokes cool.

Pull off all the dark green outer leaves of the lettuce, reserving for another use. Use only the pale green inner leaves (the "heart"). Each heart should weigh 6 to 8 ounces. Cut off the core, leaving the leaves whole. Rinse well with cold water and pat thoroughly dry.

Arrange romaine hearts on a large serving platter in a sunburst pattern. Using a slotted spoon to lift them out of the marinade, arrange artichokes at the base of the hearts. Crisscross strips of red pepper over the romaine leaves, then drizzle the leaves with the remaining artichoke marinade.

*Serving size: ½ head romaine, 6 artichoke hearts, ¼ red bell pepper,*
   *¼ of the dressing*
Calories: 98
Fat: 0.5 g
Cholesterol: 0 mg
Carbohydrate: 20.7 g
Protein: 6.1 g
Sodium: 270.0 mg

> **TIP**
>
> An aluminum or iron pot can discolor artichokes; cook them in a nonreactive pot, such as enameled cast iron or stainless steel.

# WHOLE WHEAT SPAGHETTI MARINARA WITH SPINACH

*High in vitamins A and C and folacin, fresh spinach gives this tomato sauce a nutritional lift. Now that so many supermarkets carry stemmed, washed, and dried spinach leaves in bags or in their salad bars, you can add them easily to salads, soups, and pasta sauces such as this one. On another occasion, omit the spinach and serve this sauce over spinach pasta (made without eggs).*

SERVES 4

*Marinara Sauce:*
¼ cup Vegetable Broth, homemade (page 18) or store-bought
1 onion, chopped
2 cloves garlic, minced
1 (28-ounce) can diced tomatoes or crushed tomatoes in puree
¼ cup tomato paste
½ teaspoon dried oregano
Salt and pepper

1 pound whole wheat spaghetti
2 cups tightly packed stemmed small spinach leaves (about 4 ounces)
¼ cup grated nonfat Parmesan cheese

Make marinara sauce: In a large skillet, bring vegetable broth to a boil over moderately high heat. Add onion and garlic and simmer until onion is softened, about 5 minutes. Add tomatoes, tomato paste, and oregano. Stir to blend. Bring to a boil, then reduce heat and simmer gently, stirring occasionally, until mixture is thick and tasty, about 10 minutes. Season to taste with salt and pepper.

Bring a large pot of salted water to a boil over high heat. Add spaghetti and cook according to package directions until al dente.

While pasta is cooking, add spinach leaves to marinara sauce and simmer, stirring, until they wilt, about 1 minute. Keep sauce warm over lowest heat.

Drain spaghetti, then transfer to a large warm bowl. Add sauce and toss well. Serve on four warm plates, topping each portion with 1 tablespoon of cheese.

*Serving size: 2 cups pasta, 1 cup sauce*
*Calories: 465*
*Fat: 3.7 g*
*Cholesterol: 3.9 mg*
*Carbohydrate: 95.9 mg*
*Protein: 21.3 g*
*Sodium: 702.9 mg*

### TIP

The basic marinara sauce in this recipe can be enhanced in many ways. Add sliced mushrooms, bell peppers, frozen artichoke hearts, broccoli or cauliflower florets, or sliced zucchini to create a new pasta sauce. The sauce keeps, refrigerated, for a couple of days, or you can freeze it for up to 6 months in quantities suitable for your family's meals.

*Everyday Cooking with Dr. Dean Ornish*

# ROASTED GARLIC TOAST

*Whole garlic cloves baked slowly become so soft and mild that you can spread them on bread like butter. Choose heads that are firm and heavy for their size. They do take a long time to cook, but it is unattended time. Go work in the garden or take a walk while they're cooking, and when you return, the house will smell marvelous.*

SERVES 4

4 heads garlic
¼ teaspoon dried thyme
¼ teaspoon salt
Pepper
1 French baguette, in ½-inch-thick slices

> **TIP**
>
> Why not bake several garlic heads while you're at it? They keep well for two or three days in the refrigerator and are good cold.

Preheat oven to 300 degrees F. Lightly spray a small baking dish with nonstick spray (see Tip, page 248).

With a sharp knife, slice ½ inch from the top (not the root end) of each garlic head. Rub the heads of garlic with your hands to remove some of the loose papery skin, taking care not to separate the cloves.

Place in baking dish cut side up. Sprinkle with thyme, salt, and pepper to taste. Add ¼ cup water, cover and bake until the garlic cloves are very tender when pierced, 1½ to 2 hours. Set aside.

Raise oven temperature to 375 degrees. Toast baguette slices until dry, about 10 minutes. Put toasts in a basket on the table. Serve each diner a whole head of roasted garlic. To eat, squeeze the soft, mild cloves from their skins onto the toasts, or use a small knife to scoop the soft garlic out of the skins and spread it thickly on toast.

> **TIP**
>
> Here's another method for making garlic that is so soft and mild, you can eat it like butter. Separate four heads of garlic into individual cloves. Discard any cloves that are too small to bother with. Peel the remaining cloves. (This is tedious, but the results are worth it.) In a small saucepan, combine the peeled cloves and ½ cup vegetable broth. Bring to a simmer over high heat, cover, and reduce heat to maintain a very gentle simmer. Cook until garlic is tender when pierced but not mushy, 18 to 22 minutes. Check once or twice during cooking, and add 2 to 3 tablespoons more broth if most of the broth has evaporated. And there you have it: unbelievably delicious, soft-as-butter garlic cloves, which you can keep in the refrigerator for a couple of days.

Serving size: ¼ of the baguette, 1 head garlic
Calories: 329
Fat: 3.4 g
Cholesterol: 0 mg
Carbohydrate: 63.5 g
Protein: 11.0 g
Sodium: 1,174.0 mg

Hearts of Butter Lettuce with Julienned Beets
**Spring Vegetable Ragout**
**Steamed Bulgur with Lemon Zest**
Crusty French Bread
**Warm Whole Wheat Crepes with Strawberries and**
**Frozen Vanilla Yogurt**

When several vegetables are braised together, each lends its own flavor to the pot and takes up flavor from the others. The result is much more than the sum of its parts, as the elegant spring vegetable stew at the heart of this menu shows. Serve it with fluffy steamed bulgur and a crusty baguette for soaking up the juices, and precede it with a simple, springtime salad: tender butter or Bibb lettuce hearts topped with beets. Buy canned beets if you're in a hurry, or bake them (page 79) if you're not. Dress them with bottled nonfat Italian salad dressing or a splash of balsamic vinegar. On a leisurely weekend evening, make strawberry crepes for dessert; if you're pressed for time, serve bowls of sliced strawberries with a dollop of frozen vanilla yogurt.

The timing: Make the crepe batter, cook the crepes, and make the strawberry puree. Dress the beets and wash and dry the lettuce hearts; set aside. Prepare the vegetables for the ragout, but don't begin cooking it yet. Steam the bulgur. While it's cooking, proceed with the ragout. Assemble the salad just before you're ready to serve it so the lettuces don't wilt. After dinner, assemble and heat the crepes.

## SPRING VEGETABLE RAGOUT

*The French call them* primeurs—*the first tender vegetables of spring—and they braise them together with just a hint of an herb to accent their sweet-*

ness. *This beautiful variation on that theme will make you wish it was spring year-round. When it's not, however, you can use this recipe as a guide for braising other seasonal vegetables. You might try a summer ragout, for example, with potatoes, zucchini, peppers, and corn. Or cut the turnips, carrots, and sugar snap peas in small pieces and serve over pasta to make an easy pasta primavera.*

## SERVES 4

½ cup Vegetable Broth, homemade (page 18) or store-bought
3 turnips (about ¾ pound), peeled and cut into 8 wedges
6 shallots, peeled and left whole
3 small carrots, peeled and sliced diagonally ¼ inch thick
1 cup sugar snap peas, strings removed
6 mushrooms, thickly sliced
1½ cups fresh green peas or thawed frozen peas
2 teaspoons chopped fresh mint
½ teaspoon lemon juice
¼ teaspoon salt

In a medium saucepan, bring broth to a boil over moderately high heat. Add turnips, shallots, and carrots and return to a boil. Cover, reduce heat to low, and cook 5 minutes.

Gently stir in snap peas, mushrooms, fresh peas (if using), mint, lemon juice, and salt. Cover and cook until vegetables are crisp-tender, about 5 minutes. If using thawed frozen peas, add them for the final 2 minutes.

*Serving size: 1 cup*
*Calories: 156*
*Fat: 0.8 g*
*Cholesterol: 0 mg*
*Carbohydrate: 31.8 g*
*Protein: 7.9 g*
*Sodium: 261.0 mg*

| TIP |
| --- |
| To keep fresh mint or parsley in good condition for several days, stand the stems in a tall glass of water and cover the leaves with a plastic bag. Refrigerate, changing the water every couple of days. |

# Steamed Bulgur with Lemon Zest

*When you add the green onions and lemon zest to the hot steamed bulgur, breathe deeply. The aroma will be absolutely heavenly.*

## Serves 4

2 cups Vegetable Broth, homemade (page 18) or store-bought
1 cup bulgur
¼ cup finely minced green onions
1 teaspoon grated lemon zest
Salt and pepper

In a medium saucepan, bring the vegetable broth to a boil over high heat. Add the bulgur, stir well, then cover and reduce the heat to maintain a gentle simmer. Cook 15 minutes, then remove from heat and let stand, covered, for 5 minutes.

Add green onions and lemon zest and fluff bulgur with a fork. Season to taste with salt and pepper.

*Serving size: approximately ¾ cup*
*Calories: 132*
*Fat: 0.4 g*
*Cholesterol: 0 mg*
*Carbohydrate: 29.6 g*
*Protein: 4.9 g*
*Sodium: 8.0 mg (with no salt added)*

---

**TIP**

Be sure to mince the green onions fine so they "cook" in the heat of the hot bulgur.

---

# Warm Whole Wheat Crepes with Strawberries and Frozen Vanilla Yogurt

*This recipe makes twice as many crepes as you need for four people, but they freeze beautifully. Or refrigerate them and use them the next day for breakfast. Just warm the crepes in a nonstick skillet and wrap them around chopped fresh fruit, or spread lightly with sugar-free jam. Note that the recipe includes only enough strawberry filling and frozen yogurt topping for four.*

## Makes 8 Crepes • Serves 4, with 4 Leftover Crepes

1 pint strawberries, hulled and quartered
1 teaspoon sugar
1 cup nonfat milk
½ cup liquid egg substitute
½ teaspoon vanilla extract
6 tablespoons whole wheat flour
¼ cup unbleached all-purpose flour
Pinch salt
½ cup nonfat frozen vanilla yogurt

Puree ¾ cup of the strawberries in a food processor or blender until smooth. Transfer to a bowl and stir in sugar. You should have about ½ cup strawberry puree.

In another bowl, combine remaining strawberries with ¼ cup strawberry puree and toss to coat.

In a large bowl, whisk together milk, egg substitute, and vanilla. In another bowl, stir together whole wheat flour, all-purpose flour, and salt. Add dry ingredients to wet ingredients and whisk lightly, just until there are no lumps.

Spray a 10-inch nonstick skillet lightly with nonstick spray (see Tip, page 251) and set over moderate heat. When hot, add ¼ cup of batter. Swirl skillet so batter covers the bottom of the skillet evenly and goes just a little way up the sides. Cook until golden, about 1 to 1½ minutes. With a rubber spatula, loosen the crepe around the edges, then slip the spatula underneath the crepe and flip it. Cook the other side until golden. Transfer to a paper towel to cool. Repeat with remaining batter. (You only need to spray the skillet once, for the first crepe.) When crepes are cool, you can stack them directly on top of each other.

Preheat oven to 400 degrees F. To assemble crepes, lay one crepe out flat on a work surface. Put one quarter of the strawberries in the center of the crepe. Fold the bottom up over the filling, then fold the sides in and the top down. Put seam side down on a baking sheet. Repeat with remaining crepes. Top each crepe with 1 tablespoon strawberry sauce and bake until warm, about 5 minutes. Serve immediately, topping each crepe with 2 tablespoons of frozen yogurt.

*Serving size: 1 crepe*
*Calories: 126*
*Fat: 0.6 g*
*Cholesterol: 1.0 mg*
*Carbohydrate: 25.4 g*
*Protein: 5.8 g*
*Sodium: 51.5 mg*

**TIP**

Crepes make terrific wrappers for a lot of different foods. For breakfast, fill them with scrambled eggs (made with liquid egg substitute) or warm applesauce. For dinner, roll them around stir-fried vegetables, sautéed mushrooms, or the creamy stroganoff filling on page 177. For an elegant dessert, spread the crepes lightly with unsweetened chestnut puree sweetened with a little vanilla sugar (see Tip, page 188) or honey, roll and bake until warm, then serve with a small spoonful of nonfat frozen vanilla yogurt.

**Wild Rice and White Bean Salad**
**Carrot-Cauliflower Soup with Tarragon**
Warm Multigrain Bread
**Sour Cherry Pudding**

W ith a substantial salad to start and a basket of chewy bread, a vegetable soup makes a satisfying supper. Satisfaction comes not only from a satiated appetite, but from the variety of colors, flavors, and textures that make the meal. Note how successfully this menu contrasts color and texture to please the senses—putting a creamy soup after a multitextured salad, for example. Try to plan these juxtapositions in your own menus, and you will find your meals are doubly appealing.

The timing: Begin by cooking the wild rice. While it cooks, make dessert. As the rice cools, prepare the soup. Assemble the rice and bean salad while the soup simmers. Serve soup and salad together or as separate courses.

# WILD RICE AND WHITE BEAN SALAD

*The bright colors of this salad make it a mouthwatering sight. And it tastes as good as it looks. To dress it up a little, line the serving bowl or salad plates with hearts of butter lettuce.*

SERVES 4

⅔ cup wild rice
1¾ cups Vegetable Broth, homemade (page 18) or store-bought
Salt
1 cup small white beans, home-cooked or canned (rinsed if canned)
¾ cup thawed frozen peas
½ cup finely diced red bell pepper
¼ cup thinly sliced green onions
3 tablespoons bottled nonfat Italian salad dressing
1 teaspoon lemon juice
⅛ teaspoon salt

Rinse wild rice in a sieve or colander with cold running water. In a 1½-quart saucepan, bring vegetable broth and 1¾ cups water to a boil over high heat. Salt lightly. Add rice, stir once, and boil, uncovered, until rice is tender, about 35 minutes. Drain, reserving broth for another use, if desired. Set rice aside to cool.

In a medium bowl, combine cooled wild rice, beans, peas, bell pepper, green onions, dressing, lemon juice, and salt to taste. Toss gently. Serve at once or refrigerate up to 24 hours.

*Serving size: 1 cup*
*Calories: 209*
*Fat: 0.6 g*
*Cholesterol: 0 mg*
*Carbohydrate: 41.5 g*
*Protein: 10.4 g*
*Sodium: 397.0 mg*

| TIP |
| --- |
| Because this salad stands up well over time, it's a good choice to take to a potluck or on a picnic. |

# CARROT-CAULIFLOWER SOUP WITH TARRAGON

*Fresh tarragon is a wonderful complement for both carrots and cauliflower; it's worth the trouble to find it. (On another occasion, try tarragon vinegar on steamed carrots or cauliflower.) Leftover soup would be delicious for lunch the next day with whole grain toast and a spinach salad; or add some cooked rice before reheating.*

FROM ELIZABETH KAPSTEIN, CHEF,
*Dr. Ornish Program for Reversing Heart Disease at Beth Israel Medical Center, New York, New York.*
SERVES 4

1 cup finely diced onion
2¼ cups Vegetable Broth, plus more if needed, homemade (page 18) or store-bought
1½ pounds carrots, peeled and cut in ½ inch dice
¾ pound russet-type baking potatoes, peeled and cut in ½-inch dice
1 pound cauliflower, in small florets
2 teaspoons chopped fresh tarragon
Salt and pepper

In a large saucepan, combine onion and ¼ cup vegetable broth. Bring to a simmer, covered, over moderate heat and simmer until onion is softened, about 5 minutes. Add carrots, potatoes, another 2 cups vegetable broth, and 2 cups water. Bring to a boil. Cover, adjust heat to maintain a simmer, and cook 5 minutes. Add cauliflower, cover, and simmer until all the vegetables are tender, 15 to 20 minutes. Cool slightly, then puree in food processor or blender until smooth. Return soup to pot. Stir in tarragon. Thin, if desired, with additional vegetable broth. Season to taste with salt and pepper. Reheat and serve.

*Serving size: 2 cups*
*Calories: 126*
*Fat: 0.4 g*
*Cholesterol: 0 mg*
*Carbohydrate: 28.9 g*
*Protein: 3.9 g*
*Sodium: 59.8 mg*

| TIP |
| --- |
| Cauliflower is available in good quality and quantity year-round, and it's a great nonfat snack. Enjoy it raw or blanched, with **Hummus** (page 152) or **Spinach and Cucumber Raita** (page 241). Chop it and add it to stir-fries and salads. And for variety, try the green broccoflower, the pale green cauliflower-broccoli hybrid. |

# SOUR CHERRY PUDDING

*This old-fashioned, homestyle dessert can be mixed up in one bowl in minutes. Put it in the oven when you sit down to dinner and enjoy it freshly baked. Be sure to use unsweetened water-packed cherries, not pie filling.*

FROM CYNTHIA J. KELLEY OF PLATTSMOUTH, NEBRASKA:
*Mike and Cynthia Kelley are in the Ornish program at Immanuel Medical Center/The Heart Institute in Omaha, Nebraska. Mike has heart disease, but both participate in the program. Mike's goal is to get off all medications; so far, he has cut them in half. "I can't believe Mike is the same man," says Cynthia. "He couldn't even walk up the stairs without angina. Now he feels so much better and has so much energy. He keeps a regular routine of working out at work."*

*Cynthia adapted this Depression-era family recipe. She says it is delicious made with other fruits; peaches are a favorite.*

MAKES ONE 9-INCH PUDDING

1 cup unbleached all-purpose flour
½ cup sugar
2 teaspoons baking powder
½ teaspoon salt
⅔ cup nonfat milk
1 (15-ounce) can sour pie cherries, drained

Preheat oven to 350 degrees F.

In a medium bowl, combine flour, sugar, baking powder, and salt. Stir to combine. Add milk and stir just until blended.

Pour half the cherries into a 9-inch cake pan, either nonstick or sprayed lightly with nonstick spray (see Tip, page 251). Pour all the batter over the cherries to cover completely. Scatter remaining cherries over the top of the batter. Bake until a toothpick inserted in the center comes out clean, 35 to 40 minutes. Serve warm (not hot) or cool.

*Serving size: ⅛ of the pudding*
*Calories: 150*
*Fat: 0.3 g*
*Cholesterol: 0.6 mg*
*Carbohydrate: 34.5 g*
*Protein: 3.4 g*
*Sodium: 167.0 mg*

> **TIP**
> Fresh pitted cherries or quartered ripe apricots would be even better than the canned cherries in this dessert.

### Julienned Spinach Salad with Jicama and Oranges
### Southwest Pizza
### Frosty Pineapple Shake
🍅

Pizza with beans? Yes, and lower your eyebrows. It's truly delicious. Created by French chef Jean-Marc Fullsack, the Southwest pizza is proof positive that pizza has much more potential than Italians realize. Top it with beans, roasted onions, chiles, cheese, and tomato and see if you don't agree. A salad of fresh spinach with crunchy jicama and orange slices makes a refreshing companion. Finish the meal with a frosty shake—a fresh pineapple shake, in this case, but you can adapt the recipe to many other fruits.

The timing: Prepare the pizza dough and, while it rises, make the pizza topping. Peel and slice the oranges for the salad and set aside. Freeze the pineapple for the shake; chop and refrigerate remaining pineapple as recipe indicates. When the dough is ready, apply the pizza topping and bake. While the pizza is baking, complete the salad. Make the shake just before you are ready for dessert.

## JULIENNED SPINACH SALAD WITH JICAMA AND ORANGES

*Juicy, colorful, and crunchy, this salad would fit in any meal with a Mexican or Southwestern flavor. You could add some cucumber slices or sliced red onion, if you like, or replace the spinach with watercress. The zesty orange-basil dressing is versatile, too: try it on sliced beets or melon, replacing the basil with chopped tarragon or mint for a different character.*

SERVES 4

*Orange-Basil Dressing:*
2 tablespoons freshly squeezed orange juice
1 teaspoon seasoned rice vinegar
½ teaspoon Dijon mustard
1 teaspoon chopped fresh basil
Salt and pepper

2 navel oranges
4 cups shredded fresh spinach leaves
½ pound peeled jicama, in ½-inch dice (see Tip below)

Make orange-basil dressing: In a small bowl, whisk together orange juice, vinegar, and mustard. Stir in basil. Season to taste with salt and pepper. Use at once or refrigerate up to 24 hours.

Slice the ends off the oranges and set them on one end on a cutting board. Using a sharp knife, cut away the peel (the orange rind and white pith) by carefully slicing from top to bottom all the way around the orange. Slice oranges crosswise into rounds.

Arrange spinach on a large serving platter. Arrange orange slices in a circle on top of the spinach, overlapping the slices slightly. Scatter jicama over the top. Drizzle with orange-basil dressing.

*Serving size: 1 cup salad,*
  *2 teaspoons dressing*
*Calories: 56*
*Fat: 0.4 g*
*Cholesterol: 0 mg*
*Carbohydrate: 12.7 g*
*Protein: 2.5 g*
*Sodium: 66.1 mg (with no salt added)*

---

**TIP**

Jicama is a sweet, crunchy root vegetable that looks like a large brown-skinned turnip. Underneath the ugly skin, however, the flesh is creamy white and as firm, crisp, and juicy as an apple. If you can't find it, substitute sliced radishes.

---

## SOUTHWEST PIZZA

*You'll never find it in Naples, but the Southwest Pizza—with its topping of beans, cheese, chiles, and fresh tomato—may become a pizza classic. If you're pressed for time, use the whole wheat pizza dough recipe on page 136, which is made with quick-rising yeast. Note that this recipe makes two large pizzas. If you are only cooking for one or two people, you may want to save half the dough for a pizza the following night. See directions accompanying Pizza with Roasted Eggplant and Peppers (page 136) for how to do that. If you want to bake both pizzas and are fortunate enough to have two ovens, bake them in separate ovens for best results. Otherwise, bake the pizzas on two racks of one oven, switching their position halfway through.*

MAKES TWO 12-INCH ROUNDS • SERVES 4

---

*Pizza Dough:*
2 teaspoons active dry yeast
1 cup warm water
2½ to 3 cups unbleached all-purpose flour
1 teaspoon sugar
¾ teaspoon salt

*Topping:*
1 cup diced Roasted Onions (page 22)
1 cup home-cooked or canned pinto or black beans (no added fat), drained
2 tablespoons canned diced mild green chiles
1 teaspoon minced garlic
½ teaspoon ground cumin
1 cup grated nonfat cheese, such as Monterey Jack, mozzarella, or a combination
3 medium tomatoes, sliced ¼ inch thick
1 teaspoon dried oregano
Salt and pepper
2 tablespoons chopped cilantro (optional)

To make dough by hand: Sprinkle yeast over warm water in a large bowl. Let stand 2 minutes to soften; whisk with a fork and let stand 10 minutes until bubbly. Stir together flour, sugar, and salt. Add flour mixture to water gradually, stirring until mixture forms a dough. You may not need all the flour. Turn dough out onto a lightly floured surface and knead until smooth and silky, 8 to 10 minutes. Transfer to a bowl, cover with plastic wrap, and let rise in a warm place until doubled, 1½ to 2 hours. Punch down and let rise again in a warm place for 30 minutes.

To make dough in the food processor: Sprinkle yeast over warm water in a small bowl. Let stand 2 minutes to soften; whisk with a fork and let stand 10 minutes until bubbly. Put 3 cups flour, sugar, and salt in work bowl of food processor fitted with steel blade. Pulse to blend. With machine running, add yeast mixture through the feed tube. Mixture should form a dough. Add a little more water if needed to form a dough. Knead dough in processor 2 minutes, then transfer to a bowl, cover with plastic wrap, and let rise in a warm place until doubled, 1½ to 2 hours. Punch down and let rise again in a warm place for 30 minutes.

Preheat oven to 450 degrees F.

Transfer dough to a lightly floured work surface. Divide it into two equal pieces. Roll each piece into a round about 12 inches in diameter. Transfer the rounds to two pizza pans or heavy baking sheets. Fold the edges over all the way around to make a rim.

Combine roasted onions, beans, chiles, garlic, and cumin. Divide the mixture between the two rounds and spread it evenly over the dough's surface. Sprinkle each round with cheese. Arrange the tomatoes in a single layer atop each round. Top each with oregano, salt, and pepper. Bake until edges are golden brown and topping is sizzling, 15 to 20 minutes. Garnish, if desired, with chopped cilantro.

*Serving size: ½ of one pizza*
*Calories: 501*
*Fat: 2.1 g*
*Cholesterol: 4.4 mg*
*Carbohydrate: 102.3 g*
*Protein: 21.0 g*
*Sodium: 249.0 mg (with no salt added to topping)*

---

**TIP**

If you're not in the mood to make pizza dough from scratch, you can make quick mini pizzas using this same topping on pita bread rounds.

---

## FROSTY PINEAPPLE SHAKE

*Frozen pineapple and nonfat sour cream blend up into a frothy "shake" in seconds. Here, it's poured over chopped fresh pineapple (bananas would also be nice) to make a refreshing finale to a Southwestern meal.*

### SERVES 4

1 small ripe pineapple
½ cup nonfat sour cream
2 tablespoons plus 2 teaspoons sugar

Cut off the leafy pineapple frond. Quarter the pineapple lengthwise. Cut away the cores. Slide a knife between the meat and skin of each quarter to remove the meat in one piece. Cut each peeled quarter into ¼-inch slices. Put 3 cups of the slices on a baking sheet in the freezer and freeze until firm, about 45 minutes.

Chop enough of the remaining pineapple to make 2 cups and set aside. Refrigerate any remaining sliced pineapple for breakfast or a snack.

Put frozen pineapple in a food processor along with sour cream and sugar. Process until smooth and frothy. Put ½ cup of chopped pineapple in each of four balloon wineglasses or compote dishes. Top with the frosty pineapple shake, dividing it evenly among the glasses.

Serving size: ½ cup fruit, ½ cup
   shake
Calories: 143
Fat: 0.88 g
Cholesterol: 0 mg
Carbohydrate: 35.2 g
Protein: 1.8 g
Sodium: 35.2 mg

> ### TIP
>
> How do you find a ripe pineapple? There are a couple of good clues. First and foremost, how does it smell? A ripe pineapple should have a powerful, sweet perfume. Avoid pineapples with no aroma or with a fermenting smell. Also note the color. A high proportion of yellow or golden-orange skin is a good sign that the flesh inside is sweet. Many markets sell already peeled and cored pineapples. These are a time-saver but you do pay a premium for them.

"EASTER BRUNCH"

**Fresh Asparagus Omelets with Herbs**
**New Potatoes Baked in Rock Salt**
**Pear-Ginger Muffins and Blueberry Muffins**
**Layered Spring Fruit Medley**

For many people, holiday meals provoke some of the most treasured childhood memories. There's no denying that these occasions contribute to our spiritual and emotional health by making us feel part of a family or community. But they don't do much for our physical health when they are occasions for overindulging in fat-laden foods.

This menu allows you to celebrate Easter with festive spring dishes that may create new memories and new traditions at your house: plump, golden omelets; creamy potatoes baked in a rock salt crust; tender fruit muffins; and a bowl of sliced fresh fruit that's pretty enough to be your table's centerpiece.

The timing: Make the fruit medley first and refrigerate. Cook the asparagus for the omelets. If you have two ovens, you can bake the potatoes and muffins simultaneously. If you don't, bake the potatoes first. When they're done, reduce the oven temperature and mix and bake the muffins. The potatoes will stay hot in their salt crust. Just before you are ready to eat, make the omelets and crack the potatoes' salt crust.

## FRESH ASPARAGUS OMELETS WITH HERBS

*A nonstick skillet in good condition is essential to success with this recipe. Otherwise, the omelet will stick. This recipe makes two large omelets, which you can make one right after the other; they take only a minute or two. Keep the first one warm in a low oven while you make the second. These big half-domes are puffy and golden on the outside, with bright green asparagus peeking out the edges.*

### MAKES 2 LARGE OMELETS TO SERVE 6

1 cup diced fresh asparagus
3 cups liquid egg substitute
⅓ cup minced fresh chives
⅓ cup minced parsley
1 teaspoon minced fresh tarragon (optional)
½ teaspoon salt
¼ teaspoon pepper

Preheat oven to lowest setting. Bring a pot of salted water to a boil over high heat. Add asparagus and cook just until tender, about 3 minutes. Drain and transfer to ice water to stop the cooking. Drain again and pat dry.

Put 1½ cups of egg substitute in each of two bowls. Add half the chives, parsley, tarragon (if using), salt, and pepper to each bowl. Whisk to blend. Add half the asparagus to each bowl and stir. Over moderately high heat, heat a 10-inch nonstick skillet lightly sprayed with vegetable oil spray. Add the contents of one bowl and raise heat to high. When mixture begins to set around the edges, push them toward the center with a rubber or plastic spatula and let the uncooked egg flow to the outer rim. As that sets, push it toward the center and let more uncooked egg flow to the edges. It should take only 1 to 2 minutes for all the egg to set.

When the egg has set but omelet still looks moist, slide it out onto a warm serving plate, tilting the skillet as you do so that the omelet folds over to make a half-moon. Put omelet in the warm oven and repeat with remaining ingredients. Serve one third of each omelet to each diner.

*Serving size: ⅓ of 1 omelet*
*Calories: 50*
*Fat: 0 g*
*Cholesterol: 0 mg*
*Carbohydrate: 2.1 g*
*Protein: 11.2 g*
*Sodium: 356.0 mg*

---

**TIP**

If you buy large asparagus, peel the stalks with a vegetable peeler before you cook them. Thin asparagus do not need peeling.

---

## SHOPPING FOR NONSTICK COOKWARE

High-quality nonstick cookware and bakeware allow you to cook easily with no added fat. Whether you're cooking pancakes, potatoes, or muffins, the food will release cleanly without sticking. That means easier cleanup, too.

If you bought your nonstick pans several years ago, chances are they are scratched and pitted and no longer releasing foods properly. It may be time to replace them. The good news is that nonstick coatings have greatly improved over the years. They are more durable, with better release ability, and in some cases, they are guaranteed for a lifetime.

Now some of the premium cookware manufacturers like All-Clad and Calphalon are offering their excellent pots and pans with nonstick coatings. The core of these pans is anodized aluminum, a hardened aluminum that conducts heat well, so the pans have no "hot spots." The composition of the coating and the way it's applied vary from manufacturer to manufacturer; be sure to read the companies' literature carefully to compare the features of each brand.

If you buy only one piece of nonstick cookware, make it a 10- or 12-inch skillet (the smaller size if you normally cook for one or two). It's less important to have a nonstick surface in pots used for soups and stews, because these high-moisture foods don't tend to stick. Nevertheless, one nonstick pot is nice to have for chili and thick bean stews. With no added fat, these thick foods can stick in conventional pots if they're not watched carefully and stirred often.

Consider buying a nonstick baking sheet, cake pan, muffin tin, and loaf pan if you enjoy baking. They eliminate the need to use nonstick spray, and you can count on a clean release. The least expensive brand may not be the best long-term buy; look for a brand with a lifetime guarantee on its coating.

Most manufacturers advise you not to use metal utensils with nonstick cookware as they can scratch the coating. Stick with plastic, rubber, or wooden utensils. And follow the manufacturer's directions for cleaning. Most advise you to wash them by hand with soapy water and a soft nylon scrubber. Don't use steel-wool scouring pads or harsh cleansers, which can damage the coating.

## NEW POTATOES BAKED IN ROCK SALT

*Baking potatoes whole in a bed of rock salt seems to seal in and intensify their flavor. It makes a dramatic presentation, too. The salt and egg white mixed together form a hard golden crust that needs to be cracked open with a mallet or the back of a knife. Children will have a fine time searching for the potatoes buried in the salt. Surprisingly, they don't taste salty—just moist and gently perfumed with garlic and rosemary.*

SERVES 6

3 pounds small new potatoes
3 pounds kosher salt
1½ cups egg whites (from approximately 12 eggs)
⅓ cup minced fresh rosemary
12 garlic cloves, whole and unpeeled

Preheat oven to 450 degrees F. Scrub potatoes and set aside. In a large bowl, combine salt, egg whites, rosemary, and garlic. Mix with your hands until well blended. Put a thin layer on the bottom of a deep baking dish large enough to hold the potatoes in one layer. Add the potatoes, then cover them completely with salt. Bake 25 minutes. The salt will turn golden brown and will look like a beautifully risen cake, but it will be quite hard. Unmold the "cake" onto a serving platter or a cutting board. Use a mallet or the back of a knife to break the brittle salt cake open. The potatoes will be nestled inside, steaming hot and lightly dusted with salt. Brush off the salt and serve.

*Serving size: ⅙ of the potatoes*
*Calories: 102*
*Fat: 0.1 g*
*Cholesterol: 0 mg*
*Carbohydrate: 23.6 g*
*Protein: 2.2 g*
*Sodium: 433.8 mg*

**TIP**

You won't regret making more of these potatoes than you need for brunch. Quartered and seasoned with freshly ground black pepper, they make a great finger-food snack.

# PEAR-GINGER MUFFINS AND BLUEBERRY MUFFINS

*From one batter, get two different muffins. Stir blueberries into one half, dried pears and candied ginger into the other half. Of course, you can make them all one flavor if you prefer. Look for dried pears in natural food stores.*

### MAKES 12 MUFFINS

1 cup whole wheat flour
1 cup unbleached all-purpose flour
3 tablespoons sugar
1 tablespoon baking powder
½ teaspoon salt
½ teaspoon ground nutmeg
½ teaspoon ground cinnamon
¼ cup liquid egg substitute or 2 egg whites
1 cup nonfat milk
¼ cup unsweetened applesauce
1 teaspoon vanilla extract
½ cup frozen blueberries
¼ cup finely diced dried pears
1 tablespoon finely chopped candied ginger (see Tip, page 78)

*Topping:*
1 tablespoon sugar
½ teaspoon ground cinnamon

Preheat oven to 375 degrees F. Spray a standard muffin pan (see Tip, page 251) lightly with nonstick spray.

In a medium bowl, combine whole wheat flour, all-purpose flour, sugar, baking powder, salt, nutmeg, and cinnamon. Stir to blend well.

In a small bowl, combine egg substitute, milk, applesauce, and vanilla. Whisk until smooth. Add to dry ingredients. Stir with a fork just until batter is blended; do not overmix.

Put half the batter (about 1¼ cups) in a small bowl and gently stir in the blueberries. Add the pears and ginger to the other half of the batter. Spoon the batter into the prepared muffin cups, filling each cup almost full.

To make topping, stir together sugar and cinnamon. Sprinkle ¼ teaspoon of the mixture over each muffin. Bake until the muffins spring back when touched lightly and the tops are golden, about 15 minutes. Cool in the pan 5 minutes, then remove and serve warm.

*Serving size: 1 muffin*
*Calories: 101*
*Fat: 0.3 g*
*Cholesterol: 0.4 mg*
*Carbohydrate: 21.5 g*
*Protein: 3.7 g*
*Sodium: 114.1 mg*

---

**TIP**

Don't thaw frozen blueberries before you use them, or their color will "bleed" throughout the batter.

---

## LAYERED SPRING FRUIT MEDLEY

*Make this colorful fruit salad the centerpiece of your Easter table. Arrange the fruit in layers in a decorative glass or crystal bowl, then put the bowl in the center of the table where it reminds guests to save room for dessert.*

SERVES 6

2 large mangoes
4 kiwi fruit
1 pint strawberries, hulled and sliced
1½ cups papaya nectar, canned or made from concentrate
1 tablespoon sugar
¾ teaspoon grated fresh ginger (see Tip, page 112)

---

To peel mangoes, cradle them in one hand and, with a small sharp knife, peel the side that's facing up. Carefully slice the flesh away from the pit in lengthwise slices. Dice the slices. Turn the mangoes over and peel, slice, and dice the other side. You should have about 3 cups diced fruit from the two mangoes. Set aside.

Cut the ends off the kiwi fruit, then peel them with a sharp knife or a vegetable peeler. Slice into rounds.

In a pretty glass or crystal bowl, arrange the mango slices on the bottom. Top with the kiwi slices, then the strawberries. Cover with plastic wrap and chill until time for brunch.

In a small bowl, whisk together papaya nectar, sugar, and ginger. Cover and refrigerate. Just before serving, pour the flavored nectar over the fruit, toss gently, and serve on dessert plates.

Serving size: about 1 cup
Calories: 121
Fat: 0.6 g
Cholesterol: 0 mg
Carbohydrate: 30.3 g
Protein: 1.1 g
Sodium: 7.8 mg

**TIP**

Use the fine holes of a hand grater to grate peeled fresh ginger. The grater will reduce the ginger to a near-puree, with no stringy bits.

"PASSOVER SEDER"
**Vegetable Broth with Matzo Balls**
**Savory Mushroom Pudding**
**Sweet and Sour Red Cabbage**
**Roasted Carrots, Parsnips, and Beets**
**Cucumber Salad with Horseradish and Dill**
**Baked Vanilla Custard**
Sliced Fresh Strawberries

This Passover Seder is a feast of colorful dishes with nothing trimmed but the fat. From the matzo ball soup to the final spoonful of vanilla custard, the meal will surprise anyone who thinks that holiday food and healthful food are mutually exclusive terms.

The timing: Make the vegetable broth and the red cabbage the day before, if possible. Make the vanilla custard several hours ahead and chill. Make the matzo balls and the cucumber salad a couple of hours before the seder. Begin roasting the root vegetables about an hour and a quarter before you plan to eat. Slice the strawberries and chill. Make the mushroom pudding mixture, but don't bake it until 20 minutes before you are ready to eat. (It can bake alongside the root vegetables.) Peel the beets. Reheat the matzo balls and enjoy!

## VEGETABLE BROTH WITH MATZO BALLS

*Eureka! It wasn't easy to develop a light and flavorful matzo ball with no added fat, but here you have it. As good as Mom's? Maybe better. To do these delicate dumplings justice, serve them in a homemade vegetable broth. Double the recipe to yield the required 8 cups broth (7 for the soup, 1 for the matzo balls).*

MAKES 7 CUPS BROTH AND 2 CUPS MATZO BALL MIXTURE,
ENOUGH FOR 24 MATZO BALLS • SERVES 8

*Matzo Balls:*
1 cup matzo meal
1 cup Vegetable Broth, preferably homemade (page 18)
1 tablespoon grated onion
1 tablespoon minced parsley
Salt and pepper
4 egg whites

7 cups Vegetable Broth, preferably homemade (page 18)

In a large bowl, stir together matzo meal, 1 cup vegetable broth, onion, and parsley. Season to taste with salt and pepper. Make sure mixture is evenly moistened with stock. It will be quite thick.

In another large bowl, beat egg whites to firm but not stiff peaks. Using a whisk, stir one third of the beaten egg whites into the matzo mixture to lighten it. Stir well until mixture is no longer lumpy. With a large rubber spatula, fold the remaining egg whites in gently. Fold until no white streaks remain, but do not overmix.

Bring a large pot of salted water to a boil over high heat. Using clean, wet hands, gently shape 1 heaping tablespoon of matzo mixture into a ball and carefully drop into boiling water. Repeat with remaining matzo mixture. Cover, lower heat to a simmer, and cook until matzo balls are cooked through, 20 to 25 minutes. Transfer with a slotted spoon to a plate and cool until ready to use.

To serve, bring 7 cups vegetable broth to a simmer over moderate heat. Add matzo balls and reheat gently until hot throughout. Serve immediately.

| | |
|---|---|
| *Serving size: 1 cup broth, 3 matzo balls*<br>*Calories: 71*<br>*Fat: 0.3 g*<br>*Cholesterol: 0 mg*<br>*Carbohydrate: 12.7 g*<br>*Protein: 3.8 g*<br>*Sodium: 27.7 mg (with no salt added)* | **TIP**<br>The matzo balls are poached in water first so as not to cloud the vegetable broth. Under pain of death don't peek into the pot while the matzo balls are cooking. You would release the steam that helps to make light dumplings. |

## SAVORY MUSHROOM PUDDING

*Baked in ramekins, custard cups, or muffin tins, these oniony mushroom flans can be unmolded on a bed of Sweet and Sour Red Cabbage. Add a drizzle of nonfat sour cream for flavor and eye appeal.*

### SERVES 8

1 cup minced yellow onion
½ cup Vegetable Broth, homemade (page 18) or store-bought
2 pounds mushrooms, minced (see Tip, page 115)
1 cup minced green onions
¼ cup plus 2 tablespoons minced parsley
¼ cup liquid egg substitute
1 cup matzo meal
2 teaspoons salt
½ teaspoon black pepper
¼ cup nonfat sour cream, whisked

*Everyday Cooking with Dr. Dean Ornish*

In a large skillet, combine onion and vegetable broth. Bring to a simmer, covered, over moderate heat and simmer until onion is softened, about 5 minutes. Add mushrooms and cook, uncovered, over moderately high heat until mushrooms are tender and all the liquid they generate has evaporated, 20 to 25 minutes. Remove from heat and stir in green onions. Transfer to a large mixing bowl and set aside to cool.

Preheat oven to 350 degrees F. When mushroom mixture is cool, stir in ¼ cup parsley, egg substitute, matzo meal, salt, and pepper. Stir well. Lightly spray eight ½-cup ramekins or muffin tins with vegetable oil spray. Divide mixture among the eight ramekins. Bake until firm, 15 to 20 minutes. Unmold onto a serving platter or individual dinner plates. Drizzle each with ½ tablespoon of sour cream and top with some of the remaining 2 tablespoons parsley. Serve immediately.

Serving size: ½ cup
Calories: 135
Fat: 1.1 g
Cholesterol: 0 mg
Carbohydrate: 25.2 g
Protein: 8.5 g
Sodium: 635.0 mg

**TIP**

The fastest way to mince mushrooms is in a food processor. Halve them if small, quarter if large, then place them, ½ pound at a time, in a processor fitted with the steel blade. Pulse until minced (not pureed!).

## SWEET AND SOUR RED CABBAGE

*You can make this dish the day before your Seder and reheat it just before serving. Some people even say that reheating improves it, although it's quite tasty when freshly made.*

### SERVES 8

8 cups finely sliced, quartered, cored red cabbage
¾ cup apple juice
1 teaspoon salt
½ cup raisins
3 tablespoons cider vinegar
Black pepper

In a large pot or Dutch oven, combine cabbage, apple juice, and salt. Cover, bring to a boil, adjust heat to maintain a gentle simmer, and cook 15 minutes. Add raisins and vinegar. Cover and simmer until cabbage is tender, about 15 minutes more. Taste and adjust seasoning with more vinegar, salt, or black pepper.

Serving size: ½ cup
Calories: 60
Fat: 0.2 g
Cholesterol: 0 mg
Carbohydrate: 15.7 g
Protein: 1.3 g
Sodium: 297.5 mg

> **TIP**
>
> If you don't like raisins, add 1 cup grated apple or pear. Red cabbage and fruit are good companions.

## ROASTED CARROTS, PARSNIPS, AND BEETS

*Roasting seems to intensify root vegetables' sweet taste, because none of the flavor (and none of the nutrients) is lost to water. It takes a little longer to roast them, but you will find the results worth the time. If desired, add some fresh thyme sprigs or bay leaves to the roasting pan. Red potatoes are also delicious prepared this way.*

SERVES 8

8 medium carrots, peeled if desired
8 medium parsnips, peeled
8 medium beets
Salt and pepper

Preheat oven to 350 degrees F.

Cut carrots into 3-inch lengths beginning at the narrow end. As you move toward the thicker end, cut the carrots in half or in quarters to keep pieces about the same size. Cut parsnips into pieces the same size as the carrots. Cut the tops off the beets, leaving 2 inches of stem still attached to prevent "bleeding." Do not cut off root.

Place beets in a roasting pan lightly sprayed with nonstick spray (see Tip, page 251) and roast 15 minutes. Add carrots and parsnips, spray vegetables lightly with nonstick spray, and roast, turning occasionally, until vegetables are tender when pierced, about 45 minutes. When beets are cool enough to handle, peel them, and slice into halves or wedges, or leave whole if small. Season vegetables to taste with salt and pepper.

*Serving size: 1 carrot, 1 parsnip,*
*1 beet*
*Calories: 104*
*Fat: 0.4 g*
*Cholesterol: 0 mg*
*Carbohydrate: 24.4 g*
*Protein: 2.4 g*
*Sodium: 74.0 mg*

| **TIP** |
| :--- |
| What other vegetables can you roast? Try fennel bulb, turnips, onions, zucchini, and winter squash. |

## CUCUMBER SALAD WITH HORSERADISH AND DILL

*Horseradish—one of the traditional bitter herbs on the Passover table—gives a kick to a simple cucumber salad. Horseradish varies in strength from brand to brand; add a little to the salad and taste before you add more. Be sure to buy bottled horseradish with no egg or cream.*

FROM ELIZABETH KAPSTEIN, CHEF,
Dr. Ornish Program for Reversing Heart Disease at Beth Israel Medical
Center, New York, New York.
SERVES 8

4 medium cucumbers, peeled, halved, and seeded, then sliced thin
2 tablespoons kosher salt (see Tip, page 118)
2 tablespoons white wine vinegar, or more to taste
1 to 2 teaspoons prepared horseradish
½ cup minced green onions
2 tablespoons minced fresh dill
Black pepper

In a large bowl, combine cucumbers and kosher salt. Mix well. Put cucumbers in a sieve set over the bowl and let stand at room temperature 30 minutes. Rinse cucumbers in three changes of water. Drain and pat dry.

In a large bowl, stir together wine vinegar and horseradish. Add cucumbers, green onions, and dill. Toss to combine. Refrigerate at least 30 minutes, stirring occasionally. Season with black pepper before serving.

*Serving size: ½ cup*
*Calories: 9*
*Fat: 0.1 g*
*Cholesterol: 0 mg*
*Carbohydrate: 2.0 g*
*Protein: 0.3 g*
*Sodium: 293.3 mg (assuming*
  *cucumbers absorb 1 teaspoon of salt)*

> **TIP**
>
> Pre-salting the cucumbers draws out their excess water and concentrates their flavor. You will rinse off most of the salt, but if you are watching your salt intake, omit the pre-salting.

## BAKED VANILLA CUSTARD

*Serve squares of this delicate golden custard with sliced ripe strawberries. Cooking it slowly in a water bath helps preserve its silky texture.*

### SERVES 8

**3 cups nonfat milk**
**1½ cups liquid egg substitute**
**⅓ cup sugar**
**2 teaspoons vanilla extract**

Preheat oven to 325 degrees F. In a large bowl, whisk together milk, egg substitute, sugar, and vanilla until sugar dissolves. Pour into a 7 by 11-inch glass baking dish. Put that dish inside a larger dish, then fill the larger dish with enough hot water to come halfway up the sides of the glass baking dish. Bake 1 hour, adding more hot water if needed to maintain water level. Custard is done when a knife inserted near the edge comes out clean. Cool, then chill for several hours or overnight.

*Everyday Cooking with Dr. Dean Ornish*

*Serving size:* ⅛ *of the custard*
*Calories: 83*
*Fat: 0.16 g*
*Cholesterol: 0 mg*
*Carbohydrate: 13.0 mg*
*Protein: 7.0 g*
*Sodium: 109.0 mg*

**TIP**

On another occasion, try replacing some of the sugar with maple syrup. You can also bake the custard in light individual custard cups, in which case it will cook more quickly. Begin testing after about 25 minutes. Custard is done when a knife inserted near the edge of the cup comes out clean. The custard will finish cooking as it cools.

# SUMMER

**Zucchini-Potato Soup**
**Angel Hair Pasta with Fresh Tomato and Basil**
Crusty Italian Bread
Sliced Nectarines and Blackberries

**The Ginsbergs' Creamy Corn Soup**
**Vegetarian Tacos**
**Fresh Tomato Salsa (page 192)**
**Watermelon Salad**

**Soupe au Pistou**
**(French Vegetable Soup with Basil)**
**Whole Wheat Bread**
Sliced Fresh Peaches
**Strawberry Sorbet**

**Arugula Salad with Corn and Red Onions**
**Pizza with Roasted Eggplant and Peppers**
Fresh Sliced Figs with Summer Berries

**Fresh Tomato Bruschetta**
**Risotto with Corn and Red Peppers**
Steamed Sugar Snap Peas
**Quick Peach Sherbet**

**Lentil, Cucumber, and Radish Salad**
**Baked Bulgur-stuffed Tomatoes**
**Herbed Yogurt Sauce**
Whole Wheat Pita Bread
Chilled Cantaloupe and Honeydew Wedges

**White Bean Salad with Zucchini, Tomato, and Basil**
**Pasta with Creamy Red Pepper Sauce**
Whole Grain Bread
**Fresh Apricot Clafouti**

**Two Middle Eastern Salads:**
**Hummus (Creamy Chickpea Puree)**
**Tabbouleh (Bulgur and Parsley Salad)**
Hearts of Romaine
**Fresh Tomato Soup**
Warm Whole Wheat Pita Bread
**Spiced Poached Peaches**

**Corn Pancakes**
**Swiss Chard with Roasted Onions**
**Cucumber and Potato Soup with Dill**
Whole Grain Bread
Fresh Blueberries and Raspberries

"INDEPENDENCE DAY BARBECUE"
**Chilled Zucchini Soup with Salsa**
**Grilled Portobello Mushroom and Onion Burgers**
Fresh Corn on the Cob
**Creamy Coleslaw**
**Old-Fashioned Potato Salad**
Vegetarian Baked Beans
Chilled Watermelon Slices
**Warm Peach Cobbler**

"AL FRESCO LUNCH"
**Gazpacho with White Beans**
**Zucchini and Cheese Quesadillas**
**Summer Fruit Salad with Lime and Mint**

Whether you patronize a farmers' market or a supermarket, shopping for summer meals can be a real treat. The tomatoes are red-ripe and fragrant, the corn sweet and juicy, and the berries and melons so perfumed that you can smell them from yards away. With fruits and vegetables this good, you don't need to do much to them. That's why summer cooking can be particularly quick and easy. Toss angel hair pasta with fresh tomatoes and basil (page 126); make a creamy fresh corn soup (page 128) or a Chilled Zucchini Soup with Salsa (page 162); or stir corn and red peppers into an Italian risotto (page 140). Set a picnic table outdoors and enjoy an al fresco meal of gazpacho (page 168) and hot-off-the-grill quesadillas (page 169); or invite the neighbors for a full-scale Fourth of July backyard barbecue, with coleslaw (page 164), potato salad (page 165), corn on the cob, and grilled mushroom-onion burgers (page 163). You'll find all these in the following menus, accompanied by imaginative salads, fresh fruit desserts, and other dishes that capture the taste of summer.

In summer, look for:

berries: blackberries, raspberries, blueberries, olallieberries
black-eyed peas
chard
cherries
corn
cucumbers
eggplant
figs
garlic
green beans
kohlrabi
melons: cantaloupe, honeydew, watermelon, casaba

nectarines
okra
onions
peaches
peppers, sweet and hot
plums
potatoes
tomatoes
yellow summer squash
zucchini

**Zucchini-Potato Soup**
**Angel Hair Pasta with Fresh Tomato and Basil**
Crusty Italian Bread
Sliced Nectarines and Blackberries

Pasta with a fresh vegetable sauce is one of the easiest, most health-ful main courses you can make. And when the vine-ripe tomatoes hit the market in summer, there's no tastier pasta sauce than tomato and onion simmered with fresh basil. Start with a quickly made veg-etable soup that gets a last-minute lift from lemon, and finish with a coupe of chilled sliced nectarines and berries.

The timing: Make the soup first. While it's simmering, prepare the tomato-basil sauce. Put a large pot of salted water on to heat for the pasta while you sit down and enjoy the soup. Cook the pasta when you have finished your soup; it cooks in just a few minutes. Slice the nec-tarines into a bowl and sprinkle with blackberries when you are ready for dessert.


## ZUCCHINI-POTATO SOUP

*Launch a summer dinner with this delicate soup, a smooth puree of summer squash and potato. On a warm evening, you may want to chill it and serve it cold, like a vichyssoise.*

FROM ELIZABETH KAPSTEIN, CHEF
*Dr. Ornish Program for Reversing Heart Disease at Beth Israel Medical Center, New York, New York*
SERVES 4 WITH LEFTOVERS

2 cups thinly sliced leeks, white part only
1 garlic clove, minced
5¼ cups Vegetable Broth, homemade (page 18) or store-bought
2 cups diced peeled russet-type baking potatoes
4 cups diced zucchini
4 cups diced yellow summer squash
2 tablespoons minced fresh chives or green onions
1 to 2 tablespoons lemon juice

---

Salt and pepper
4 thin lemon slices (optional)

In a large saucepan, combine leeks, garlic, and ¼ cup vegetable broth. Bring to a simmer, covered, over moderate heat and simmer until vegetables are softened, about 3 minutes. Add potatoes and remaining 5 cups broth. Bring to a boil, cover, adjust heat to maintain a simmer, and cook until potatoes are tender, 12 to 15 minutes.

Add zucchini and summer squash, cover and simmer until tender, 8 to 10 minutes. Cool slightly, then puree soup in blender or food processor until smooth. Return soup to pot; stir in chives and lemon juice to taste. Season to taste with salt and pepper. Reheat and serve, garnishing each serving with a thin slice of lemon, if desired.

*Serving size: 1 cup*
*Calories: 68*
*Fat: 0.35 g*
*Cholesterol: 0 mg*
*Carbohydrate: 15.25 g*
*Protein: 2.7 g*
*Sodium: 21.5 mg*

> **TIP**
>
> Leeks are a mild member of the onion family. Most recipes call for using the white part only—the part that grows underground—because it is tender and sweet. The dark green leaves, which grow aboveground, can be tough and are usually discarded or saved for making vegetable broth. Leeks need careful cleaning. Slit them to within a couple of inches of the root end and rinse under cold running water, letting the water run between the layers. For a delicious salad, steam leeks until tender, then chill them. Dress them with bottled nonfat Italian dressing, chopped egg white, and herbs, or with a dash of tarragon vinegar.

## ANGEL HAIR PASTA WITH FRESH TOMATO AND BASIL

*With fragrant vine-ripe tomatoes, you can make a superb pasta sauce in minutes. In fact, when you can get your hands on some great tomatoes, you may want to make a lot of this sauce and freeze it. Here, it's tossed with delicate angel hair noodles, but it would complement whole wheat spaghetti or spaghettini, too. Or pull it from the freezer throughout the year for use in soups, bean dishes, or vegetable stews.*

SERVES 4

1¼ cups Vegetable Broth, homemade (page 18) or store-bought
2 medium onions, chopped
1½ teaspoons minced garlic
3½ pounds fresh tomatoes, peeled, seeded, and diced (see Tip below)
¼ cup chopped fresh basil
⅛ teaspoon hot red pepper flakes, or more to taste
Salt
1 pound dried angel hair pasta

In a large nonstick skillet, heat broth over moderately high heat until boiling. Add onions and garlic and cook, stirring, until softened, 3 to 5 minutes. Stir in tomatoes, basil, hot red pepper flakes, and salt to taste. Adjust heat to maintain a simmer and simmer, stirring occasionally, until sauce thickens slightly, 10 to 15 minutes.

Meanwhile, bring a large pot of salted water to a boil over high heat. Add pasta and cook according to package directions until al dente. Drain, then transfer to a large warm bowl. Add sauce and toss well. Serve immediately.

*Serving size: 2 cups pasta, 1 cup*
  *sauce*
*Calories: 531*
*Fat: 3.2 g*
*Cholesterol: 0 mg*
*Carbohydrate: 109.1 g*
*Protein: 20.5 g*
*Sodium: 43.0 mg*

**TIP**

To peel and seed tomatoes easily, bring a large pot of water to a boil over high heat. Cut a shallow "X" in the rounded end of each tomato, then boil for 30 seconds (a little less if tomatoes are very ripe, longer if they are not quite ripe). Transfer them to a bowl of ice water to stop the cooking. Lift them out when cool. The skin should peel back easily from the "X." Core tomatoes, halve crosswise, and squeeze gently to remove the seeds, using the fingers of one hand to pry the seeds out of their cavities.

The Ginsbergs' Creamy Corn Soup
Vegetarian Tacos
Fresh Tomato Salsa (page 192)
Watermelon Salad
👁

Corn, tomatoes, peppers, watermelon . . . it must be summer. Set a table outdoors and exploit the summer harvest in a dinner with a Mexican accent. If you're short on time, buy store-bought salsa; if not, try making your own.

The timing: Make the corn soup and set it aside. Prepare all the ingredients for the watermelon salad, but don't assemble it yet. Make the salsa, if desired. Prepare the garnishes for the tacos, then sauté the peppers and heat the tortillas. While the peppers are cooking, assemble the watermelon salad and reheat the corn soup.

## THE GINSBERGS' CREAMY CORN SOUP

*A spoonful of diced green chiles gives this sweet, velvety soup a kick. You can make it several hours ahead, but it will get spicier as it sits.*

FROM HANK AND PHYLLIS GINSBERG OF MILL VALLEY, CALIFORNIA: *Hank and Phyllis are original research participants in the Ornish study. Phyllis has become an expert in Ornish cooking. This recipe of hers is a favorite at Ornish retreats in California.*
SERVES 4

1 cup finely diced onion
¼ cup Vegetable Broth, homemade (page 18) or store-bought
3 cups fresh or frozen corn kernels (see Tip, page 141), or 2 (15-ounce) cans corn kernels, drained
2 tablespoons diced mild canned green chiles
2 tablespoons diced red pimiento
2 cups nonfat milk
Salt and pepper
Cayenne pepper (optional)
1 tablespoon cilantro leaves (optional)

In a large saucepan, combine onion and vegetable broth. Bring to a simmer, covered, over moderate heat and simmer until onion is softened, about 5 minutes.

Put ½ cup corn in a small bowl with chiles and pimiento. Stir to combine.

Add remaining 2½ cups corn and the milk to the onion. Bring to a boil. Cover, adjust heat to maintain a simmer, and cook until corn is tender, about 5 minutes. Cool slightly, then puree in blender or food processor until smooth. Return soup to pot. Stir in corn/chile/pimiento mixture. Reheat gently; season to taste with salt and pepper. Add a pinch of cayenne pepper if you like more heat. Serve hot, garnishing each portion with cilantro, if desired.

*Serving size: 1 cup*
*Calories: 158*
*Fat: 1.65 g*
*Cholesterol: 2.2 mg*
*Carbohydrate: 31.4 g*
*Protein: 8.3 g*
*Sodium: 81.6 mg (with fresh corn and no salt added)*

> **TIP**
>
> If you have leftovers, reheat the soup the following day with diced cooked potato to make a corn chowder.

# VEGETARIAN TACOS

*Pile sweet sautéed bell peppers and onions into steamed tortillas to make a juicy soft taco. Let diners serve themselves to optional condiments such as shredded romaine, cheese, tomato salsa, or nonfat sour cream. Set out chopped cilantro if you like it, and some sliced pickled jalapeños if you're a chile fan.*

## SERVES 4

1 large green bell pepper, ribs and seeds removed, thinly sliced
1 large red bell pepper, ribs and seeds removed, thinly sliced
1 large onion, thinly sliced
1 teaspoon chili powder
Salt and pepper
8 corn tortillas
1 (16-ounce) can nonfat refried beans
1 cup Fresh Tomato Salsa, homemade (page 192) or store-bought

½ cup grated nonfat cheese
½ cup nonfat sour cream
Shredded romaine lettuce

Preheat oven to 300 degrees F.

Combine peppers and onion in a large nonstick skillet. Cover and cook over moderate heat until the vegetables begin to soften, about 5 minutes. Uncover and cook, stirring occasionally, until the vegetables are tender but not mushy, 5 to 10 minutes more. Season with chili powder and with salt and pepper to taste.

Stack tortillas and wrap them in aluminum foil. Heat in oven until hot throughout, 8 to 10 minutes. Heat the beans in a saucepan over moderately low heat. Set out bowls of salsa, cheese, sour cream, and lettuce. To assemble tacos, spread about 3 tablespoons of the hot beans on each tortilla. Top with ¼ cup of the vegetable mixture and fold in half to enclose the filling. Serve immediately.

*Serving size: 2 tacos*
*Calories: 297*
*Fat: 2.8 g*
*Cholesterol: 4.4 g*
*Carbohydrate: 55.7 g*
*Protein: 13.6 g*
*Sodium: 657 mg (with no salt added)*

> **TIP**
>
> Don't be concerned if the nutrition label on packaged corn tortillas indicates that the tortillas are not fat-free. Corn naturally contains a small amount of fat, which is a source of essential fatty acids. More important: read the list of ingredients to make sure there is no *added* fat.

## WATERMELON SALAD

*Here's a salad of inviting contrasts: cool, refreshing melon and mint juxtaposed with piquant onion, vinegar, and pepper. It's just the right zippy partner for tacos or other spicy Mexican foods.*

### SERVES 4

4 cups ½-inch cubes seeded, peeled watermelon
½ cup diced red onion
4 tablespoons rice vinegar (not seasoned)
2 tablespoons chopped fresh mint
½ teaspoon pepper

Combine all ingredients in a large bowl. Serve immediately.

*Serving size: 1 cup*
*Calories: 50*
*Fat: 0.7 g*
*Cholesterol: 0 mg*
*Carbohydrate: 11.5 g*
*Protein: 1.0 g*
*Sodium: 3.0 mg*

> **TIP**
>
> You can make several different permutations of this perky salad by substituting honeydew or cantaloupe for the watermelon; tarragon or basil for the mint; or raspberry vinegar for the rice vinegar. You could also mix two or three types of melon for a more colorful dish.

**Soupe au Pistou**
**(French Vegetable Soup with Basil)**
**Whole Wheat Bread**
Sliced Fresh Peaches
**Strawberry Sorbet**
🍅

If you have a large, pretty soup tureen, now's the moment for it. Put boiling water in it to heat it, then empty out the water and fill the tureen with a chunky, aromatic *soupe au pistou*, the beloved vegetable soup from southern France. Ladle the soup into warm bowls at the table and pass a basket of thick-sliced homemade bread. For dessert, spoon some sliced peaches into balloon wineglasses or compote dishes, and top with a spoonful of just-made strawberry sorbet.

The timing: Make the bread and freeze the strawberries several hours ahead. Start the soup 25 minutes before you want to sit down for dinner. While the soup is simmering, slice and chill the peaches. Make the sorbet just before you are ready to eat it.

## SOUPE AU PISTOU
### (French Vegetable Soup with Basil)

*This is the classic summer vegetable soup of Provence, where basil and garlic are used as freely as salt and pepper. Pistou, like Italian pesto, is an herb paste—in this case, a paste of basil, beans, and garlic that's stirred into the soup at the last minute to thicken and flavor it.*

SERVES 4

½ cup diced onion

½ cup diced carrots

½ cup diced celery

½ cup diced turnips

½ cup diced peeled russet-type baking potato

½ cup diced leeks, white part only

½ cup diced, peeled tomato, fresh or canned

4 cups Vegetable Broth, homemade (page 18) or store-bought

½ cup 1-inch lengths dried whole wheat spaghetti

1 (15-ounce) can navy beans, or 2 cups home-cooked navy beans in
   ¾ cup liquid

1 cup tightly packed basil leaves (see Tip below)

3 garlic cloves, minced

Salt and pepper

In a large pot, combine onion, carrots, celery, turnips, potato, leeks, tomato, and vegetable broth. Bring to a simmer over moderate heat. Cover and adjust heat to maintain a simmer. Cook 10 minutes. Add spaghetti and 1 cup beans with their liquid. Cover and simmer until spaghetti is tender, 10 to 12 minutes.

To make pistou, combine remaining beans with their liquid, basil, and garlic in a food processor and puree until smooth. Add the puree to the soup and stir until blended. Season to taste with salt and pepper.

Serving size: 1¾ cups

Calories: 271

Fat: 0.88 g

Cholesterol: 0 mg

Carbohydrate: 53.7 g

Protein: 14.6 g

Sodium: 58.0 mg (with no salt
   added)

> **TIP**
>
> Basil leaves tend to blacken and go limp in the refrigerator. To extend their life, wrap them in damp paper towels and then tuck that package in a plastic bag. They will keep for several days.

# WHOLE WHEAT BREAD

*Even if you have access to a good local bakery, you may want to make your own bread occasionally for the sheer pleasure of it. This easy bread has that sweet aroma and wholesome, nutty taste of a 100 percent whole grain loaf.*

MAKES TWO 8½-INCH LOAVES

⅔ cup instant nonfat dry milk
2 (¼-ounce) packages active dry yeast
¼ cup sugar
1 tablespoon salt
6½ to 7½ cups whole wheat flour

In a large bowl, stir together 3 cups warm (not hot) water, dry milk, and yeast. Let stand 3 to 4 minutes to dissolve the yeast.

Add the sugar, salt, and 4½ cups of the flour. Beat vigorously until you have a smooth, heavy batter, about 2 minutes. Add 1½ cups of the remaining flour and stir vigorously to make a manageable dough.

Turn the dough out onto a generously floured surface and knead for 2 minutes, adding additional flour as necessary to keep dough from sticking. Let dough rest 10 minutes. Resume kneading until the dough is smooth and elastic, about 8 minutes, adding enough of the remaining flour as necessary to keep the dough manageable.

Spray a large bowl with nonstick spray (see Tip, page 251). Put the dough in the bowl, cover with a clean towel, and let rise until doubled, 1 to 2 hours.

Punch the dough down, divide it in half, and form each half into a loaf. Transfer to two 8½ by 4½ by 2½-inch loaf pans, either nonstick or lightly sprayed with nonstick spray. Cover loosely with a towel and let rise until doubled, 45 to 60 minutes. Preheat oven to 350 degrees F. Bake loaves until firm and nicely browned, 55 to 60 minutes. Remove from the pans and cool on a rack before slicing.

*Serving size: ¹/₁₂ loaf*
*Calories: 123*
*Fat: 0.6 g*
*Cholesterol: 0.1 mg*
*Carbohydrate: 26.0 g*
*Protein: 5.0 g*
*Sodium: 293 mg*

> **TIP**
>
> Breads without fat tend to go stale more quickly than breads with fat. It's best to freeze what you can't eat within a day or two. It will keep for a month if well wrapped.

# STRAWBERRY SORBET

*Finish a summer dinner with the refreshing taste of a fruit sorbet, whipped up in a flash in a blender or food processor. (Note that the directions vary slightly for these two machines.) If you can't find ripe strawberries, use other fruit in season: blackberries, raspberries, apricots, peaches, pears, or nectarines.*

FROM MRS. JOHN H. MARTIN OF MOUNT DORA, FLORIDA

*Bunny Martin has attended the Ornish Residential Lifestyle Retreat in California. When she had heart surgery nine years ago, doctors told her she had six to ten years to live. Today she feels better than ever and says she walks four miles and swims fifty laps a day. She has learned to be assertive in restaurants, asking for exactly what she wants; now she says chefs enjoy pleasing her with Ornish food.*

SERVES 4

**1 pound (1 pint) strawberries, quartered**
**1½ cups apple juice**
**4 fresh mint sprigs**

Food processor method: Put quartered strawberries in a shallow metal pan or loaf pan and pour apple juice over to cover. Cover pan with plastic wrap. Freeze until solid. Remove from freezer 20 to 30 minutes before serving to defrost slightly. Transfer to food processor and blend until mixture is the consistency of sherbet. Serve immediately, garnishing each portion with a sprig of fresh mint.

Blender method: Freeze quartered berries on a baking sheet. Place frozen berries in blender with enough apple juice to allow blender to work. With blender running, add more juice until mixture reaches a sherbet consistency. Serve immediately, garnishing each portion with a sprig of fresh mint.

*Serving size: ¾ cup*
*Calories: 66*
*Fat: 0.4 g*
*Cholesterol: 0 mg*
*Carbohydrate: 16.0 g*
*Protein: 0.5 g*
*Sodium: 3.5 mg*

**TIP**

Many store-bought fruit sorbets contain no added fat (check the label), but they are almost always high in sugar and, therefore, in calories. As this recipe shows, sorbet doesn't need additional sugar if you start with ripe fresh fruit and apple juice.

**Arugula Salad with Corn and Red Onions**
**Pizza with Roasted Eggplant and Peppers**
Fresh Sliced Figs with Summer Berries

There's no reason to go out for pizza when you can make even tastier pizza at home with fresh seasonal vegetables. Serve this roasted-eggplant version with a picture-pretty salad, a toss of bright green arugula, red onion, and sweet corn. End your meal with ripe figs, sliced and topped with the best available berries. If you can't find fresh figs, substitute sliced melon.

The timing: Make the pizza dough. While it is rising, roast the eggplant and prepare the other pizza-topping ingredients. Assemble and bake the pizzas. While they are baking, prepare the salad. When you are ready for dessert, slice the figs into halves or quarters and place in four dessert bowls. Mix together raspberries, blueberries, blackberries, or other summer berries and spoon over the figs.

## ARUGULA SALAD WITH CORN AND RED ONIONS

*Arugula is a leafy salad green with an appealing nutty taste. Look for young, tender leaves; older ones can be peppery-hot. Because it has so much flavor, it's a good idea to "stretch" it by mixing it with other salad greens, such as the prewashed mix of baby greens that many markets now sell in bulk or bags. Tossed with corn kernels and fine slivers of red onion, these greens make a beautiful salad that you will want to have often in summer.*

SERVES 4

4 cups mixed baby salad greens
1 bunch arugula (about 4 ounces), stems removed
1½ cups fresh or thawed frozen corn kernels (see Tip, page 141)
½ red onion, thinly sliced
2 tablespoons seasoned rice vinegar
1 tablespoon nonfat bottled Italian salad dressing

In a medium bowl, combine mixed greens, arugula, corn, red onion, vinegar, and nonfat dressing. Toss gently to coat all ingredients with dressing. Serve immediately.

Serving size: 2 cups
Calories: 76.5
Fat: 0.72 g
Cholesterol: 0 mg
Carbohydrate: 17.0 g
Protein: 3.8 g
Sodium: 87.5 mg

---

**TIP**

Add a handful of dark green arugula to your mixed green salads for a tasty dose of beta-carotene and vitamin C. This flavorful and nutritious salad green is easy to grow and increasingly available in markets. Wilt it in a skillet with garlic and toss with whole wheat spaghetti, or stir it into bean soup.

---

## PIZZA WITH ROASTED EGGPLANT AND PEPPERS

Adding some whole wheat flour to the dough gives this pizza crust a nutty flavor and a nutritional boost. Seek out the long, slender Japanese or Chinese eggplants for the topping. They cook more quickly, have fewer seeds, and are less bitter than the large globe eggplants. Note that this recipe makes two pizzas, so you will need two pizza pans or baking sheets. If you don't have two ovens, you can bake them on different racks of a single oven. In that situation, it's better to use pizza pans than baking sheets so the heat can circulate better.

If you are only cooking for two, you may not want to make two pizzas at once. Divide the dough in half before the first rise and refrigerate one half until the next day. Before baking, punch it down, bring it to room temperature, allow it to rise twice more as directed in the recipe, and top as desired.

MAKES TWO 12-INCH ROUNDS

SERVES 4

**Whole Wheat Pizza Dough:**
1¼ cups warm water
1 package (1 tablespoon) quick-rising yeast (see Tip, page 138)
1½ cups unbleached all-purpose flour
1½ cups whole wheat flour
1 teaspoon sugar
¾ teaspoon salt

**Topping:**
2½ pounds Japanese or Chinese eggplant

2 cups canned tomato sauce
2 teaspoons minced fresh oregano
2 cups sliced mushrooms
1 red bell pepper, ribs and seeds removed, sliced into thin rings
1 green bell pepper, ribs and seeds removed, sliced into thin rings
4 ounces grated nonfat cheese
Salt and pepper
1 tablespoon minced parsley

To make dough in a food processor: Put water in a small bowl. Whisk in yeast and 2 tablespoons all-purpose flour. Let proof until bubbly, about 10 minutes. In food processor, combine remaining all-purpose flour, whole wheat flour, sugar, and salt. Pulse to blend. With motor running, add proofed mixture gradually through the feed tube. Keep machine running until dough forms a ball. Add a little more flour if dough seems sticky. Transfer dough to a bowl; cover with plastic wrap and let rise in a warm place for 20 minutes. Punch down, cover, and let rise again in a warm place until doubled, about 30 minutes.

To make dough by hand: In a large bowl, whisk together warm water, yeast, and 2 tablespoons all-purpose flour. Let proof 10 minutes. In another bowl, stir together remaining all-purpose flour, whole wheat flour, sugar, and salt. Add flour mixture to water gradually, stirring until mixture forms a dough. You may not need all the flour. Turn dough out onto a lightly floured surface and knead until smooth and silky, 8 to 10 minutes. Transfer to a bowl, cover with plastic wrap, and let rise in a warm place 20 minutes. Punch down, cover and let rise again in a warm place until doubled, about 30 minutes.

To make topping: Preheat oven to 450 degrees F. Cut eggplants in half lengthwise. Arrange cut side down on a nonstick or lightly sprayed baking sheet. Roast until tender, about 25 minutes. With a spoon, scrape the soft flesh away from the skin. You should have about 3 cups eggplant.

Stir together tomato sauce and oregano.

To assemble and bake pizza: Preheat oven to 450 degrees F. Divide dough in two equal pieces. With a rolling pin, roll each piece out one at a time on a lightly floured surface into a 12-inch round. Transfer to two pizza pans, either nonstick or lightly sprayed with nonstick spray (see Tip, page 251). Put half the sauce on each round, spreading it evenly with the back of a spoon to within ½ inch of the edge. Divide the eggplant evenly between the two rounds. Top with mushrooms, then alternating rings of red and green bell pepper. Sprinkle with cheese and with salt and pepper to taste. Bake until crust is golden brown on the bottom and edges, about 25 minutes. If you are baking the pizzas on two different racks of a single oven, switch their position halfway through baking. When done, sprinkle with parsley.

*Serving size: ½ of one 12-inch pizza*
*Calories: 446.5*
*Fat: 1.9 g*
*Cholesterol: 4.4 mg*
*Carbohydrate: 93.5 g*
*Protein: 18.0 g*
*Sodium: 389.0 mg (with no salt*
*added to topping)*

---

**TIP**

Quick-rising yeast is a high-activity yeast strain that can cut dough-rising time in half. You can use regular yeast, but expect the rising times to be about twice as long as indicated in the recipe.

---

**Fresh Tomato Bruschetta**
**Risotto with Corn and Red Peppers**
Steamed Sugar Snap Peas
**Quick Peach Sherbet**

Think of risotto—like pasta—as a showcase for whatever vegetables are in season. Once you have mastered the risotto-making technique (it isn't hard), you will be able to adapt the dish throughout the year to the vegetables you have at hand. In summer, add sweet corn kernels and diced red peppers for a particularly colorful variation. Then contrast the creamy risotto with crisp steamed sugar snap peas, the sweet peas with the edible shell. While you stir the risotto, enjoy an Italian appetizer of juicy seasoned fresh tomatoes on toasted bread. Conclude the meal with a fresh peach sherbet that is so creamy, guests might think it is ice cream.

The timing: Freeze the peaches several hours ahead or the day before. About 45 minutes before you are ready to eat, make the tomato *bruschetta*. You can nibble on them in the kitchen while you prepare the risotto and peas. First trim the peas, removing the strings, and put them in a bamboo or collapsible metal steamer. Then make the risotto. About 5 minutes before the risotto is ready, put the steamer basket over simmering water, cover and steam the peas until crisp-tender. Make the sherbet just before you are ready to eat it.

---

*Everyday Cooking with Dr. Dean Ornish*

# FRESH TOMATO BRUSCHETTA

*Italians make bruschetta (pronounced brew-sketta) whenever they can get their hands on sweet, vine-ripe tomatoes. They chop the tomatoes, season them, and then pile them on crisp toast for an easy summer first course. Capers make a nice addition. Be sure to squeeze out all the juice before you chop the tomatoes so the toasts don't get soggy.*

FROM BETTY CRISAFI OF BAY VILLAGE, OHIO:
*Frank and Betty Crisafi have attended the week-long Ornish retreat in California. Frank has lost more than fifty pounds on the program, and Betty has become adept at cooking Reversal Diet foods. In fact, she has taught local chefs a thing or two. She gave the chef at her favorite restaurant a recipe and asked him to prepare it for her. Next thing she knew it was on the menu. The recipe? Here it is for you.*

SERVES 4

8 French baguette slices, ½ inch thick, cut on the diagonal
2 large ripe tomatoes or 4 to 5 plum (Roma) tomatoes
¼ cup minced red onion
6 to 8 fresh basil leaves, torn into small pieces
1 tablespoon red wine vinegar
2 teaspoons minced garlic
Salt and pepper

Toast the baguette slices on both sides until dry. Set aside.

Halve tomatoes and squeeze out juice and seeds. Chop tomatoes into ¼-inch dice and transfer to small bowl. Add onion, basil, vinegar, and garlic. Stir to combine. Season to taste with salt and pepper.

Divide tomato mixture evenly among the eight toasts. Serve immediately.

**TIP**

Here's another bruschetta idea from Lydia Karpenko of Danville, California. Top baguette slices with a little nonfat mayonnaise and toast in a 350 degree F. oven until browned, 10 to 15 minutes. Spread with a little fat-free cream cheese mixed with garlic, then top with a thin tomato slice, a thin cucumber slice, and some fresh basil. Lydia and Vic Karpenko were in the original group of Ornish research participants. Lydia has become an expert in Reversal Diet cooking. Her dishes are always favorites at the cooking demonstrations at the Ornish retreats in California.

*Serving size: 2 pieces*
*Calories: 178*
*Fat: 2.2 g*
*Cholesterol: 0 mg*
*Carbohydrate: 34.5 g*
*Protein: 5.7 g*
*Sodium: 323.3 mg*

# RISOTTO WITH CORN AND RED PEPPERS

*Italian cookbooks tell you to add the broth a little at a time when making risotto, but this method works just as well and is less trouble. The result is a creamy rice dish, studded with kernels of sweet corn and red bell pepper.*

### SERVES 4

5 cups Vegetable Broth, homemade (page 18) or store-bought, or more as needed
1½ cups Arborio rice (page 54)
1 cup diced red bell pepper
½ cup diced Roasted Onions (page 22)
1 garlic clove, minced
1 cup fresh corn kernels, cut from the cob (see Tip, page 141)
¼ cup fresh basil chiffonade (see Tip, page 211)
Salt and pepper

Put broth in a saucepan and bring to a simmer; adjust heat to keep broth barely simmering. In a saucepan, combine rice, bell pepper, onion, garlic, and 3 cups hot broth. Bring mixture to a simmer over moderately high heat, adjust heat to maintain a simmer, and cook, stirring occasionally, until most of the liquid has been absorbed, about 10 minutes, stirring occasionally. Add more hot broth 1 cup at a time, stirring often and waiting until rice has absorbed most of the liquid before adding more. After 8 more minutes, the rice should still be a little firm to the bite, and it should have absorbed about 5 cups total liquid. Add corn and cook 2 minutes more, adding a little more liquid if rice seems underdone or mixture seems dry. Risotto should be creamy, but not soupy. Remove from heat and stir in basil. Season with salt and pepper. Serve immediately.

*Serving size: 1¼ cups*
*Calories: 317 g*
*Fat: 0.7 g*
*Cholesterol: 0 mg*
*Carbohydrate: 71.0 g*
*Protein: 6.5 g*
*Sodium: 35.0 mg*

> **TIP**
>
> One large ear of corn yields about 1 cup of corn kernels. Cut the stem off, set the ear on the stem end, and slice down, from tip to stem, all the way around the ear to remove the kernels.

## QUICK PEACH SHERBET

*If you start with sweet, ripe fruit, you don't need to add much sugar to make a tasty fruit sherbet. Just freeze the cut-up fruit, then puree it with a little sugar and nonfat sour cream—no ice cream freezer required. This makes a soft, creamy sherbet that should be served immediately.*

### SERVES 4

**4 medium peaches, peeled, pitted, and coarsely chopped**
**½ cup nonfat sour cream**
**2 tablespoons plus 2 teaspoons sugar**
**2 teaspoons lemon juice**
**1 teaspoon vanilla extract**
**4 sprigs fresh mint (optional)**

Freeze the chopped peaches on a baking sheet until frozen hard, several hours or overnight.

In a small bowl, whisk together sour cream, sugar, lemon juice, and vanilla.

Transfer frozen peaches to a food processor and pulse until mixture is like snow. Add sour cream mixture and blend until smooth and creamy, stopping the machine and scraping down the sides of the bowl once or twice. Serve immediately, garnishing each portion with a mint sprig, if desired.

> **TIP**
>
> This recipe works beautifully with other fresh fruit (try mangoes, strawberries, or blackberries) and with store-bought frozen fruit.

*Serving size: ¾ cup*
*Calories: 84.5*
*Fat: 0.7 g*
*Cholesterol: 0 mg*
*Carbohydrate: 21.0 g*
*Protein: 1.6 g*
*Sodium: 60.0 mg*

## HOLD ON TO THOSE NUTRIENTS

You can minimize vitamin and mineral loss in fresh produce by storing, handling, and cooking it properly. Here are a few pointers to help you hold on to all the nutrients you can:

- To maintain maximum nutrients, limit the foods' exposure to light, air, heat, and water.
- Don't chop or slice fruits and vegetables until you are ready to use them.
- Wash your produce under running water, or let stand briefly in several changes of water. Soaking fruits and vegetables in water can cause loss of the water-soluble vitamins.
- Since most nutrients are just under the skin, it's best to cook fruits and vegetables with their skin on. If you can't eat the skin, peel it after cooking.
- If you can't steam vegetables, then cook them in the smallest amount of water possible, in a covered pot or in the microwave (page 144), for the shortest amount of time possible. Then "retrieve" the nutrients by adding the cooking water to a soup, sauce, or stew.
- From the standpoint of safeguarding nutrients, it's better to undercook than overcook.

## STEAM IT RIGHT

Vegetables cooked by steam retain more of their nutrients than vegetables cooked in a large quantity of boiling water. That's because vitamin C and the B vitamins, which are both water-soluble, leach into the boiling water. You can "retrieve" some of the vitamins by using the cooking water in another dish, but it's often easier just to steam. Here are a few guidelines for doing it properly.

For maximum nutrient retention, before steaming, cut vegetables into chunks but not into small pieces. By cutting up the vegetables, you shorten the cooking time and thus minimize nutrient loss. But cutting them up also exposes more surfaces to air, speeding up nutrient loss. So the best approach is the middle path: cut them up, but not too much.

You can steam vegetables on a conventional stove top or in your microwave. Here's how:

### Conventional Stove-Top Method:

Steam in a covered pot with the food above—not in—boiling water. If the water touches the food, it can leach out nutrients.

For best results, use either a bamboo steamer or a collapsible metal steamer.

Bamboo steamers are sold in cookware stores and in markets catering to a Chinese clientele. They come in a range of sizes, but a 12-inch steamer is probably the most useful. You need only one lid, but you may want two baskets; they stack neatly in tiers, allowing you to steam a couple of different things at once.

These bamboo steamers are designed to fit inside a wok, with boiling water underneath. Make sure your steamer is about 2 inches smaller than your wok so it will fit inside properly. You can also set a steamer over a Dutch oven or a pot that is slightly smaller in diameter. Be careful that the steamer doesn't get too close to the heat source, or it could burn.

You can put vegetables in two tiers of the steamer, although the food in the upper tier will cook more slowly. Or you can use the lower tier for steaming and the upper tier for reheating something that's already cooked, such as corn tortillas.

You can also set a bamboo steamer over a pot of simmering soup or stew so that foods can cook or reheat in that flavorful steam.

Most foods can be placed directly on the woven strips of the steamer. This is particularly convenient for long vegetables like asparagus and broccoli spears, which can lay flat in the steamer. To reheat leftover grains in a steamer, put them on a heatproof dinner plate or in a heatproof glass pie pan that can fit inside the steamer.

To steam, fill your wok or pot with an inch or so of water—enough so that it won't boil away during the cooking. Bring water to a boil, then set the covered steamer over the water. Keep water simmering, adding more hot water if it threatens to boil away before the food is cooked. Some people put a penny in the water so they can hear it rattle. When the penny stops "dancing," the water is about to boil away.

You can put bay leaves, parsley stems, thyme sprigs, coriander seed, lemon peel, wine, or other seasonings in your steaming liquid to flavor it. The steam will impart those flavors to the food subtly.

Clean bamboo steamers after use with hot water (no soap) and a scrub brush. Dry thoroughly. Store them in a well-ventilated spot so they don't mildew. (They look pretty hanging on a kitchen wall.)

Collapsible metal steamers fit inside almost any size pot, adjusting themselves to fit the pot. They are inexpensive and easy to clean. Their main disadvantage is that they tend to have short "legs," so you can't put much water under them. If you are steaming something that takes more than a few minutes, you may need to add more boiling water at some point. Take care to keep the water level below the food.

To use a collapsible metal steamer, bring water to a boil in the appropriate pot. Fill the steamer basket with the trimmed vegetables. Carefully lower the steamer into the pot, making sure it is over, not in, the water. Cover the pot and adjust heat to keep water simmering. When vegetables are done to your liking, uncover (stand back—the steam will be hot) and, with a potholder, lift the steamer out by its center ring.

### Microwave Method:
Place cut-up vegetables in a microwave-safe baking dish with 2 tablespoons water per pound. Cover with a lid or plastic wrap and microwave on high until done to your taste. Most vegetables will take 5 to 10 minutes, depending on their size and shape and the power of your oven. Stir or rearrange the vegetables halfway through for more even cooking. Remember that the food will continue to cook from internal heat after it's removed from the oven, so undercook slightly.

Or consider buying an electric rice cooker/food steamer. Several manufacturers now make this electrical appliance, which you can use to steam rice and vegetables or make soups. These convenient appliances are virtually foolproof, keep your stove burners free for other cooking, and keep food warm. Drip trays in these steamers keep food away from the cooking water, which means fewer vitamins and minerals are leached into the water.

**Lentil, Cucumber, and Radish Salad**
**Baked Bulgur-stuffed Tomatoes**
**Herbed Yogurt Sauce**
Whole Wheat Pita Bread
Chilled Cantaloupe and Honeydew Wedges

Stuffing vegetables with grains is a common practice in Greek, Turkish, Lebanese, and other eastern Mediterranean kitchens. When large, vine-ripe tomatoes appear in your market, try stuffing and baking them with the richly spiced bulgur and corn pilaf in the following menu. (The pilaf is also excellent on its own.) A creamy yogurt sauce makes the perfect accompaniment, both for the tomatoes and for the cool lentil salad. Serve the melon afterward, but if you have yogurt sauce left over, keep it on the table. It is surprisingly appealing with melon.

The timing: Cook the lentils first. While they are cooking and then cooling, stuff and bake the tomatoes. While the tomatoes are baking, marinate the cucumbers and radishes for the salad and make the yogurt sauce. Assemble the salad just before serving. At dessert time, halve and seed the chilled melons, then cut into thin wedges. Serve with wedges of lemon or lime.

## LENTIL, CUCUMBER, AND RADISH SALAD

*Marinating the cucumber and radish slices briefly in seasoned rice vinegar gives this beautiful summer salad its refreshing character. Take care not to overcook the lentils. They should maintain their shape. Taste them frequently toward the end of the cooking time to catch them when they are done but still firm.*

SERVES 4

1 cup dried lentils
2 cups Vegetable Broth, homemade (page 18) or store-bought
1 ½ cups thinly sliced halved cucumbers, peeled if necessary (see Tip, page 146)
½ cup thinly sliced radishes
¼ cup seasoned rice vinegar
2 tablespoons chopped fresh chives

2 teaspoons nonfat bottled Italian salad dressing
Salt and pepper

Rinse the lentils in a sieve. Combine lentils and broth in a medium pot and bring to a boil over high heat. Reduce heat to moderately low and cook, partially covered, until lentils are just tender, 25 to 30 minutes. Drain and let cool.

Combine cucumbers, radishes, and vinegar in a medium bowl and toss to mix. Let marinate 15 to 20 minutes. Gently stir in lentils, chives, and salad dressing. Season to taste with salt and pepper.

Serving size: 3/4
Calories: 169
Fat: 0.6 g
Cholesterol: 0 mg
Carbohydrate: 29.0 mg
Protein: 14.0 g
Sodium: 21.3 mg (with no salt added)

**TIP**

The hothouse-grown English cucumbers don't need peeling, but you should peel waxed cucumbers. To make English cucumber slices even prettier, "score" them with a fork: Draw the tines of a fork the length of the cucumber just deep enough to pierce the skin. Repeat all the way around the cucumber, then slice.

## BAKED BULGUR-STUFFED TOMATOES

*The tomatoes can be stuffed up to 4 hours in advance, refrigerated, and baked just before serving. If you can find tomatoes with some of the stem still attached, they'll make this dish look particularly pretty.*

SERVES 4

4 large tomatoes
Salt to taste, plus 1/2 teaspoon
Black pepper
1 cup Vegetable Broth, homemade (page 18) or store-bought
1/2 teaspoon turmeric
1/2 teaspoon ground cumin
Cayenne pepper
1 small zucchini, in 1/4-inch dice
1/4 cup chopped onion
2 teaspoons minced jalapeño chile (see Tip, page 19)

½ teaspoon minced garlic

½ cup bulgur

¾ cup corn kernels, fresh or thawed frozen (see Tip, page 141)

Cut a horizontal slice about ½ inch from the stem end of each tomato, reserving the tops. Using a spoon or melon baller, remove the seeds and pulp from each tomato. Season the insides of the tomatoes lightly with salt and black pepper and place upside down on paper towels to drain.

In a medium saucepan, combine broth, turmeric, cumin, ½ teaspoon salt, and a pinch of cayenne pepper. Bring to a boil over high heat. Stir in zucchini, onion, jalapeño, garlic, and bulgur and return to a boil. Cover, reduce heat to low, and cook until liquid has been absorbed and bulgur is tender, about 15 minutes. Stir in corn kernels.

Preheat oven to 350 degrees F. Choose a baking dish just large enough to hold the tomatoes and spray with nonstick spray (see Tip, page 251). Place tomatoes cut side up in the dish. Fill each with ½ cup of the bulgur filling. Replace tomato tops. Bake until tomatoes are heated through but not falling apart, 25 to 30 minutes.

*Serving size: ½ cup*
*Calories: 133*
*Fat: 1.0 g*
*Cholesterol: 0 mg*
*Carbohydrate: 30.0 g*
*Protein: 5.2 g*
*Sodium: 13.0 mg*

> **TIP**
>
> Most of a chile's heat isn't in the seeds, as many people think, but in the white tissue that holds the seeds. If you want a milder chile flavor, halve the chile and scrape out the white ribs and seeds. (Wear gloves if you are sensitive to the chile's heat.) If you can take the heat, mince the whole chile.

## HERBED YOGURT SAUCE

*A dollop of this lively sauce complements both the lentil salad and the stuffed tomatoes. You may decide it's something you want to keep in your refrigerator all the time for drizzling on sandwiches, sliced tomatoes, steamed vegetables, or salad greens.*

SERVES 4

¾ cup nonfat plain yogurt
2 tablespoons chopped fresh cilantro
1 tablespoon chopped fresh mint
2 teaspoons minced jalapeño chile (see Tip, page 147)
1 teaspoon fresh lime juice
1 teaspoon brown sugar

In a small bowl, combine yogurt, cilantro, mint, chili, lime juice, and sugar. Stir until well mixed. Serve immediately or refrigerate up to 2 days.

*Serving size: ¼ cup*
*Calories: 26.5*
*Fat: 0.7 g*
*Cholesterol: 0.77 mg*
*Carbohydrate: 4.0 g*
*Protein: 2.4 g*
*Sodium: 32.7 mg*

> **TIP**
>
> It may sound unlikely, but this creamy sauce makes an irresistible dip for fresh melon or pineapple.

### White Bean Salad with Zucchini, Tomato, and Basil
### Pasta with Creamy Red Pepper Sauce
Whole Grain Bread
### Fresh Apricot Clafouti

Apricots have such a short season that it's wise to enjoy them while they last. Here, they star in an old-fashioned French dessert, a simple baked custard called a *clafouti* (cla-foo-tee). On the way to dessert, you'll find an easy white bean salad enhanced with zucchini, tomato, garlic, and herbs; and pasta tossed with a delightful red pepper sauce that's made in 15 minutes. Instead of serving the salad and pasta together, serve them in courses. Intentionally slowing the meal down gives you a chance to relax more with friends and family at the table. What's more, when you eat slowly, you are less likely to overeat because you give your body the chance to tell you it's full.

The timing: Make the bean salad first, up to the point of putting it on the spinach leaves. Make the red pepper sauce and set aside while you heat a large pot of salted water for the pasta. While the water is heating, prepare and bake the dessert. Arrange the bean salad on its spinach bed, then sit down and enjoy it; cook the pasta when you have finished your salad.

# WHITE BEAN SALAD WITH ZUCCHINI, TOMATO, AND BASIL

*Contrasting textures, colors, and flavors give this salad its appeal. To save time, buy washed and dried spinach leaves, available in bags, in bulk, or in your supermarket's salad bar. If you prefer, you can make this salad with chickpeas, kidney beans, pinto beans, black beans, or whole hominy.*

SERVES 4

2 (15-ounce) cans small white beans, rinsed and drained, or 3 cups
    home-cooked white beans
1 cup diced zucchini
½ cup diced fresh tomato
2 tablespoons nonfat bottled Italian salad dressing
1 teaspoon red wine vinegar
1 clove garlic, minced
6 fresh basil leaves, in chiffonade (see Tip, page 211)
Salt and pepper
4 cups shredded fresh spinach leaves

In a medium bowl, combine beans, zucchini, tomato, salad dressing, vinegar, garlic, basil, and salt and pepper to taste. Toss gently.

Arrange spinach leaves on a serving platter. Mound bean salad in the center.

*Serving size: 1 cup spinach, 1 cup
    bean salad
Calories: 256
Fat: 0.9 g
Cholesterol: 0 mg
Carbohydrate: 50.0 g
Protein: 16.6 g
Sodium: 520.0 mg (with canned
    beans)*

> **TIP**
>
> Bean salads are a nutritionally sound addition to summer meals and picnics. Experiment with different bean varieties and with vegetable and herb additions. Try combining beans with fresh corn, cucumbers, celery, red and green peppers, or chopped fresh green beans. Season with dill, mint, or cilantro. Add chopped chives, green onions, or red onions for a bit of a bite. Beans are high in protein and complex carbohydrates and low in fat. And don't worry that you are tossing out nutrients when you rinse canned beans. Most of the nutrients are retained in the cooked bean.

# PASTA WITH CREAMY RED PEPPER SAUCE

*The best pasta choices for this dish are shapes with grooves or holes that can trap the luscious sauce. Try fusilli (spirals), rotelle (wagon wheels), conchiglie (shells), or penne rigate (ridged tubes). On another occasion, make a batch of the sauce to drizzle on steamed cauliflower, broccoli, or potatoes.*

## SERVES 4

2 large red bell peppers, seeds and ribs removed, then diced
1 cup diced onion
1 garlic clove, minced
½ teaspoon minced fresh thyme
2 cups Vegetable Broth, homemade (page 18) or store-bought
½ cup nonfat sour cream
Salt and cayenne pepper
1 pound dried pasta (see suggestions above)

In a large skillet, combine bell peppers, onion, garlic, thyme, and ½ cup vegetable broth. Bring to a simmer over moderate heat and simmer 5 minutes. Add remaining 1½ cups broth, cover, and simmer until peppers are tender, about 10 minutes. Whisk in sour cream and return to a simmer, then remove from heat.

Puree mixture in a food processor or blender until smooth. Strain through a fine sieve to remove bits of pepper skin. Return to skillet. Season with salt and cayenne pepper. Reheat and keep warm.

Bring a large pot of salted water to a boil over high heat. Add pasta and cook until al dente according to package directions. Drain and transfer to a warm bowl. Add sauce and toss to coat. Serve on warm plates.

*Serving size: 2 cups pasta, ½ cup sauce*
*Calories: 462*
*Fat: 1.9 g*
*Cholesterol: 0 mg*
*Carbohydrate: 94.0 g*
*Protein: 16.3 g*
*Sodium: 220.3 mg*

| TIP |
| --- |
| Red bell peppers were formerly green bell peppers, but they stayed on the plant long enough to ripen. They are great sources of vitamins A and C. Take advantage of their relatively low price in summer and enjoy them often. Sliced into strips, they make a sweet and satisfying summer snack. |

# FRESH APRICOT CLAFOUTI

*A clafouti is a classic French fruit dessert, a cross between a pudding and a custard. This version is particularly delicate, a creamy custard surrounding nuggets of soft-cooked apricots.*

SERVES 6

1 pound fresh apricots
2 tablespoons flour
1 cup nonfat milk
2 tablespoons plus 2 teaspoons sugar
1 teaspoon vanilla extract
½ cup liquid egg substitute

Preheat oven to 375 degrees F. Cut the apricots in quarters if small, or in sixths if large, discarding the pit. Set aside.

Put flour in a small saucepan. Whisk in enough of the milk to form a paste, then gradually whisk in the remaining milk, sugar, and vanilla. Bring to a boil, whisking constantly, over high heat. Mixture will thicken considerably. Remove from heat, cover, and let cool 10 minutes, then whisk in liquid egg substitute.

Put apricots in a 9-inch pie pan, either nonstick or lightly sprayed with nonstick spray (see Tip, page 251). Pour in milk mixture and bake until firm and lightly colored, about 25 minutes. The clafouti will be handsomely puffed but will fall a little as it cools. Serve warm.

*Serving size: ⅙ of the clafouti*
*Calories: 112*
*Fat: 0.5 g*
*Cholesterol: 0 mg*
*Carbohydrate: 23.0 mg*
*Protein: 5.3 g*
*Sodium: 88.0 mg*

| TIP |
| --- |
| Use this recipe to make clafouti with other fruits in season, such as pitted cherries, sliced peaches, or prune plums, or with canned apricots with no sugar added. |

**Two Middle Eastern Salads:**
**Hummus (Creamy Chickpea Puree)**
**Tabbouleh (Bulgur and Parsley Salad)**
Hearts of Romaine
**Fresh Tomato Soup**
Warm Whole Wheat Pita Bread
**Spiced Poached Peaches**

Hummus and tabbouleh—both Lebanese appetizers—are now so popular in this country that you find them in many American delis. But they can be high in fat, especially the hummus. It takes only half an hour to make both of these low-fat versions, and together, they are an inviting opener for a summer meal. Serve them with hearts of romaine for dipping and scooping and with wedges of pita bread, then follow with a simple fresh tomato soup that is the essence of summer. Whole poached peaches in a gently spiced syrup end the meal on a satisfying sweet note.

The timing: Make the peaches first and chill, if desired. Then prepare the soup, hummus, and tabbouleh in whatever order you like. The timing is not critical in this menu; all the finished dishes can stand to wait for the others with no loss of quality.

## HUMMUS
### (Creamy Chickpea Puree)

*You won't miss the high-fat tahini (sesame seed paste) in this version of hummus; it tastes plenty rich and flavorful without it. Once you see how easy it is to make, you'll probably want to have it on hand often. Hummus is a terrific dip for raw or steamed vegetables and an excellent sandwich spread.*

SERVES 4

1 (15-ounce) can chickpeas (garbanzo beans)
2 tablespoons lemon juice
¼ teaspoon ground cumin
1 small garlic clove, minced
Pinch cayenne pepper
2 tablespoons minced parsley
1 tablespoon minced red onion

Drain chickpeas, reserving juice. Do not rinse. Transfer peas to a food processor or blender and blend with ½ cup reserved chickpea juice, lemon juice, cumin, garlic, and cayenne. Add parsley and red onion and pulse briefly just to mix.

*Serving size: ½ cup*
*Calories: 134.5*
*Fat: 2.1 g*
*Cholesterol: 0 mg*
*Carbohydrate: 22.5 g*
*Protein: 7.2 g*
*Sodium: 359.0 mg*

> **TIP**
>
> For a real summer treat, make a hummus and tomato sandwich on toasted whole wheat bread or a whole wheat bagel. Spread bread with hummus; add sliced tomato, sprouts, and thinly sliced red onion and green pepper.

# TABBOULEH
## (Bulgur and Parsley Salad)

*Spoon this Lebanese salad into pale green romaine spears or scoop it up with wedges of warm whole wheat pita bread. You might want to double this recipe and have the remainder for lunch the next day. Tabbouleh makes a great sandwich: pile it into pita bread along with shredded lettuce, sliced tomato, and a spoonful of Hummus (page 152) or nonfat yogurt.*

SERVES 4

1 cup bulgur
½ cup diced, seeded, peeled cucumber
Salt to taste, plus ½ teaspoon
3 tablespoons lemon juice
1 teaspoon minced garlic
Pepper
1 cup diced fresh tomato
1 cup chopped parsley
1 tablespoon chopped fresh mint

Bring 1 cup water to a boil in a small saucepan. Add bulgur, cover, remove from heat, and let stand 25 minutes.

Sprinkle cucumber with ½ teaspoon salt. Place in a sieve set over a

---

bowl and let drain 20 minutes. Press lightly on the cucumber to release moisture.

In a small bowl, whisk together lemon juice, garlic, and salt and pepper to taste. Transfer bulgur to a large bowl, add lemon juice mixture, and fluff with a fork to blend. Stir in tomatoes, cucumbers, parsley, and mint. Taste and adjust seasoning.

*Serving size: 1 cup*
*Calories: 166*
*Fat: 0.85 g*
*Cholesterol: 0 mg*
*Carbohydrate: 36.2 g*
*Protein: 6.4 g*
*Sodium: 296.8 mg*

---

**TIP**

Be sure to buy bulgur and not plain cracked wheat. Bulgur is cracked wheat that has been steamed, then dried, so it needs only to soak in hot water to soften.

---

## THINK PLANNED-OVERS, NOT LEFTOVERS

You can get a running start on many meals by regularly cooking extra. Are you making minestrone? It takes maybe 10 percent more time to make twice as much soup, an impressive return on your investment. The next day, the extra soup can be thickened with pureed beans and served over pasta or polenta, or pureed and seasoned with herbs to make it taste fresh and new.

Avoid the temptation to make huge quantities or you will likely tire of the dish before you finish it. (Vegetable broth excepted—you can't have too much in your freezer.) But a second day's supply of last night's grains, beans, or vegetables can give you a leg up on meal preparation. Bean dishes even seem to improve overnight.

Be sure to pack the extra food in airtight plastic containers. Otherwise, they can lose moisture and pick up odors from the refrigerator.

Extra cooked broccoli? Serve it as a chilled salad with nonfat Italian dressing and diced pimiento; or slice and add to a mixed green salad; or chop and add to steamed brown rice or millet; or reheat with sautéed onions and garlic and serve over pasta.

Extra cooked turnips, carrots, sweet potatoes, corn? Leftover vegetables can be pureed with vegetable broth to make soup. Add nonfat milk or yogurt for a creamier texture. Season with herbs, sun-dried tomatoes, or ground ginger. For a heartier soup, add small pasta shapes or cooked rice.

Extra bean or vegetable stew? Reheat and stuff a pita with it or make a burrito, adding shredded lettuce or cabbage, chopped fresh tomato, and cilantro.

Extra chili? Ladle it into a warm bun for a "sloppy Joe"; or stretch it with canned beans and diced squash and spoon it over rice; or serve it over whole grain toast and top with grated nonfat cheese to make a hearty open-face sandwich.

Extra rice? Simmer in nonfat milk and thicken with cornstarch to make rice pudding; or reheat for breakfast with nonfat milk, brown sugar, and raisins or chopped dates.

Extra cooked greens? Add chopped cooked kale, chard, beet greens, or collards to tomato sauce for pasta; toss with steamed wild rice or couscous; stir into a pot of braised beans; or dress with Herbed Yogurt Sauce (page 147) and serve as a salad.

Extra cooked beans? Add vegetable broth, pasta, and chopped vegetables to make a soup; or puree and use as a sandwich spread or dip.

---

## FRESH TOMATO SOUP

*This basic but flavorful tomato soup can be "accessorized" to suit your mood. Serve it hot or cold, with a splash of balsamic vinegar or a dollop of nonfat sour cream or yogurt, or add chopped fresh herbs such as basil, cilantro, oregano, or parsley. You could also add cooked pasta or float Homemade Croutons (page 186) on top.*

SERVES 4

**4 pounds fresh tomatoes, peeled, seeded, and coarsely chopped (see Tip, page 127)**
**½ cup Vegetable Broth, homemade (page 18) or store-bought**
**¼ cup chopped onion**
**Salt**

In a medium nonreactive saucepan, combine tomatoes, broth, onion, and salt to taste. Bring to a boil over high heat. Reduce heat to moderate and cook until onion is tender, about 15 minutes.

---

*Serving size: 1 cup*
*Calories: 77.5*
*Fat: 1.2 g*
*Cholesterol: 0 mg*
*Carbohydrate: 17.1 g*
*Protein: 3.1 g*
*Sodium: 30.0 mg (with no salt added)*

> **TIP**
>
> Make a double or triple batch of this soup and enjoy it over two or three nights, in different guises. Try it one night as is; the next night with pasta shells, white beans, and diced zucchini; the third night, with rice and spinach.

# SPICED POACHED PEACHES

Candied ginger, cinnamon, and vanilla flavor the poaching liquid for these peaches. If you can't find candied ginger (usually available on the supermarket spice rack), substitute a pinch of ground ginger. You could use the same delicious poaching liquid for apricots, nectarines, or pears.

### SERVES 4

2 tablespoons sugar
1 tablespoon lemon juice
2 teaspoons minced candied ginger (see Tip, page 78)
1 teaspoon cornstarch
1 cinnamon stick
½ vanilla bean, quartered lengthwise
4 medium peaches, peeled (see Tip, page 157)

In a medium saucepan, combine 2 cups water with sugar, lemon juice, ginger, cornstarch, cinnamon, and vanilla bean. Whisk to dissolve cornstarch. Bring to a boil over moderately high heat. Add the peaches and adjust heat to maintain a gentle simmer. Cook peaches, turning them over with a spoon occasionally, until they are tender when pierced with a knife, about 10 minutes. Transfer them to a serving bowl with a slotted spoon. Raise heat to high and bring poaching liquid to a boil. Boil until reduced to 1 cup, about 5 minutes. Cool, then pour over peaches. Serve each peach with ¼ cup of the flavorful poaching liquid.

*Everyday Cooking with Dr. Dean Ornish*

*Serving size: 1 peach, ¼ cup sauce*
*Calories: 70*
*Fat: 0.7 g*
*Cholesterol: 0 mg*
*Carbohydrate: 18.0 g*
*Protein: 0.6 g*
*Sodium: 0.6 mg*

---

**TIP**

This recipe calls for cooking and serving the peaches whole. If you can find free-stone peaches, you can halve them, remove the pit, and poach the halves. Note that the halves will cook more quickly.

---

**Corn Pancakes**
**Swiss Chard with Roasted Onions**
**Cucumber and Potato Soup with Dill**
Whole Grain Bread
Fresh Blueberries and Raspberries

The combination of airy corn pancakes with well-seasoned chard is one of the most popular dishes chef Jean-Marc Fullsack makes at the week-long retreats for Ornish program participants. They are easy to reproduce at home; serve them as a first course before bowls of delicate cucumber-potato soup. For dessert, alternate layers of blueberries and raspberries in a pretty compote dish or individual wineglasses.

The timing: Make the soup first, then make the Swiss chard. Set both aside. Make the pancakes, reheating the chard just before the pancakes are ready. Serve pancakes hot off the griddle, with the chard alongside. Then reheat the soup for a second course with a basket of whole grain bread. Assemble the berry dessert just before serving.

## CORN PANCAKES

*These are some of the lightest pancakes you'll ever eat, thanks to the aerating power of egg whites. Eat them hot off the griddle with Swiss Chard with Roasted Onions (page 159) or with a favorite salsa. And don't just reserve them for dinner; they would be a nice treat for Sunday breakfast with a little fat-free fruit chutney or maple syrup.*

SERVES 4

---

1½ cups fresh, canned, or thawed frozen corn kernels (see Tip, page 141)
3 large egg whites
⅓ cup soft tofu
¼ cup unbleached all-purpose flour
1 tablespoon chopped parsley
½ teaspoon baking powder
½ teaspoon salt
¼ teaspoon black pepper

Set aside ½ cup corn kernels. In a food processor or blender, blend remaining 1 cup corn with 1 egg white, tofu, flour, parsley, baking powder, salt, and pepper until smooth, stopping once to scrape down the sides of the container. Transfer mixture to a bowl and stir in reserved whole corn.

In another bowl, beat the remaining 2 egg whites to soft, moist peaks that droop slightly when the beater is lifted. Scoop the egg whites onto the corn batter and fold them in gently with a rubber spatula.

Preheat oven to low. Spray a nonstick skillet lightly with nonstick spray (see Tip, page 251) and place over moderate heat. When the skillet is hot enough to make the batter sizzle, make pancakes, using ¼ cup batter per cake. Cook until browned on the bottom, 2 to 3 minutes, then turn and cook until cakes are golden brown on the other side, about 2 more minutes. Transfer to a platter and keep warm in oven. Continue until all batter is used.

*Serving size: 3 three-inch pancakes*
*Calories: 124*
*Fat: 2.3 g*
*Cholesterol: 0 mg*
*Carbohydrate: 19.8 g*
*Protein: 8.5 g*
*Sodium: 333.5 mg*

> **TIP**
>
> If you're short on time, replace the corn pancakes with corn on the cob served Mexican style: with a swipe of nonfat sour cream and a dash of chili powder.

# SWISS CHARD WITH ROASTED ONIONS

*You can adapt this recipe to whatever greens you have: spinach, kale, collards, or beet greens, for example. Just adjust the boiling time (spinach takes seconds to cook; collards take several minutes), and make sure to transfer the boiled greens to ice water to stop the cooking and preserve the nutrients. The roasted onion and softened red pepper add a pleasing sweetness to the dish. On another evening, serve these savory greens as a sauce for spaghetti.*

SERVES 4

½ bunch Swiss chard (about 10 ounces total)
1 cup diced red bell pepper
2 garlic cloves, minced
½ cup Vegetable Broth, homemade (page 18) or store-bought
1 large Roasted Onion (page 22), peeled and diced
Salt and pepper

Bring a large pot of salted water to a boil. Separate chard ribs from leaves. Coarsely chop leaves and ribs separately. Boil the ribs until tender, about 4 minutes. Scoop them out with a slotted spoon or sieve and run under cold water to stop the cooking. Boil leaves in same water until tender, about 3 minutes. Drain and transfer to a bowl of ice water. Drain and gently squeeze leaves to remove excess water.

Combine bell pepper, garlic, and vegetable broth in a skillet over moderate heat. Cover and cook until peppers are softened, about 4 minutes. Stir in diced onion, chard ribs and leaves, and salt and pepper to taste. Cook until hot throughout.

*Serving size: ½ cup*
*Calories: 40*
*Fat: 0.18 g*
*Cholesterol: 0 mg*
*Carbohydrate: 8.8 g*
*Protein: 2.4 g*
*Sodium: 159.4 mg (with no salt added)*

**TIP**

Cold cooked greens make an inviting salad when seasoned with a splash of vinegar. Make a double batch of these greens so you can have some chilled the next day with hot pepper vinegar, red wine vinegar, or the mild balsamic vinegar from Italy.

# Cucumber and Potato Soup with Dill

*Cucumbers and dill are a marriage made in heaven. Add vegetable broth and a little potato for body, and you can make a smooth and delicate soup in half an hour. On a hot day or for lunch, consider serving it chilled. If you can't find fresh dill, substitute 2 tablespoons minced green onion.*

### SERVES 4

3 cucumbers, about 2 pounds total
1 onion, diced
4 cups Vegetable Broth, homemade (page 18) or store-bought
1 small russet-type baking potato (about 6 ounces), peeled and diced
1½ teaspoons minced fresh dill
Salt and pepper
4 teaspoons nonfat sour cream or yogurt (optional)

Peel the cucumbers, halve them lengthwise, and scrape out the seeds with a small spoon. Dice enough to make 1 cup finely diced cucumber. Coarsely chop the remaining cucumber.

In a saucepan, combine onion and ½ cup vegetable broth. Bring to a simmer over moderate heat and simmer 5 minutes. Add remaining 3½ cups stock, coarsely chopped cucumber, and potato. Cover and simmer until vegetables are tender, about 15 minutes. Puree in a blender or food processor until smooth. Return to saucepan and bring to a simmer over moderate heat. Add finely diced cucumber and simmer until cucumber softens slightly, about 5 minutes. Stir in dill and season to taste with salt and pepper. Serve in warm mugs or bowls, topping each portion, if desired, with a teaspoon of sour cream or yogurt.

*Serving size: 1¼ cups*
*Calories: 57*
*Fat: 0.17 g*
*Cholesterol: 0 mg*
*Carbohydrate: 12.8 g*
*Protein: 1.8 g*
*Sodium: 20.0 mg (with no salt added)*

### TIP

Greenhouse cucumbers (the long ones that come wrapped in plastic) tend to have fewer seeds and less bitterness than the common slicing cucumbers. They are a good choice for this soup and great to have on hand for snacking. In summer, look for the pale green Armenian cucumbers and the skinny, dark green Japanese cucumbers. Both have a firm, crisp flesh and superior flavor.

"INDEPENDENCE DAY BARBECUE"
**Chilled Zucchini Soup with Salsa**
**Grilled Portobello Mushroom and Onion Burgers**
Fresh Corn on the Cob
**Creamy Coleslaw**
**Old-Fashioned Potato Salad**
Vegetarian Baked Beans
Chilled Watermelon Slices
**Warm Peach Cobbler**

Invite friends and plan a feast on the Fourth of July with this collection of all-American dishes—everyone's favorite barbecue food traditions in fat-trimmed versions. Pass around mugs of chilled zucchini soup, then arrange the side dishes on a buffet, and put the "burgers" on the grill. Portobello mushroom burgers are showing up on trendy restaurant menus now, and the giant portobello mushrooms are becoming staples in supermarkets. People love their firm texture and meaty taste, and grilling suits them to perfection. Put the corn on the grill, too, if you like: peel back (but don't remove) the husks, remove the silk, and soak the corn in cold water for 20 minutes. Then replace the husks and tie them at the top with a thin husk ribbon. Grill until hot throughout, 15 to 20 minutes.

Most supermarkets carry fat-free vegetarian baked beans, and here's the perfect setting for them. Add them to the buffet alongside two revised American classics: a fat-free coleslaw and potato salad. For dessert: chilled watermelon and an irresistible fresh fruit cobbler.

The timing: You can make the potato salad and the zucchini soup a day ahead. In any case, you should make the soup several hours ahead so it has time to chill. Slice and chill the watermelon and make the salsa several hours ahead; make the coleslaw at least an hour ahead. Prepare the mushrooms, peppers, and onions for the burger and set aside. Trim and soak the corn a half-hour ahead, if grilling; otherwise, husk the corn and set it aside. Prepare the cobbler and put it in the oven shortly before the meal is served so that it will be warm when it's time for dessert. When it's time to eat, heat the beans, boil or grill the corn, and grill the vegetables for the mushroom burger.

---

# CHILLED ZUCCHINI SOUP WITH SALSA

*Adapted from a recipe that appeared in* Bon Appétit *magazine, this refreshing soup hits the spot on a hot day. You can make it a day ahead, but the salsa is best if made no more than a few hours before serving.*

SERVES 8

*Zucchini Soup:*

½ cup diced onion

3 cups Vegetable Broth, homemade (page 18) or store-bought

2 pounds zucchini, in ½-inch dice

1 cup sliced green onions

2 cups nonfat plain yogurt

½ cup chopped fresh basil

Salt and pepper

*Salsa:*

1 cup diced, seeded, peeled tomato (see Tip, page 127)

⅓ cup diced, seeded, peeled cucumber

⅓ cup fresh corn kernels (see Tip, page 141)

2 tablespoons minced red onion

2 tablespoons minced jalapeño chile

2 tablespoons cider vinegar

2 teaspoons chopped cilantro

Make zucchini soup: In a large skillet or saucepan, combine onion and ½ cup vegetable broth. Bring to a simmer, covered, over moderate heat and simmer until onion is softened, about 5 minutes. Add zucchini and remaining 2½ cups vegetable broth. Bring to a boil, cover, adjust heat to maintain a simmer and cook until zucchini is tender, 10 to 12 minutes. Remove from heat and stir in green onions.

Puree zucchini mixture, yogurt, and basil in a blender or food processor until smooth, in batches if necessary. Transfer to serving bowl and refrigerate until cold, or up to 24 hours. Just before serving, season to taste with salt and pepper.

Make salsa: In a small bowl, stir together tomato, cucumber, corn, onion, jalapeño, and vinegar. Refrigerate until chilled. Just before serving, drain off any accumulated juices and stir in cilantro. Put 1 cup of soup in each bowl and top with 3 tablespoons salsa.

Serving size: 1 cup soup,
  3 tablespoons salsa
Calories: 52
Fat: 0.2 g
Cholesterol: 1.0 mg
Carbohydrate: 8.8 g
Protein: 4.2 g
Sodium: 99.0 mg (with no salt added)

<table>
<tr><td>

**TIP**

You'll want to make this chopped vegetable salsa again for use in other dishes. Serve it on black bean soup; in warm corn tortillas spread with nonfat refried beans; or over chopped romaine for a summer salad.

</td></tr>
</table>

## GRILLED PORTOBELLO MUSHROOM AND ONION BURGERS

*Look for the cultivated portobello mushrooms in your market's produce section, where they may be sold whole or already sliced and packaged. These giant mushrooms (the caps may be five inches across) are just common brown mushrooms that have been allowed to mature. They are wonderfully meaty in taste and texture, and grilling brings out their best.*

### SERVES 8

2 French-style baguettes (each about 24 inches long and 2 inches in
  diameter)
4 portobello mushrooms (about 6 ounces each)
1½ cups nonfat bottled Italian salad dressing
5 tablespoons chopped fresh thyme
¼ cup Worcestershire sauce
2 large red onions, in ½-inch-thick slices
2 large red bell peppers, quartered, stems and ribs removed
8 lettuce leaves

Cut each baguette into four equal sections, then cut each section in half horizontally.

Wipe the mushrooms clean with a damp paper towel, remove the stems, and slice the caps into ½-inch-thick slices.

In a small bowl, whisk together salad dressing, thyme, and Worcestershire sauce.

Preheat oven to low and prepare a medium-hot charcoal fire. Place grilling rack 4 to 6 inches from the coals.

Brush mushrooms, onions, and bell peppers with herbed dressing. Grill, turning once or twice, until nicely browned on the outside and tender, 6 to 8 minutes total. Remove from grill and keep warm in oven.

Brush the cut sides of the baguettes with remaining herbed dressing. Place cut side down over indirect heat (not directly over the coals) and grill until rolls are just heated through and beginning to brown at the edges.

For each "burger," place a baguette bottom cut side up on a plate. Top with an onion slice, 4 to 5 mushroom slices, one quarter of a bell pepper, and a lettuce leaf. Cover with the top of the baguette, pressing down gently to form a sandwich. Repeat with remaining ingredients. Serve immediately.

*Serving size: 1 burger*
*Calories: 235*
*Fat: 2.2 g*
*Cholesterol: 0 mg*
*Carbohydrate: 45.0 g*
*Protein: 8.3 g*
*Sodium: 233.0 mg*

**TIP**

It's not easy to find a whole grain hamburger bun with no fat added, but a specialty bakery may be willing to make them for you. If you can find buns, they will make your mushroom burger even more inviting. And don't forget to set out the other condiments that people like to put on burgers: mustard, nonfat mayonnaise, pickles, and sliced tomato.

## CREAMY COLESLAW

*Packaged coleslaw mix, available in many supermarket produce sections, makes it easy to whip up a quick slaw. Of course you can also slice your own red and white cabbage and grate some carrots to make the 8 cups of undressed slaw mix you need for this recipe. The tangy dressing takes only a moment to make. Like most slaws, this one improves with an hour's rest.*

SERVES 8

**Creamy Tofu Dressing:**
¾ cup soft tofu
¼ cup cider vinegar
1 tablespoon plus 1 teaspoon honey
1 teaspoon prepared horseradish

½ teaspoon celery seed
½ teaspoon salt
¼ teaspoon pepper

8 cups packaged coleslaw mix

Combine all dressing ingredients in a food processor or blender and blend until smooth.

Toss dressing with coleslaw in a large bowl. Refrigerate at least 1 hour before serving.

*Serving size: 1 cup slaw,*
  *¼ of the dressing*
*Calories: 63*
*Fat: 1.9 g*
*Cholesterol: 0 mg*
*Carbohydrate: 8.2 g*
*Protein: 4.0 g*
*Sodium: 253.0 mg*

> **TIP**
>
> You can also use Creamy Tofu Dressing on steamed broccoli, cauliflower, or green beans, or drizzled over salad greens.

## OLD-FASHIONED POTATO SALAD

*The Fourth of July would seem incomplete without a creamy potato salad. Fortunately, it's easy to remodel the classic recipe, which is typically a minefield of fat and calories. You won't miss them.*

SERVES 8

3 pounds red-skinned potatoes
1 cup diced celery
1 cup diced red onion
¼ cup cider vinegar
1½ teaspoons salt
¼ teaspoon pepper
3 tablespoons sweet pickle relish
3 hard-boiled egg whites, chopped (see Deviled Eggs, page 224)
¾ cup nonfat mayonnaise
1 tablespoon minced parsley

In a bamboo steamer or collapsible metal steamer, steam the potatoes over boiling water, covered, until tender when pierced, 30 to 40 minutes. When cool enough to handle, peel, then cut into ½- to ¾-inch dice.

In a large bowl, stir together potatoes, celery, onion, vinegar, salt, and pepper. Add relish, egg whites, and mayonnaise and stir gently to combine. Taste and adjust seasoning with salt and pepper. Transfer to a serving bowl and sprinkle with parsley.

Serving size: ¾ cup
Calories: 84
Fat: 0.17 g
Cholesterol: 0 mg
Carbohydrate: 18.0 g
Protein: 3.3 g
Sodium: 523.0 mg

> **TIP**
>
> You can make this salad a day ahead and refrigerate it. Before serving, taste and adjust seasoning with salt, pepper, or vinegar.

## WARM PEACH COBBLER

*Choose ripe, fragrant peaches to make this homespun dessert, or substitute 4 cups juicy blackberries or olallieberries. A mixture of peaches and berries would be nice, too.*

### SERVES 8

6 medium peaches (see Tip, page 167)
⅓ cup sugar
¾ cup unbleached all-purpose flour
¾ teaspoon baking powder
Pinch salt
6 tablespoons nonfat milk
6 tablespoons liquid egg substitute
½ teaspoon vanilla extract

Preheat oven to 400 degrees F. Peel and slice peaches. You should have about 4 cups. Sprinkle with 2 teaspoons sugar taken from the ⅓ cup.

In a bowl, stir together remaining sugar, flour, baking powder, and salt. In a large bowl, whisk together milk, egg substitute, and vanilla.

Add dry ingredients to wet ingredients and stir just to blend. Batter will be thick.

Put peaches in a 9-inch nonstick pie pan. Spoon the batter over the peaches, smoothing it with the back of the spoon. It doesn't need to cover the peaches completely; in fact, it looks nice if some of the peaches are poking through. Bake until the peaches are bubbly and the topping is browned, about 30 minutes.

*Serving size: ⅛ of the cobbler*
*Calories: 110*
*Fat: 0.18 g*
*Cholesterol: 0.2 mg*
*Carbohydrate: 25.0 g*
*Protein: 2.9 g*
*Sodium: 20.0 mg*

> ### TIP
>
> If your peaches are nice and ripe, you should be able to peel them easily with a small knife. If not, it will help to blanch them. Bring a large pot of water to a boil. Cut an "X" in the rounded end of each peach. Add peaches to the boiling water and boil 30 seconds. Transfer to ice water with a slotted spoon. Lift them out when they are cool. The skins will slip right off.

## "AL FRESCO LUNCH"

### Gazpacho with White Beans
### Zucchini and Cheese Quesadillas
### Summer Fruit Salad with Lime and Mint

Eating outdoors is one of life's simple pleasures, whether it's lunch by a swimming pool or a picnic on the grass. Take advantage of good summer weather to set your table (or blanket!) outdoors and treat guests to this tantalizing lunch: chilled Spanish gazpacho with hot Mexican quesadillas, followed by a photogenic fruit salad with the zing of fresh lime. The meal could just as easily be a light summer supper, eaten with friends on a patio or terrace after the sun goes down. You can prepare the quesadillas indoors, or outdoors on a gas or charcoal grill. Just be sure to have plenty of them if there are kids around.

The timing: Make the soup up to 12 hours ahead. Make the fruit salad up to 4 hours ahead. Prepare all the quesadilla ingredients but do not cook them until you are ready to eat. They should be served hot from the oven or grill as a companion to the gazpacho. Follow with the fruit salad.

---

# GAZPACHO WITH WHITE BEANS

*This chilled Spanish soup is great for summer parties because you can make it hours ahead. For best flavor, use vine-ripe tomatoes and fresh herbs. The white beans are an unconventional but likable addition to this classic dish; they contribute body and a generous dose of fiber and calcium.*

FROM ELIZABETH KAPSTEIN, CHEF
*Dr. Ornish Program for Reversing Heart Disease at Beth Israel Medical Center, New York, New York*
SERVES 6

3 cups tomato juice
1 (15-ounce) can cannellini or navy beans, drained and rinsed, or 2 cups home-cooked white beans
1½ cups diced tomatoes
1 cup diced, seeded, peeled cucumber
1 cup diced green pepper
1 cup thinly sliced green onion
½ cup diced celery
¼ cup thinly sliced fresh basil leaves
2 tablespoons minced parsley
2 teaspoons minced fresh oregano, or 1 teaspoon dried oregano
2 teaspoons red wine vinegar
1 garlic clove, minced
¼ teaspoon ground cumin
Salt and pepper

In a large serving bowl, combine tomato juice, beans, tomatoes, cucumber, green pepper, green onion, celery, basil, parsley, oregano, wine vinegar, garlic, and cumin. Stir to combine. Season to taste with salt and pepper. Refrigerate 4 to 12 hours before serving. Serve chilled.

*Serving size: 1 cup*
*Calories: 149*
*Fat: 0.7 g*

> **TIP**
>
> On another occasion, when you're not serving quesadillas, serve the gazpacho with a bowl of Homemade Croutons (page 186). You can also make a smooth gazpacho by pureeing all the ingredients except the beans; stir the beans in after pureeing.

Cholesterol: 0 mg
Carbohydrate: 30.0 g
Protein: 8.6 g
Sodium: 500.4 mg (*with canned tomato juice and canned beans*)


## ZUCCHINI AND CHEESE QUESADILLAS

These cheesy Mexican restaurant favorites are easy to make at home, even without a griddle. You can bake them in a hot oven or grill them over charcoal or gas outdoors. If you're just making one for yourself, you can toast it in a nonstick skillet sprayed lightly with nonstick spray (see Tip, page 251), cooking it on both sides over moderate heat until the cheese melts.

### SERVES 6

3 small zucchini
⅜ teaspoon kosher salt
12 nonfat flour tortillas
1½ cups grated nonfat mozzarella cheese
3 tablespoons minced red onion
2 tablespoons canned diced mild chiles
1 tablespoon minced cilantro

Trim ends from zucchini and grate in a food processor or on the coarse side of a hand grater. Put grated zucchini in a sieve or colander and toss with salt to wilt slightly. Let drain 5 minutes, then squeeze dry.

Preheat oven to 500 degrees F. or prepare a medium-hot charcoal fire. Spray 1 or 2 large baking sheets lightly with nonstick spray (see Tip, page 251). Lay 6 tortillas flat on the baking sheet(s). Spread each tortilla evenly with ¼ cup zucchini, ¼ cup cheese, 1½ teaspoons onion, 1 teaspoon diced chiles, and ½ teaspoon cilantro. Top each with one of the remaining tortillas, pressing down gently to form a sandwich.

Oven method: Bake quesadillas until cheese is melted and tortillas begin to brown, 5 to 7 minutes.

Grill method: Grill quesadillas carefully over indirect heat (not directly over coals), turning once or twice, until cheese has melted and tortillas begin to brown, 3 to 4 minutes.

With a large spatula, transfer quesadillas to a cutting board. Using a pizza wheel or large knife, cut each quesadilla into quarters and serve immediately.

*Serving size: 1 quesadilla*
*Calories: 138*
*Fat: 0.1 g*
*Cholesterol: 4.4 mg*
*Carbohydrate: 23.3 g*
*Protein: 3.2 g*
*Sodium: 550 mg*

> **TIP**
>
> Create your own quesadilla variations by adding such ingredients as cooked black beans or nonfat refried beans; roasted red peppers; chopped tomato; or fresh corn.

## SUMMER FRUIT SALAD WITH LIME AND MINT

*It would be hard to imagine a more refreshing end to a meal than this lovely fruit salad. Choose a pretty platter or shallow bowl to serve it in.*

### SERVES 6

1 Crenshaw, cantaloupe, or honeydew melon
¾ cup fresh raspberries
¾ cup fresh blackberries or blueberries
1 lime
6 fresh mint leaves, shredded

Quarter melon and remove seeds. Using a thin, sharp knife, remove the skin from the melon quarters. Cut each quarter crosswise into ½-inch-thick slices and place in a medium serving bowl. Scatter raspberries and blackberries over the top.

Grate the lime zest (green part only). You should have about 1 teaspoon. Scatter the zest over the fruit and squeeze the lime juice over the top. Scatter mint leaves over the top and serve at once, or cover and refrigerate up to 4 hours.

*Serving size: 1 cup*
*Calories: 48.8*
*Fat: 0.4 g*
*Cholesterol: 0 mg*
*Carbohydrate: 11.89 g*
*Protein: 1.0 g*
*Sodium: 9.1 mg*

---

**TIP**

Take advantage of whatever fresh summer fruit is available to you to vary this salad. Replace the melon with peaches or nectarines, for example. Replace the blackberries with figs. Aim for contrasting textures and colors.

---

# Autumn

**Creamy Mushroom Stroganoff**
**Broccoli Florets with Honey Mustard Dressing**
Warm Nine-Grain Bread
Crisp Fall Apples

**Corn Lover's Vegetable Stew**
**Braised Kale with Garlic**
**Perfect Fat-Free Corn Bread**
Fresh Pears

**Mushroom and Spinach Lasagne**
**Caesar Salad with Homemade Croutons**
Crusty Italian Bread
**Vanilla Poached Pears**

**Two-Bean Enchiladas**
**Spicy Mexican Rice**
**Green Pea Guacamole**
**Fresh Tomato Salsa**
**Cabbage and Green Apple Slaw**
Pineapple with Pomegranate Seeds

**Rigatoni with Rich Tomato-Mushroom Sauce**
Mixed Garden Salad
**Ranch Dressing**
Crusty Italian Bread
**Apple-Raisin Strudel**

**Marinated Mushrooms and Sweet Peppers**
**Gary's Broccoli Manicotti**
Crusty Italian Bread
**Zucchini Brownies**

**Jo's Chili**
Creamy Coleslaw (page 164)
**Spicy Corn Muffins**
Sliced Persimmons with Lime *or* Chilled Red and Green Grapes

**Chickpea Stew with Couscous**
**Cucumber-Yogurt Sauce with Mint**
Warm Whole Wheat Pita Bread
Orange Segments with Chopped Dates

**Greek Bean Salad**
**Harvest Vegetable Soup**
Whole Wheat Bread
**Baked Apples with Apricot Jam**

**Mixed Grains Loaf with Spinach**
Herbed Yogurt Sauce (page 147)
**Jean-Marc's Oven "Fries"**
Steamed Fresh Green Beans
**Homemade Chunky Applesauce**

"CASUAL DINNER WITH FRIENDS"
**Sweet Potato Soup with Lime**
**Rice-Stuffed Bell Peppers**
**Black Bean Sauce**
Steamed Swiss Chard
**Carrot Cake with Cream Cheese Frosting**

"A THANKSGIVING GROANING BOARD"
Relish Tray: **Deviled Eggs,** Pickled Cherry Peppers, Baby Carrots, Celery Hearts
**Autumn Vegetables in a Squash**
White and Wild Rice Pilaf
**Glazed Holiday Yams**
**Old-Fashioned Bread Dressing**
**Brandied Cranberry Relish**
Watercress and Beet Salad
**Apple Cranberry Cake**

When the autumn leaves turn color, the produce market changes color, too. In come the hard-shelled squash in forest green, orange, and gold; the new-crop apples with their shiny red skins; the inky-purple eggplants and green-gold pears; and, for those lucky enough to find them, tart quince and sweet persimmons. These alluring fruits and vegetables can inspire some delicious autumn meals, enhanced with grains, beans, salads, and whole grain breads. The cooler weather means appetites gear up for heartier fare, like Creamy Mushroom Stroganoff (page 177), Rigatoni with Rich Tomato-Mushroom Sauce (page 194), chili (page 205) with Spicy Corn Muffins (page 206), and Chickpea Stew (page 208). And yes, you can entertain guests within Reversal Diet guidelines. With the menus in this chapter, you can welcome friends to an informal dinner party featuring Sweet Potato Soup with Lime (page 218) and Rice-Stuffed Bell Peppers (page 219); or set an old-fashioned Thanksgiving groaning board, with many of the traditional dishes in slimmed-down editions.

In autumn, look for:
apples
beans, shelling
broccoli
brussels sprouts
cranberries
eggplants
grapes
jerusalem artichokes
pears
peppers, sweet and hot

persimmons
quince
squash, hard-shelled
sweet potatoes and yams
wild mushrooms

**Creamy Mushroom Stroganoff**
**Broccoli Florets with Honey Mustard Dressing**
Warm Nine-Grain Bread
Crisp Fall Apples
☙

A mushroom stroganoff might sound like a time-consuming dish to make, but this one isn't. You can have dinner on the table in half an hour: fettuccine noodles with a creamy mushroom sauce, chilled broccoli florets drizzled with a zesty mustard dressing, and sturdy nine-grain bread for soaking up the last bits of sauce. Buy several different kinds and colors of apples—a farmers' market is a good source—and cut them in wedges so every diner can have a little of each.

The timing: Blanch and chill the broccoli first and make the honey mustard dressing. Then prepare the mushroom stroganoff.

## Creamy Mushroom Stroganoff

*If your market carries fresh shiitake or other exotic mushrooms, use them in place of some or all of the familiar button mushrooms. Even with the usual supermarket mushrooms, this stroganoff is a satisfying meatless rendition of the classic Russian dish. On another evening, serve the sauce over a brown and wild rice pilaf or over steamed kasha (buckwheat groats).*

Serves 4

6 (2.5-ounce) patties Boca Burger "No Fat Original" or other textured
   soy protein
1 cup chopped onion
1 teaspoon minced garlic
1 teaspoon soy sauce
4 cups sliced mushrooms
2 cups Vegetable Broth, homemade (page 18) or store-bought
2 cups nonfat sour cream
2 tablespoons cornstarch
1 tablespoon brandy (optional)
¼ cup minced parsley
Salt and pepper
1 pound dried fettuccine (without egg)

Cook Boca Burger according to package directions. Chop into ¾-inch dice.

In a large nonstick skillet, combine onion, garlic, soy sauce, and ¼ cup water. Bring to a simmer over moderate heat and simmer until liquid evaporates and onions are translucent, 3 to 5 minutes. Add mushrooms, stock, and Boca Burger. Simmer gently until mushrooms are cooked, 15 to 20 minutes. Stir in sour cream and bring mixture to a simmer. In a small bowl, whisk together cornstarch and 2 tablespoons cold water until smooth. Add to sauce, whisking it in well. Simmer until thickened, about 3 minutes. Stir in brandy and half the parsley and season to taste with salt and pepper. Keep warm.

Bring a large pot of salted water to a boil over high heat. Add noodles and cook according to package directions until al dente. Drain. Divide noodles among four warm plates. Ladle mushroom stroganoff over noodles. Top each serving with some of the remaining minced parsley.

*Serving size: 1½ cups*
*Calories: 547*
*Fat: 2.5 g*
*Cholesterol: 0 mg*
*Carbohydrate: 124.0 g*
*Protein: 22.0 g*
*Sodium: 621.0 mg (with no salt added)*

---

**TIP**

Boca Burger, a soy-based meat substitute, imparts a smoky flavor to cooked dishes. If you use another meat substitute, you may want to enhance the seasoning with herbs or spices. Note that some textured soy proteins and some formulations of Boca Burger contain added fat. Look for nonfat formulations.

---

## BROCCOLI FLORETS WITH HONEY MUSTARD DRESSING

*This lovely, light dressing also complements cooked cauliflower, green beans, beets, and leeks. You can use whole broccoli spears instead of the more expensive florets, if you prefer. To get the thick broccoli stalks to cook as quickly as the florets do, peel the stalks with a vegetable peeler down to the pale green heart, then slit the thickest part.*

SERVES 4

½ pound broccoli florets (2 generous cups)

*Honey Mustard Dressing:*
1 tablespoon white miso (page 57)
1 tablespoon honey
1 tablespoon Dijon mustard
1 teaspoon lemon juice
¼ cup water
Pinch black pepper

Bring 2 quarts of salted water to a boil over high heat. Add broccoli and cook until crisp-tender, about 2 minutes. Drain and transfer to a bowl of ice water to stop the cooking, or cool under cold running water. Drain well and pat dry.

Make honey mustard dressing: Combine all ingredients in a small bowl and whisk to blend.

Toss broccoli with honey mustard dressing just before serving, or pass sauce separately. It's best not to dress the broccoli in advance because the sauce will dull the vegetable's bright green color.

*Serving size: ½ cup broccoli,*
  *2 tablespoons dressing*
*Calories: 37*
*Fat: 0.42 g*
*Cholesterol: 0 mg*
*Carbohydrate: 7.9 g*
*Protein: 1.8 g*
*Sodium: 169.5 mg*

> **TIP**
>
> Whenever you blanch or boil vegetables in water, try to use the blanching water in another dish. It's full of water-soluble nutrients—vitamin C, the B vitamins, and minerals—that have leached into it. Use it to make soup, for example, or to cook brown rice or couscous.

**Corn Lover's Vegetable Stew**
**Braised Kale with Garlic**
**Perfect Fat-Free Corn Bread**
Fresh Pears

## CORN LOVER'S VEGETABLE STEW

*There are two kinds of corn in this colorful autumn stew: whole sweet corn and whole hominy. Braise them with butternut squash, bell peppers, and* tomatoes to make a sweet, brothy stew that just begs to be served Southern-style over halved corn bread. If you don't like hominy, substitute kidney beans or pinto beans. This stew reheats well.

SERVES 4

2½ cups Vegetable Broth, homemade (page 18) or store-bought
1 onion, thinly sliced
2 garlic cloves, minced
4 cups 1-inch cubes peeled butternut squash (see Tip below)
1 (16-ounce) can diced peeled tomatoes
1¼ cups fresh or thawed frozen corn kernels (see Tip, page 141), or
    1 (15¼-ounce) can whole corn kernels, drained
1 tablespoon chopped fresh thyme, or 1 teaspoon dried thyme
1 teaspoon salt
¼ teaspoon pepper
1 (14½-ounce) can golden or white hominy
1 red or green bell pepper, seeds and ribs removed, in 1-inch squares

In a Dutch oven or 4-quart saucepan, bring ½ cup of the broth to a boil over moderate heat. Add onion and garlic and cook until onion softens, about 5 minutes. Add squash, tomatoes, corn, thyme, salt, pepper, and remaining 2 cups broth. Stir to combine. Bring to a boil, then cover, reduce heat to maintain a simmer, and cook 10 minutes. Add the hominy and the bell pepper and return to a simmer. Cover and simmer until the squash and bell pepper are tender when pierced but not mushy, about 10 minutes.

*Serving size: 2 cups*
*Calories: 201*
*Fat: 1.5 g*
*Cholesterol: 0 mg*
*Carbohydrate: 47.0 g*
*Protein: 5.8 g*
*Sodium: 916.0 mg*

**TIP**

Can't find butternut squash? Substitute acorn, kabocha, delicata, banana, or any other hard-skinned, orange-fleshed sweet winter squash. Butternut is preferable because its skin is thin and easy to peel, but the others will work in this dish.

                                                   *Everyday Cooking with Dr. Dean Ornish*

# BRAISED KALE WITH GARLIC

*You can cook any sturdy greens this way, although some take longer than others. Fresh spinach, for example, wilts in just a minute or two. If you can find them fresh in your market, you can substitute mustard, collard, turnip or beet greens, or chard. These dark leafy greens are rich sources of vitamins A and C and are packed with flavor, too.*

FROM ELIZABETH KAPSTEIN, CHEF
*Dr. Ornish Program for Reversing Heart Disease at Beth Israel Medical Center, New York, New York*
SERVES 4

**3 bunches fresh kale (3 to 4 pounds)**
**2 tablespoons soy sauce**
**6 large garlic cloves, thinly sliced**

Wash greens well. Remove and discard tough ribs and stems. Slice leaves into ½-inch-wide ribbons.

Bring 1½ cups water and soy sauce to a boil in a large pot over moderate heat. Add garlic and simmer, uncovered, for 1 minute; do not let garlic brown. Add greens, toss to coat with seasonings, cover, and cook until greens are wilted and tender, about 5 minutes. If too much liquid remains in the pan, uncover and simmer until juices are reduced and concentrated.

*Serving size: ¾ cup*
*Calories: 39*
*Fat: 0.4 g*
*Cholesterol: 0 mg*
*Carbohydrate: 7.7 g*
*Protein: 2.6 g*
*Sodium: 128.8 mg*

---

**TIP**

To wash any leafy greens, such as kale or spinach, fill a sink with cold water. Add the greens, swish them several times, then lift them out to a sieve or colander, leaving dirty water behind. Repeat with fresh water if necessary.

---

Whether cooked or eaten raw, dark leafy greens are nutritional superstars. For salads, buy arugula, watercress, spinach, chicory, and escarole. For cooking, try collards, kale, mustard greens, turnip greens, or dandelion greens. Here's a scorecard.

**Best for beta-carotene and other carotenoids:**

arugula
beet greens
dandelion greens
kale
mustard greens
spinach
turnip greens

A four-ounce serving of any of these supplies enough beta-carotene to meet the RDA for vitamin A.

**Best for vitamin C:**

arugula
kale
mustard greens
turnip greens

A four-ounce serving of any of these supplies enough vitamin C to meet the RDA.

**Best for calcium:**

arugula
dandelion greens
turnip greens

Four ounces of any of these supplies at least as much calcium as a half a cup of milk.

**Best for iron:**

beet greens
dandelion greens

kale
spinach
Swiss chard

**Best for fiber:**
kale
mustard greens
spinach
turnip greens

Don't forget curly endive, collards, escarole, and watercress. They may not be tops in any particular nutrient, but they have plenty to offer.

*(Source: Reprinted by permission from the University of California at Berkeley Wellness Letter, © Health Letter Associates, 1995.)*

---

## PERFECT FAT-FREE CORN BREAD

*This easy corn bread will probably become a regular part of your repertoire. Enjoy it with bean stews, vegetable soups, hearty chilis, fat-free refried beans, and coleslaw, or for breakfast with a drizzle of honey.*

FROM LINDA CARLSON OF OGDEN, IOWA:
*Linda and Gerald Carlson are participants in the Ornish program at Mercy Hospital Medical Center/Iowa Heart Center in Des Moines, Iowa. Jerry has lost more than twenty pounds and reduced his medications. And Linda says she has learned that she can adapt favorite family recipes such as this corn bread with good results.*
MAKES ONE 8-INCH SQUARE

1 cup unbleached all-purpose flour
1 cup yellow cornmeal
2 tablespoons sugar
2 teaspoons baking powder
1 teaspoon salt
1 cup nonfat milk

¼ cup unsweetened applesauce
2 egg whites

Preheat oven to 425 degrees F. Spray an 8-inch nonstick pan lightly with nonstick spray (see Tip, page 251).

In a medium bowl, stir together flour, cornmeal, sugar, baking powder, and salt. In a large bowl, whisk together milk, applesauce, and egg whites.

Put the prepared pan in the oven to preheat for a minute or two while you combine the ingredients; take care not to overheat as spray burns easily.

Add dry ingredients to liquid ingredients. Stir lightly just to blend; do not overmix. Pour into prepared preheated pan. Bake until top is lightly browned and springs back when touched, about 20 minutes.

*Serving size: ⅛ of the corn bread*
*Calories: 152*
*Fat: 0.5 g*
*Cholesterol: 0.5 mg*
*Carbohydrate: 31.3 g*
*Protein: 5.0 g*
*Sodium: 323.3 mg*

> **TIP**
>
> **Putting the cornmeal batter in a hot pan helps to give it a crisp crust.**

---

### Mushroom and Spinach Lasagne
### Caesar Salad with Homemade Croutons
Crusty Italian Bread
### Vanilla Poached Pears

Lasagne has been so thoroughly adopted by Americans that it hardly seems Italian anymore. It is widely loved and typically wildly high in fat, thanks to generous portions of cheese, olive oil, and ground meat. This first-rate low-fat vegetarian version fills a critical need, because no one wants to give up lasagne. Accompany it with a crisp romaine salad in a creamy Caesar dressing and a basket of hot crusty bread. For dessert, serve pears poached in a light vanilla syrup or, if time is short, whole fresh pears.

---

*Everyday Cooking with Dr. Dean Ornish*

The timing: Poach the pears first and chill. Make and bake the lasagne. While it bakes, make the Caesar dressing and croutons, and wash and dry the lettuce. Assemble the salad just before you are ready for dinner.

## Mushroom and Spinach Lasagne

*Here's an excellent low-fat version of a high-fat dish that everyone loves, especially children. Note that the recipe makes enough for six, but lasagne reheats well. Enjoy any leftovers for lunch or dinner the next day.*

### Serves 6

2 cups diced mushrooms
1 cup diced onion
1 teaspoon minced garlic
1 (10-ounce) package frozen chopped spinach
1 cup nonfat ricotta cheese
½ cup liquid egg substitute
¼ cup fresh basil chiffonade (see Tip, page 211)
½ teaspoon salt
⅛ teaspoon ground nutmeg
½ pound dried lasagne noodles (no egg)
3 cups nonfat Marinara Sauce, homemade (page 92) or store-bought
2 ounces (½ cup) grated nonfat mozzarella cheese
1 tablespoon grated nonfat Parmesan cheese

In a saucepan, combine mushrooms, onion, garlic, and ¼ cup water. Simmer, covered, until onion is soft, about 5 minutes. Uncover and simmer until liquid evaporates, about 3 minutes.

Put frozen spinach in a bowl and microwave until hot throughout, about 5 minutes. Do not drain. Transfer to a large bowl and stir in ricotta, egg substitute, basil, salt, nutmeg, and the cooked mushrooms, onion, and garlic. Stir well.

Preheat oven to 425 degrees F.

Cook lasagne in a large pot of boiling salted water until just tender. (Check package directions for timing.) Drain well. Spread 1 cup marinara sauce in bottom of a rectangular baking dish approximately 8 by 12 inches. Top with a layer of noodles, arranging them side by side without overlapping. (If noodles are sticking to each other, rinse briefly with cold water, then pat dry.) Top with half the filling, spreading it evenly, then another layer of noodles. Top with remaining filling and a final layer of noodles. Spread 2 cups marinara sauce evenly over the surface. Top with mozzarella and Parmesan. Bake, uncovered, until hot throughout, about 30 minutes. Let stand 10 minutes before slicing.

*Serving size: ⅙ of the lasagne*
*Calories: 263*
*Fat: 2.0 g*
*Cholesterol: 4.4 mg*
*Carbohydrate: 50.0 g*
*Protein: 15.1 g*
*Sodium: 1,192.0 mg*

| TIP |
|---|
| Use the same spinach-mushroom filling to fill jumbo pasta shells. Top with tomato sauce and cheese and bake as you would for lasagne. |

## CAESAR SALAD WITH HOMEMADE CROUTONS

*With crisp hearts of romaine, crunchy croutons, and a creamy nonfat Caesar dressing, you can re-create the flavor of the high-fat restaurant classic. This recipe yields more croutons and dressing than you need for one meal. Save the extra croutons in an airtight container and use them for soups and salad throughout the week. The leftover dressing will also keep, covered and refrigerated, for 3 or 4 days. Enjoy it as a dip with raw or blanched vegetables.*

SERVES 4

**Homemade Croutons:**
1 day-old nonfat baguette, in ³⁄₈-inch dice

**Caesar Dressing:**
½ cup nonfat mayonnaise
2 tablespoons grated nonfat Swiss cheese
1 tablespoon lemon juice
1 tablespoon red wine vinegar
2 teaspoons Dijon mustard
1 garlic clove, minced
⅛ teaspoon black pepper
1 large head romaine, washed, dried, and chopped into bite-size pieces

Make croutons: Preheat oven to 375 degrees F. Put diced baguette on a baking sheet and bake until golden brown, about 10 minutes.

Make Caesar dressing: Put all dressing ingredients in a bowl and whisk to blend.

To assemble salad, put romaine in a salad bowl. Add 1 cup croutons and half the dressing. Toss well to coat leaves evenly with dressing. Serve immediately.

*Serving size: ¼ head romaine,*
  *¼ cup croutons, 2 tablespoons*
  *dressing*
*Calories: 40*
*Fat: 0.3 g*
*Cholesterol: 0.9 mg*
*Carbohydrate: 7.0 g*
*Protein: 2.0 g*
*Sodium: 128.0 mg*

> **TIP**
>
> Invest in an inexpensive plastic salad spinner so you can dry lettuce better and faster. These handy tools work like a centrifuge. You put the washed lettuce in a perforated basket that fits inside a plastic bucket. Then you spin the basket with a drawstring or crank until the water flies out the sides. Empty the bucket of water and spin again to make sure lettuce is dry. To get the best results, don't overload the basket. If you make lettuce-drying easy and fast, you will probably make salads a lot more often.

## VANILLA POACHED PEARS

*If you like the flavor of vanilla extract, you'll love the character of real vanilla bean. Look for it in jars in your supermarket's spice rack.*

SERVES 4

1 tablespoon frozen apple juice concentrate
1 tablespoon sugar
1 (3-inch) piece vanilla bean, halved
4 pears, preferably Anjou or Bosc

In a large saucepan, combine 1½ cups water, apple juice concentrate, and sugar. Scrape the vanilla bean seeds into the water with a knife, then add the bean pods to the water, too. Bring mixture to a simmer over moderate heat and simmer 2 minutes.

Peel, quarter, and core the pears. Add to poaching liquid, return to a simmer, cover, and adjust heat to maintain a gentle simmer. Cook until pears are just tender when pierced, 5 to 10 minutes. Cool in liquid, then chill. To serve, put four pear quarters in each bowl and top with some of the poaching liquid.

*Serving size: 1 pear, ¼ cup poaching*
   *liquid*
*Calories: 117*
*Fat: 0.7 g*
*Cholesterol: 0 mg*
*Carbohydrate: 30.0 g*
*Protein: 0.67 g*
*Sodium: 1.0 mg*

---

**TIP**

This recipe uses only a part of the bean. Split the remainder of the bean in half lengthwise and put in a jar. Fill with sugar, cover, and let stand for a few days. The bean will perfume the sugar. Use a little of this aromatic vanilla sugar as a special treat on yogurt or sliced fruit.

---

**Two-Bean Enchiladas**
**Spicy Mexican Rice**
**Green Pea Guacamole**
**Fresh Tomato Salsa**
**Cabbage and Green Apple Slaw**
Pineapple with Pomegranate Seeds

If you love Mexican food, you will be pleased to know how easy it is to "slim down" popular dishes. The enchiladas in this menu are packed with fiber and calcium—and no added fat—thanks to a savory, well-spiced filling of beans and corn. Serve with tomato-flavored rice, a dollop of mock guacamole, and your own homemade or store-bought salsa. A crunchy slaw provides a cooling contrast. If you can find fresh pomegranates, sprinkle the juicy red seeds over sliced pineapple for dessert; otherwise, enjoy the chilled pineapple on its own.

The timing: Peel and slice a pineapple. (To save time, buy your pineapple already peeled; some markets have a machine to peel and core it for you on the spot.) With a knife, cut around the circumference of the pomegranate just deep enough to pierce the skin. Carefully open the fruit and remove the seeds from the membranes. Refrigerate pineapple and pomegranate seeds. Make the slaw and refrigerate. Make

---

the enchilada filling but don't assemble enchiladas yet. Make the guacamole and the salsa, but don't salt the salsa until just before dinner is ready. Prepare the rice. While the rice is cooking, fill and bake the enchiladas. At dessert time, arrange the pineapple slices on a platter and sprinkle with pomegranate seeds.

# Two-Bean Enchiladas

*Packed with a savory bean and corn filling, these plump enchiladas will appeal to all who love Tex-Mex flavors. Spoon some Green Pea Guacamole (page 191) on top and pass a store-bought salsa or your own Fresh Tomato Salsa (page 192).*

SERVES 4

1 cup finely diced onion
1 cup finely diced green bell peppers
1 teaspoon minced garlic
1 tablespoon chili powder
1 teaspoon ground cumin
¼ cup Vegetable Broth, homemade (page 18) or store-bought
1 (15-ounce) can black beans, or 1½ cups home-cooked beans with
   ¾ cup liquid
1 (15-ounce) can kidney beans, or 1½ cups home-cooked beans with
   ¾ cup liquid
1 cup canned tomato sauce
1 cup corn kernels, fresh or frozen (see Tip, page 141)
8 corn tortillas

Preheat oven to 450 degrees F. Spray a 9 by 13-inch baking dish lightly with cooking spray.

In a saucepan, combine onion, bell peppers, garlic, chili powder, cumin, and vegetable broth. Bring to a simmer over moderately high heat and cook until onion and peppers are tender, 3 to 5 minutes. Add black beans and kidney beans with their liquid, and the tomato sauce. Bring to a boil, cover, reduce heat to maintain a simmer, and cook 10 minutes to blend flavors. Stir in corn and simmer 2 minutes. Put mixture into a strainer set over a bowl. Reserve the liquid.

Steam tortillas: Put a stack between damp paper towels and

microwave on high until they are soft and pliable, about 1 minute. Or wrap them in a dishtowel and steam them in a bamboo steamer until soft and pliable.

Put ½ cup drained filling in each tortilla, then roll and place side by side in prepared baking dish. Drizzle filled tortillas with reserved bean-tomato juices. Cover dish with foil and bake until hot throughout, about 15 minutes. Serve immediately.

*Serving size: 2 enchiladas*
*Calories: 374*
*Fat: 3.4 g*
*Cholesterol: 0 mg*
*Carbohydrate: 73.5 g*
*Protein: 17.4 mg*
*Sodium: 1,045.0 mg (with canned
    beans)*

### TIP

When nutritionist Carol Throckmorton, R.D., C.D.E., of Mercy Hospital Medical Center/Iowa Heart Center in Des Moines began teaching the importance of beans in the Reversal Diet, she gathered a collection of varieties and displayed them in clear glass jars. "I found that most participants were familiar with, at most, three varieties of beans and peas," said Carol. "Displaying them in jars helped participants become familiar with the large selection available, and also suggested a convenient and decorative way to store them." Keep your dried beans, peas, and small pasta shapes in decorative glass jars on a shelf in your kitchen or pantry. Their beautiful colors and odd shapes are a pleasing sight, and when they are always in view, you will think about using them more often.

## SPICY MEXICAN RICE

*Store-bought salsa and diced fresh vegetables flavor this version of the Mexican restaurant classic.*

### SERVES 4

½ cup canned ground tomatoes, or diced tomatoes diced finer by hand
½ cup diced green bell pepper
½ cup diced onion
¼ cup diced carrots
¼ cup Fresh Tomato Salsa, homemade (page 192) or store-bought
2 garlic cloves, minced
¼ teaspoon salt
1 cup long-grain rice (see Tip, page 191)

In a saucepan, combine tomatoes, bell pepper, onion, carrots, salsa, garlic, salt, and 1 cup water. Bring to a simmer over moderate heat. Add rice, stir once with a fork, cover, and reduce heat to lowest setting. Cook 25 minutes. Let stand, covered, 5 minutes, then uncover, transfer to a serving bowl, and fluff with a fork.

*Serving size: 1 cup*
*Calories: 194*
*Fat: 1.5 g*
*Cholesterol: 0 mg*
*Carbohydrate: 40.9 g*
*Protein: 4.5 g*
*Sodium: 216.0 mg*

### TIP

In a hurry? Fragrant long-grain basmati rice cooks even faster than converted rice. If using basmati rice, cook this dish 18 minutes, then let stand 5 minutes. Look for basmati in supermarkets, natural food stores, and Indian markets.

## GREEN PEA GUACAMOLE

*This bright green sauce looks remarkably like "the real thing" and delivers a tangy blend of Mexican flavors. Spoon it on soy burgers or atop nonfat refried black beans, or use it as a dressing for sliced tomatoes. Make it no more than 2 hours ahead for best appearance and flavor.*

MAKES A GENEROUS 1 CUP

1 cup frozen green peas (no need to thaw)
¼ cup nonfat plain yogurt
2 teaspoons lime juice
1 garlic clove, minced
⅛ teaspoon ground cumin
2 tablespoons Fresh Tomato Salsa, homemade (page 192) or
   store-bought
Salt

Put peas, yogurt, lime juice, garlic, and cumin in food processor or blender. Blend ingredients but stop machine before mixture is completely smooth; it should have a slightly coarse texture. Transfer to a bowl and stir in salsa and salt to taste.

Serving size: ¼ cup
Calories: 37
Fat: 0.17 g
Cholesterol: 0.25 mg
Carbohydrate: 6.2 g
Protein: 2.8 g
Sodium: 91.0 mg (with homemade salsa, no salt added)

**TIP**

Use hot or mild tomato salsa here, as you prefer. A green tomatillo salsa would also be a good choice.

## FRESH TOMATO SALSA

*This easy salsa may become one of your favorite toppings. Try it on a baked potato, in an omelet (page 107), on a soy burger, or stirred into bean soup. Like all fresh tomato salsas, this is best right after it's made. If you need to make it ahead, salt it just before using. The salt draws out the tomato juices.*

MAKES 1½ CUPS

1 cup diced fresh tomato
2 tablespoons finely diced white onion
1 jalapeño chile, seeds and white ribs removed, minced (see Tip, page 147)
1 tablespoon chopped cilantro
2 teaspoons lime juice
½ teaspoon minced garlic
Salt to taste

Combine all ingredients in a bowl; stir to blend.

Serving size: ½ cup
Calories: 12
Fat: 0.1 g
Cholesterol: 0 mg
Carbohydrate: 2.8 mg
Protein: 0.5 g
Sodium: 23.0 mg (with no salt added)

**TIP**

What's the difference between minced, diced, and chopped? Although many recipe writers don't draw rigorous distinctions, here's what you can expect these terms to mean in this book: To mince means to cut something very small, as with garlic. To dice means to cut something neatly, usually in ⅛- or ¼-inch squares. To chop means to cut something coarsely, when neatness doesn't matter so much.

*Everyday Cooking with Dr. Dean Ornish*

# CABBAGE AND GREEN APPLE SLAW

*Many supermarkets now carry pre-cut undressed cabbage slaw—usually a combination of sliced green and red cabbage and carrots. If you can't find this time-saving packaged mix, make your own by finely slicing green and red cabbage and grating carrots, either by hand or in a food processor. The proportions aren't too important, but you should have 4 cups total. Tossed with crisp green apple and a sweet-tart dressing, this refreshing salad improves with an hour's rest.*

SERVES 4

4 cups store-bought cabbage slaw mix
1 large tart green apple

*Sweet and Sour Dressing:*
¼ cup cider vinegar
¼ cup apple juice concentrate
1 teaspoon sugar
½ teaspoon salt
¼ teaspoon celery seed

Pepper

Put slaw mix in a large bowl. Set the apple on end and slice the flesh away from the core. Cut the apple, unpeeled, into neat matchstick-sized pieces. Add to cabbage.

Combine dressing ingredients in a small saucepan. Bring to a boil over moderate heat, then pour over cabbage mixture. Toss to coat. Season to taste with pepper.

*Serving size: 1¼ cups*
*Calories: 68*
*Fat: 0.3 g*
*Cholesterol: 0 mg*
*Carbohydrate: 17.0 g*
*Protein: 0.97 g*
*Sodium: 304.0 mg*

## TIP

Are the pre-cut vegetables that many supermarkets sell these days less nutritious than their whole counterparts? All vegetables lose nutrients in the days after harvest, and you might think that pre-cut vegetables—like broccoli florets or coleslaw—would lose more. But at least one study shows that pre-cut vegetables can lose nutrients more slowly if they are packed in the special "breathing" plastic that most processors use. The plastic, which lets oxygen and carbon dioxide pass in and out, helps keep nutrients in. According to the *Tufts University Diet & Nutrition Letter,* one university researcher found that broccoli florets in this modified packaging retained nutrients better than whole broccoli exposed to air. This doesn't mean you should switch to wrapped pre-cut vegetables, but it does mean you can enjoy their convenience without concern about nutrient loss.

**Rigatoni with Rich Tomato-Mushroom Sauce**
Mixed Garden Salad
**Ranch Dressing**
Crusty Italian Bread
**Apple-Raisin Strudel**

A pasta and salad dinner is just the ticket on busy weeknights. When you have a repertoire of quick sauces, such as the one in this menu, you can assemble a healthful dinner in little more than the time it takes to heat the water and boil the pasta. Toss a green salad with the "fixings" you like—the list that begins on page 197 should give you some fresh ideas—warm some bread, and sit down to dinner. If you have a little extra time, you can make the easy Apple-Raisin Strudel that follows; when you're out of energy, just offer the best available seasonal fruit, such as a basket of grapes and ripe pears.

The timing: Wash and dry the salad greens of your choice and prepare the dressing. Prepare the Tomato-Mushroom Sauce and set aside. Heat the water for the pasta. While it heats, prepare and bake the strudel. When the strudel goes into the oven, cook the pasta and reheat the sauce.

## RIGATONI WITH RICH TOMATO-MUSHROOM SAUCE

*As satisfying as any Italian meat sauce for pasta, this chunky blend of tomatoes, mushrooms, and soy burger is suitable for any pasta shape you like. Try it with penne, linguine, or farfalle (butterflies). If you can find fresh shiitake mushrooms, use them in place of half the regular mushrooms. This recipe makes a generous amount of sauce. You can use it all on a pound of pasta, or reserve some and enjoy it the next day over steamed brown rice.*

SERVES 4

*Tomato-Mushroom Sauce:*
6 (2.5-ounce) patties Boca Burger "No Fat Original" (see Tip, page 178)
    or other textured soy protein
1 cup canned diced tomato
1-½ cups canned tomato sauce
3 cups sliced fresh mushrooms

*Everyday Cooking with Dr. Dean Ornish*

½ cup diced Roasted Onions (page 22)
1 garlic clove, minced
½ teaspoon dried oregano
2 tablespoons chopped fresh basil
Salt and pepper
1 pound dried rigatoni or penne pasta

Cook Boca Burgers according to package directions. Chop into ½-inch dice.

In a large saucepan, combine chopped Boca Burger, diced tomato, tomato sauce, mushrooms, roasted onions, garlic, and oregano. Bring to a simmer, cover, and adjust heat to maintain a simmer. Cook, stirring occasionally, until sauce is thick and tasty, about 15 minutes. Stir in basil; season to taste with salt and pepper. Keep warm.

Bring a large pot of salted water to a boil over high heat. Add pasta and cook according to package directions until al dente. Drain and transfer to a large warm bowl. Add sauce, using as much as you like, and toss to coat. Serve immediately on warm plates.

*Serving size: 2 cups pasta,*
*  2 cups sauce*
*Calories: 630*
*Fat: 2.75 g*
*Cholesterol: 0 mg*
*Carbohydrate: 115.0 g*
*Protein: 37.3 g*
*Sodium: 340.0 mg (with no salt added)*

> **TIP**
>
> Omit the Boca Burger to make a lighter tomato-mushroom sauce. Or replace the Boca Burger with 1 cup chopped zucchini or 1 cup chopped green peppers.

## RANCH DRESSING

*This recipe makes a thick dressing to use as a dip with crisp raw vegetables or as a topping for a baked potato. To use as a salad dressing, thin to desired consistency with water. Extra dressing will keep in the refrigerator for a couple of days.*

*Shallots are a mild member of the onion family. Buy shallots that feel firm, not soft or mushy. Peel back the papery outer skin before chopping. If you can't find shallots, substitute 2 teaspoons minced green onions.*

MAKES 1 CUP

½ cup nonfat mayonnaise
¼ cup nonfat plain yogurt
¼ cup nonfat sour cream
1½ teaspoons lemon juice
1 teaspoon chopped shallots (see Headnote above)
½ teaspoon minced garlic
Salt, black pepper, and cayenne pepper

In a small bowl, whisk together mayonnaise, yogurt, sour cream, lemon juice, shallots, and garlic. Season to taste with salt, black pepper, and cayenne pepper. Whisk in a little water to thin to consistency of salad dressing.

*Serving size: ¼ cup*
*Calories: 16*
*Fat: 0.1 g*
*Cholesterol: 1.0 mg*
*Carbohydrate: 2.6 g*
*Protein: 1.3 g*
*Sodium: 135.0 mg (with no salt added)*

---

**TIP**

Wash, dry, and refrigerate lettuce when you bring it home from the market so it's ready for salads when you are. Swish the lettuce leaves in a sink full of cold water, then spin dry in a salad spinner, or drain in a colander and pat dry between towels. Wrap the dried lettuce in paper towels or a dishtowel and put the bundle in a plastic bag in the refrigerator crisper. The lettuce will stay fresh for 2 or 3 days.

---

## SALAD BARS AREN'T JUST FOR RESTAURANTS

You don't have to go out for dinner to enjoy the pleasures of a well-stocked salad bar. You can assemble your own home version and make it the centerpiece of dinner. Here are some ideas for items to have on your self-serve salad bar. Or use this list to jog your thinking about foods you can add to daily salads to take them out of the lettuce-and-tomato rut.

If you keep your refrigerator stocked with washed and dried lettuces (see Tip above) and with a variety of these salad fixings in plastic containers, you can make a "mini salad bar" in minutes.

## Greens:

arugula
bibb or Boston lettuce
curly endive (chicory)
escarole
fresh spinach
Italian parsley leaves
mixed baby lettuces (*mesclun*)
radicchio
red and green leaf lettuce
romaine
watercress

## Additions:

artichoke hearts (canned or frozen and thawed)
asparagus tips, blanched
baby corn
bean sprouts
blanched sugar snap peas
broccoli florets, raw or blanched
cauliflower florets, raw or blanched
cherry tomatoes
chilled boiled potatoes
chopped hard-cooked egg whites
cooked black beans
cooked chickpeas
cooked kidney beans
corn kernels
fat-free crackers
fat-free croutons (page 186)
fat-free tortilla chips
fresh tomato salsa
grated nonfat cheese
grated or sliced beets
grated or sliced carrots
green, red, and yellow bell pepper strips
orange or grapefruit sections
peperoncini (mild pickled peppers)
pre-cut coleslaw (undressed)

---

raisins
Roasted Garlic (page 93)
roasted sweet potatoes
shredded red cabbage
sliced celery
sliced cucumbers
sliced green onions
sliced jicama
sliced mushrooms
sliced radishes
sliced red onions
sliced water chestnuts
sliced zucchini or yellow squash
sprouts: mung bean, soybean, alfalfa, or sunflower
thinly sliced fennel
three-bean salad (no fat added)

**Dressings:**
Buttermilk Dressing (page 258)
Ranch Dressing (page 195)
Orange-Basil Dressing (page 102)
Creamy Tofu Dressing (page 164)
Honey-Mustard Dressing (page 179)
Sweet and Sour Dressing (page 193)
Bottled nonfat dressings

# APPLE-RAISIN STRUDEL

*Phyllo dough makes a crisp, flaky strudel crust even without the considerable quantity of butter that most recipes call for. You should serve this strudel while hot, however, as it loses crispness as it cools. Candied ginger adds a seductive spicy note to the filling, but you can omit it. Add a dash of cinnamon instead.*

MAKES 1 TWELVE-INCH STRUDEL

**1 tablespoon raisins**
**½ cup hot water**
**4 apples, preferably Rome Beauty or Golden Delicious**

1 tablespoon plus 1 teaspoon sugar

1 tablespoon cornstarch

1 tablespoon plus 1 teaspoon minced candied ginger (see Tip, page 78), or dash of cinnamon

1 teaspoon vanilla extract

3 (14 by 18-inch) sheets phyllo dough

1 tablespoon liquid egg substitute

Preheat oven to 375 degrees F. Put raisins in a small bowl and cover with ½ cup hot water. Let soften 20 minutes, then drain.

Peel, quarter, core, and dice the apples into small pieces. In a large bowl, stir together 1 tablespoon sugar and the cornstarch. Add the apples, ginger, and vanilla. Stir to blend. Stir in raisins.

On a large work surface, stack the phyllo sheets one on top of the other, with the longer side nearest you. Leaving a 2-inch border along the bottom and 1-inch border along the sides, spoon the apple filling onto the bottom third of the phyllo in a long 2-inch-wide cylinder. Starting from the bottom edge, roll the phyllo up and over the filling to make a long fat rope. Squeeze the short sides shut with your fingers. In a small bowl, whisk together the liquid egg substitute and remaining 1 teaspoon sugar. Brush over phyllo. Carefully transfer the "rope" to a baking sheet, either nonstick or lightly sprayed with nonstick spray (see Tip, page 251). Bake until golden brown, about 30 minutes. Slice and serve immediately.

*Serving size: ¼ of the strudel*

*Calories: 143*

*Fat: 0.7 g*

*Cholesterol: 0 mg*

*Carbohydrate: 54.5 g*

*Protein: 3.5 g*

*Sodium: 76.0 mg*

### TIP

Look for phyllo in the supermarket freezer case. Be sure to read the label to find phyllo that has less than 0.5 gram of fat per ounce. Athens Pastries and Frozen Foods (see "Where to Find Products," page 327) makes a phyllo that meets this standard. Thaw it in the refrigerator.

**Marinated Mushrooms and Sweet Peppers**
**Gary's Broccoli Manicotti**
Crusty Italian Bread
**Zucchini Brownies**

An Italian-American favorite, manicotti is a proven child-pleaser and can easily be multiplied to serve a crowd. The marinated vegetables can be made in large quantity, too, making this a good menu to turn to for casual entertaining. Another plus: both the manicotti and the vegetables can be made ahead (and the vegetables should be—they need to marinate 8 hours). The cakelike brownies, however, are best within a few hours of baking.

The timing: Make the marinated mushrooms and sweet peppers first, at least 8 hours ahead. Assemble the manicotti next, but don't bake them ahead. Refrigerate them if you need to hold them more than an hour before baking. Make the zucchini brownies last; if possible, time the baking so the brownies will be warm when served.

## MARINATED MUSHROOMS AND SWEET PEPPERS

*Balsamic vinegar and oregano give these marinated vegetables an Italian flavor. Note that they need to marinate for at least 8 hours. For best results, choose small button mushrooms that are firm and tightly closed, with no gills showing. If you can't find baby greens, use fresh spinach or soft hearts of butter lettuce.*

FROM ELIZABETH KAPSTEIN, CHEF
*Dr. Ornish Program for Reversing Heart Disease at Beth Israel Medical Center, New York, New York*
*A former Washington, D.C., caterer, Elizabeth now cooks for Ornish research participants in New York. "Most of these people have outcooked me for years, but they only knew how to make high-fat foods," says Elizabeth. "I teach them to look at food in a whole new way. It's not about restriction. It's about learning to make new dishes with flavor and zest."*
SERVES 4

¼ cup balsamic vinegar
1 tablespoon lemon juice

½ teaspoon dried oregano

Salt and pepper

¾ pound small whole mushrooms, stems removed, or larger mushrooms, halved

½ red bell pepper, seeds and ribs removed, very thinly sliced

½ green bell pepper, seeds and ribs removed, very thinly sliced

½ cup thinly sliced red onion

4 handfuls mixed baby salad greens

In a large bowl, whisk together vinegar, lemon juice, oregano, and 2 teaspoons water. Season to taste with salt and pepper. Add mushrooms, red and green bell peppers, and red onion. Toss well. Cover and refrigerate 8 hours, stirring occasionally.

Taste and adjust seasoning just before serving. Serve on a bed of baby greens.

*Serving size: 1 cup*
*Calories: 40.5*
*Fat: 0.5 g*
*Cholesterol: 0 mg*
*Carbohydrate: 7.8 g*
*Protein: 3.0 g*
*Sodium: 7.4 mg*

> **TIP**
>
> A large Ziploc bag is a convenient container for marinating vegetables. Just shake the bag occasionally to redistribute the seasonings.

## GARY'S BROCCOLI MANICOTTI

*You don't have to forswear all your favorite dishes on a low-fat vegetarian diet; just learn to adapt them. That's what Gary Fingert did with the standard manicotti recipe. Substituting nonfat dairy products for high-fat ones and filling the shells with fresh broccoli and mushrooms instead of ground meat yields a dish with all the pleasure and none of the fat of the more familiar version.*

*You can fill the shells in advance and refrigerate, but bake them just before serving. (Figure a little more time if they've been refrigerated.) Note that you need to undercook the shells before filling them as they will cook more in the oven.*

*Gary and Loretta Fingert were instrumental in getting the Ornish program started at Mercy Hospital Medical Center/Iowa Heart Center in Des Moines, Iowa. They attended the Ornish retreat in California, then convinced their own physician to begin the program in their town. "I wanted to continue the program and felt I needed the group support from others who were having similar experiences with heart disease," says Gary.*

*Now a retired dentist, Gary had a heart attack and bypass surgery at the age of forty-seven. His father and a brother died of heart attacks at forty-seven. Gary says the program gives him a feeling of being more in control of his life.*

SERVES 4

½ cup diced onion
2 garlic cloves, minced
¼ cup Vegetable Broth, homemade (page 18) or store-bought
½ cup diced mushrooms
2 cups thawed and squeezed dry frozen chopped broccoli, or 2 cups well-drained chopped cooked fresh broccoli
1 cup nonfat cottage cheese
½ cup liquid egg substitute
¼ cup plus 2 tablespoons grated nonfat mozzarella cheese
1 teaspoon salt
½ teaspoon black pepper
Pinch ground nutmeg
8 manicotti shells (half a 9-ounce package)
1 cup nonfat Marinara Sauce, homemade (page 92) or store-bought

Preheat oven to 350 degrees F.

In a small skillet, combine onion, garlic, and broth. Bring to a simmer, covered, over moderate heat and simmer until onion is softened, about 5 minutes. Add mushrooms and cook, uncovered, until mushrooms are tender and their liquid has evaporated, 3 to 5 minutes. Let cool.

In a bowl, combine mushroom mixture with broccoli, cottage cheese, egg substitute, ¼ cup mozzarella, salt, pepper, and nutmeg. Stir well.

Bring a large pot of salted water to a boil over high heat. Add manicotti shells and cook according to package directions until half-done. Drain.

Divide filling among manicotti shells and place in an 8 by 12-inch baking dish, either nonstick or lightly sprayed with nonstick spray (see Tip, page 251). Cover shells evenly with marinara sauce. Sprinkle with remaining 2 tablespoons mozzarella. Cover with foil and bake until hot throughout, about 30 minutes.

*Serving size: 2 filled pasta shells*
*Calories: 211*
*Fat: 0.5 g*
*Cholesterol: 2.9 mg*
*Carbohydrate: 33.0 g*
*Protein: 20.0 g*
*Sodium: 262.0 mg*

> **TIP**
>
> Manicotti shells are easier to fill if you place the filling in a large Ziploc bag. Cut off a corner and squeeze out the filling as if you were using a pastry bag.

## ZUCCHINI BROWNIES

*Carob powder gives these easy brownies an appetizing "chocolaty" aroma and color. Moist and cakelike, they are a remarkably satisfying alternative to the traditional high-fat, high-sugar favorite. Look for carob powder in natural food stores.*

FROM SHARON HAYDEN OF INDIANOLA, IOWA:
*Maynard and Sharon Hayden are participants in the Ornish program at Mercy Hospital Medical Center/Iowa Heart Center, Des Moines, Iowa. Sharon follows the program along with husband Maynard, who has heart disease. She believes the spousal support is important to his success and is happy to reap the benefits of the program herself.*

*"I cooked according to the American Heart Association guidelines and thought I was doing really well," says Sharon, "but this was a big change. Maynard is very content with the Reversal Diet; I miss meat every once in a while, but when I do, I have beans. They help me feel satisfied."*

*Sharon adjusted her favorite brownie recipe by substituting carob for chocolate.*

MAKES 24 TWO-INCH-SQUARE BROWNIES

**2 cups grated zucchini**
**½ cup mashed ripe banana**

2 teaspoons vanilla extract
2 cups unbleached all-purpose flour
¾ cup sugar
⅓ cup carob powder
1½ teaspoons baking soda
1 teaspoon salt
Confectioners' sugar, sifted

Preheat oven to 350 degrees F.

In a large bowl, combine zucchini, banana, vanilla, and 1 tablespoon water.

In a medium bowl, stir together flour, sugar, carob powder, baking soda, and salt. Add dry ingredients to wet ingredients and mix until well blended. Batter will be very stiff. Spread in a 9 by 13-inch baking dish, either nonstick or lightly sprayed with nonstick spray (see Tip, page 251). Bake until a toothpick inserted in the center comes out clean, about 35 minutes. Cool. Dust lightly with sifted confectioners' sugar before slicing.

*Serving size: 1 two-inch-square*
  *brownie*
*Calories: 70*
*Fat: 0.9 g*
*Cholesterol: 0 mg*
*Carbohydrate: 102.0 mg*
*Protein: 8.0 g*
*Sodium: 98.8 mg*

> **TIP**
>
> For a celebration cake, bake these brownies in two 8-inch rounds at 350 degrees F. for 25 to 30 minutes. Cool, then frost with nonfat cream cheese frosting (page 222) and decorate with sliced strawberries.

**Jo's Chili**
Creamy Coleslaw (page 164)
**Spicy Corn Muffins**
Sliced Persimmons with Lime *or* Chilled Red and Green Grapes

You can never have too many chili recipes, especially unusual recipes such as this one with bulgur and squash. Jo is Joanne Shipe, who had the bright idea to thicken her chili with high-fiber bulgur and to add a variety of colorful vegetables for textural contrast. Maybe it wouldn't pass for chili in Texas, but this is a downright tasty vegetable stew by any definition. Serve it with spicy corn muffins and a cooling cabbage slaw. If you can find Fuyu persimmons in your market—they usually turn up in late autumn—peel and slice them for dessert; Fuyu persimmons are the small, squat ones that you can eat when firm, not the large, heart-shaped ones that turn soft when ripe. Fresh grapes would be a good replacement.

The timing: Make the coleslaw first and refrigerate for at least an hour to allow the flavors to blend. Make the chili next. While it's simmering, mix and bake the muffins. You can peel and slice the persimmons ahead if you have time, or slice them just before you are ready for dessert.

# Jo's Chili

*You can make this chunky bean chili a few hours ahead, but it will thicken as it stands. When you reheat it, thin it as needed with vegetable broth or water.*

FROM JOANNE SHIPE AND ROBERT RIEGEL OF BIRDSBORO, PENNSYLVANIA: *Joanne Shipe and Robert Riegel have attended the Ornish retreat in California. At home, Jo does the cooking and Bob throws in ideas. Their suggestion about succeeding on the Reversal Diet: "Have an open mind and see it as an adventure." Jo and Bob also have great ideas for breakfast (see page 289).*

SERVES 4

2 cups halved and sliced mushrooms
1 cup diced onion
1 cup diced yellow summer squash
½ cup diced red bell pepper
½ cup diced green bell pepper
2 tablespoons chili powder
One (15-ounce) can kidney beans, or 2 cups home-cooked kidney beans, with ¾ cup liquid
2 cups nonfat Marinara Sauce, homemade (page 92) or store-bought
¼ cup bulgur
Salt and pepper

In a pot, combine mushrooms, onion, squash, red and green bell peppers, chili powder, and ¼ cup water. Bring to a simmer over moderate heat and simmer until vegetables are slightly softened, about 5 minutes. Add kidney beans with their liquid and the marinara sauce. Bring to a simmer and cook 8 minutes to blend flavors, stirring occasionally. Add bulgur and cook, stirring often, until grains are tender, about 10 minutes. If mixture gets too thick, thin with water. Season to taste with salt and pepper.

*Serving size: 1½ cups*
*Calories: 232*
*Fat: 1.4 g*
*Cholesterol: 0 mg*
*Carbohydrate: 47.0 g*
*Protein: 12.8 g*
*Sodium: 1,181.0 mg (with canned*
*beans and store-bought sauce)*

> **TIP**
>
> Washing mushrooms improperly can make them soggy because they quickly soak up water. To wash them, swish them vigorously in a sink or large bowl filled with cold water, then lift them out and pat them dry quickly. Or brush them clean with a mushroom brush.

## SPICY CORN MUFFINS

*Corn kernels, red bell pepper, and a hint of salsa give these golden muffins an appealing Southwestern flavor. They're perfect with a spicy chili, or enjoy with a favorite vegetable soup, black bean stew, or braised collard greens.*

### MAKES 8 MUFFINS

1 cup unbleached all-purpose flour
1 cup yellow cornmeal
1 tablespoon baking powder
½ cup egg whites (from approximately 4 large eggs) or liquid egg substitute
½ teaspoon salt
½ cup corn kernels, fresh or frozen (see Tip, page 141)
½ cup diced red bell pepper
¼ cup tomato salsa (no added fat)
2 tablespoons chopped cilantro or parsley
½ cup unsweetened applesauce
½ cup nonfat plain yogurt

Preheat oven to 375 degrees F. In a bowl, stir together flour, corn-meal, and baking powder.

In a large bowl, whisk egg whites with salt just to break up the whites. Stir in corn, bell pepper, salsa, cilantro, applesauce, and yogurt. Add dry ingredients and mix lightly just to blend; do not overmix.

Divide mixture evenly among eight 2½-inch-wide muffin cups, either nonstick or lightly sprayed with nonstick spray (see Tip, page 251). Batter should come just to the top of the cups. Bake until nicely risen and lightly browned, about 25 minutes.

*Serving size: 2 muffins*
*Calories: 152.5*
*Fat: 0.56 g*
*Cholesterol: 0.24 mg*
*Carbohydrate: 30.6 mg*
*Protein: 6.0 g*
*Sodium: 186.0 mg*

> **TIP**
>
> Muffins made without fat can easily become tough if you overmix them after adding the dry ingredients. Stirring the batter vigorously would develop the gluten in the flour, which would give the muffins a sturdy structure—just what you don't want. The best approach is to mix the dry ingredients in with a rubber spatula, stirring and folding gently just until there are no white clumps left.

**Chickpea Stew with Couscous**
**Cucumber-Yogurt Sauce with Mint**
Warm Whole Wheat Pita Bread
Orange Segments with Chopped Dates

Flavored with the warm spices beloved in Morocco, this full-bodied chickpea stew will make your kitchen smell divine. Served over steamed couscous, it is essentially a meal in itself, thanks to the protein in the chickpeas and the variety of vitamin-rich vegetables used. The chickpea protein is incomplete (as protein from plant sources always is), but yogurt offers the complementary amino acids needed. Offer the yogurt sauce on the side, for drizzling over the stew or to use as a dipping sauce for the pita bread. For dessert, peel and segment four oranges (see directions, page 238), working over a bowl to catch the juices. Put the segments in the bowl with a pinch of cinnamon, then add ¼ cup chopped pitted dates and toss.

The timing: Make the chickpea stew a day ahead, if desired (see Tip, page 209). Several hours before dinner, peel and slice the oranges and chill them. Prepare the cucumber-yogurt sauce while you reheat the stew gently. Steam the couscous just before you are ready for dinner. Add dates to oranges just before you are ready to serve them.

## CHICKPEA STEW WITH COUSCOUS

*Don't be put off by the long list of ingredients. This is an easy Moroccan-style vegetable stew that cooks in about 20 minutes. Serve it over a fluffy mound of steamed couscous or brown rice.*

FROM JUDITH ELIAS OF BROOKLYN, NEW YORK:
*Judy and Joe Elias attended the Ornish retreat in California, then joined the Ornish program at Beth Israel Medical Center, New York, New York. Joe has had bypass surgery and follows the program to avoid "bypassing the bypass."*

SERVES 4

1 medium onion, diced
3 garlic cloves, minced
2 cups Vegetable Broth, homemade (page 18) or store-bought
1½ cups diced zucchini
1 large sweet potato, peeled, in ½-inch dice
1 cup diced red bell pepper
1 cup diced green bell pepper
1 cup diced peeled tomato, canned or fresh, with juice
1 teaspoon cinnamon
1 teaspoon ground coriander
½ teaspoon ground cumin
Pinch cayenne
½ teaspoon salt
¼ teaspoon black pepper
1 tablespoon lemon juice
1 (15-ounce) can chickpeas (garbanzo beans), drained, or 1½ cups
   home-cooked chickpeas

2 cups couscous

2 tablespoons minced parsley or cilantro

In a large pot, combine onion, garlic, and ¼ cup vegetable broth. Cook over moderate heat until liquid evaporates and onion is transparent, about 5 minutes. Add zucchini, sweet potato, red and green bell peppers, tomato, cinnamon, coriander, cumin, cayenne, salt, and pepper. Simmer 5 minutes. Add remaining 1¾ cups vegetable broth and lemon juice. Bring to a simmer, cover, lower heat, and simmer gently until vegetables are just tender, about 5 more minutes. Stir in chickpeas and cook until chickpeas are hot. Keep stew warm.

Make couscous: Bring 2 cups water and a large pinch of salt to a boil in a medium saucepan. Add couscous, cover, and remove from heat. Let stand 5 minutes. Uncover, transfer to a bowl, and fluff with a fork to separate the grains.

To serve, make a bed of couscous on a serving platter. Spoon chickpea stew over the top. Garnish with minced parsley.

*Serving size: 1¾ cups*
*Calories: 515*
*Fat: 1.9 g*
*Cholesterol: 0 mg*
*Carbohydrate: 115.2 g*
*Protein: 18.5 g*
*Sodium: 315.0 mg*

---

**TIP**

You can cook this vegetable stew a day ahead; in fact, the flavors will improve overnight. Be sure to undercook the vegetables slightly to allow for further cooking when you reheat the stew. Make the couscous just before serving.

---

## CUCUMBER YOGURT SAUCE WITH MINT

*Fresh mint gives this pale green sauce a refreshing, cooling taste. It would make a sublime topping for steamed cauliflower, broccoli, spinach, or green beans.*
MAKES 1¼ CUPS

½ cup chopped, seeded, peeled cucumber

½ cup nonfat plain yogurt

1 tablespoon chopped fresh mint

1-½ teaspoons lemon juice

½ teaspoon minced garlic

⅛ teaspoon ground cumin
Pinch cayenne pepper
Salt

Put all ingredients except the salt in a food processor or blender and blend until completely smooth. Transfer to a bowl. Season to taste with salt.

*Serving size: ⅓ cup*
*Calories: 18*
*Fat: 0.07 g*
*Cholesterol: 2.0 mg*
*Carbohydrate: 11.2 g*
*Protein: 6.9 g*
*Sodium: 88.0 mg (with no salt added)*

---

**TIP**

Keep Yogurt Cheese on hand as a dip for vegetables or a spread for bagels. To make it, line a sieve with a coffee filter or dampened cheesecloth and set it over a bowl. Put plain nonfat yogurt in the sieve, cover with plastic wrap, refrigerate, and let drain several hours or overnight until thick. Discard the liquid that drains from the yogurt. Season the Yogurt Cheese with salt, pepper, and minced fresh herbs. It will keep in the refrigerator for 3 to 4 days.

---

**Greek Bean Salad**
**Harvest Vegetable Soup**
Whole Wheat Bread
**Baked Apples with Apricot Jam**

After a brisk autumn walk or an afternoon spent raking leaves, vegetable soup hits the spot. This is also a highly portable meal (put the soup in a wide-mouth thermos) for a tailgate party or fall picnic. For those occasions, you might serve the soup in mugs and spoon the bean salad into whole wheat pita bread pockets with a spoonful of yogurt to make a more informal meal. Follow with juicy baked fall apples flavored with jam.

The timing: Bake the apples first, then make the soup. While the soup is simmering, assemble the bean salad.

*Everyday Cooking with Dr. Dean Ornish*

# GREEK BEAN SALAD

*Pinto beans replace the feta cheese in this variation on the classic Greek salad. With its crisp cucumber, tomato, onion, and basil, the dish has an appealing freshness you rarely find in canned bean salads.*

FROM LEONA AND KHEM SHAHANI OF LINCOLN, NEBRASKA: *The Shahanis participated in the Ornish program at Immanuel Medical Center/The Heart Institute in Omaha, Nebraska. A professor of food science and technology at the University of Nebraska, Khem has many speaking engagements that take him on the road often and sometimes out of the country. He plans ahead, informing his hosts of his dietary needs.*

SERVES 4

1 (15-ounce) can pinto beans or kidney beans, drained and rinsed
1 medium cucumber, peeled, seeded, and diced
1 medium fresh tomato, halved, seeded, and diced
¼ cup diced red onion
2 tablespoons fresh basil chiffonade (see Tip below)
¼ cup bottled nonfat Italian salad dressing
Salt and pepper to taste

Combine all ingredients in a large bowl and stir to blend.

*Serving size: 1 cup*
*Calories: 86*
*Fat: 0.45 g*
*Cholesterol: 0 mg*
*Carbohydrate: 16.6 mg*
*Protein: 4.6 g*
*Sodium: 508.0 mg*

> **TIP**
>
> Chiffonade is a French cooking term that refers to very fine ribbons. The easiest way to chiffonade basil is to stack several leaves together, roll them up like a jelly roll, and then slice thinly across the roll. Always chiffonade basil at the last moment with a sharp knife to keep it from browning.

# HARVEST VEGETABLE SOUP

*Butternut squash, carrots, turnips, leeks—these fresh vegetables have a natural sweetness that infuses this delicate soup. The smaller you cut the vegetables, the faster the soup will cook. To make it heartier, add macaroni, wild rice, or brown rice, or ladle it into bowls over steamed couscous.*

FROM FRANK D. HOBLE OF POMPANO BEACH, FLORIDA:
*Frank's daughter is Darla Erlich, R.N., with the Ornish program at North Broward Hospital District/Broward General Hospital in Fort Lauderdale, Florida. Frank does a lot of cooking and has learned to adapt high-fat recipes. The Harvest Vegetable Soup is a good example of his expertise.*

SERVES 4

1 cup diced peeled turnips
1 cup diced onion
¾ cup chopped leek, white part only
½ cup diced carrots
½ cup diced celery
1 tablespoon minced garlic
7 to 8 cups Vegetable Broth, homemade (page 18) or store-bought
2½ cups diced peeled butternut squash, or other sweet winter squash
2 cups chopped cabbage, preferably savoy
1 jalapeño chile, seeded, deveined, and minced (see Tip, page 147)
2½ cups bite-size pieces broccoli florets
½ cup diced peeled broccoli stems
Salt and pepper

In a large soup pot, combine turnips, onion, leek, carrots, celery, garlic, and ½ cup vegetable broth. Bring to a simmer over moderate heat and simmer 5 minutes. Add butternut squash, cabbage, jalapeño, and 6½ cups vegetable broth. Bring to a simmer, adjust heat to maintain a gentle simmer, and cook until vegetables are tender, 20 to 30 minutes. Stir in broccoli florets and stems and cook until they are tender, about 5 minutes. If soup is too thick, add an additional 1 cup broth. Season to taste with salt and pepper.

*Serving size: 1¾ cups*
*Calories: 104*

Fat: 0.5 g
Cholesterol: 0 mg
Carbohydrate: 24.2 g
Protein: 4.7 g
Sodium: 95.3 mg

<table>
<tr><td>TIP</td></tr>
</table>

> **TIP**
>
> When a recipe calls for broccoli florets only, you can save money by buying the whole broccoli stalk. Cut off the florets for the recipe. Then use a vegetable peeler to peel the thick broccoli stems. Underneath the green skin, the pale broccoli stem is sweet and delicious. Eat it raw, or steam it and drizzle it with Honey-Mustard Dressing (page 179).

## BAKED APPLES WITH APRICOT JAM

*Make a double batch of these easy baked apples and enjoy the extras for breakfast or brunch. There's a surprise in the apples' center—a soft spoonful of creamy oats sweetened with jam.*

### SERVES 4

2 large apples, preferably Rome Beauty or Golden Delicious
4 teaspoons no-sugar-added apricot jam
4 teaspoons quick-cooking (not instant) oatmeal
2 cinnamon sticks
⅓ cup apple juice
1 teaspoon sugar
1 teaspoon lemon juice

Preheat oven to 400 degrees F.

Halve the apples and core them with a melon baller. In a small bowl, mix jam and oats into a paste. Divide the paste among the four apple cavities. Put the apples, cut side down, in a baking dish. Put the cinnamon sticks in the baking dish. Whisk together apple juice, sugar, and lemon juice. Pour around the apples. Cover and bake until apples are tender when pierced, about 30 minutes. Serve apples cut side up and spoon the pan juices over them.

*Serving size: 1 apple*
*Calories: 136*
*Fat: 0.5 g*

Cholesterol: 0 mg
Carbohydrate: 32.0 g
Protein: 2.4 g
Sodium: 6.0 mg

**Mixed Grains Loaf with Spinach**
Herbed Yogurt Sauce (page 147)
**Jean-Marc's Oven "Fries"**
Steamed Fresh Green Beans
**Homemade Chunky Applesauce**

Sometimes you'd rather have "comfort food" than the fanciest restaurant meal. Here's a dinner like Mom used to make—or like Mom would have made if she had had the information we have now about dietary fat and heart disease. Knowing what we know, it makes sense to forgo the meat loaf in favor of a high-fiber mixed grains loaf that delivers just as much taste and satisfaction, and to replace the gravy with a creamy yogurt sauce. The yogurt sauce does triple duty: it complements the grains loaf, the crusty "fries," and the steamed green beans. For dessert, enjoy a bowl of chilled applesauce made with fragrant fall apples.

The timing: Make the applesauce and chill. Mix and bake the mixed grains loaf. While it's baking, make the yogurt sauce. Prepare the "fries," timing the baking so that they come out of the oven when the grains loaf is ready to be sliced. While the potatoes are baking, trim and steam the green beans.

## MIXED GRAINS LOAF WITH SPINACH

*This savory vegetarian version of a meat loaf packs a lot of nutrition, with high-fiber grains and vitamin-rich spinach. Moist and well seasoned, it makes neat firm slices that would be right at home in a sandwich with tomato and sprouts the following day.*

SERVES 4

1 cup bulgur
1 cup quick-cooking (not instant) oatmeal
2 cups Vegetable Broth, homemade (page 18) or store-bought
2 cups diced day-old bread
1 cup diced onion
1 (10-ounce) package chopped frozen spinach, thawed
½ cup liquid egg substitute
½ cup minced parsley
1 teaspoon minced garlic
¼ teaspoon salt
⅛ teaspoon black pepper
½ cup nonfat Marinara Sauce, homemade (page 92) or store-bought
Herbed Yogurt Sauce (page 147)

Preheat oven to 450 degrees F.

In a bowl, combine bulgur and oatmeal. Bring vegetable broth to a boil and pour over grains. Cover and let stand 8 minutes to soften.

Add bread, onion, spinach, egg substitute, parsley, garlic, salt, and pepper. Blend lightly but well. Spoon into a 9 by 5-inch loaf pan, either nonstick or lightly sprayed with nonstick spray (see Tip, page 251). Spread marinara sauce evenly over the top. Bake until firm and hot throughout, about 35 minutes. Let stand 15 minutes before serving with herbed yogurt sauce.

Serving size: 1 cup
Calories: 472
Fat: 4.8 g
Cholesterol: 0 mg
Carbohydrate: 89.5 g
Protein: 22.5 g
Sodium: 821.2 mg

**TIP**

You may think of parsley as just a garnish, but it's loaded with vitamin C. The ½ cup parsley in this dish contains 27 milligrams of vitamin C, which is about half the RDA for men (50 grams) and women (60 grams). Cooking destroys some of the vitamin C, however. To get the full benefit, add generous portions of raw chopped parsley to salads and vegetable dishes.

## JEAN-MARC'S OVEN "FRIES"

*Life without french fries would be sad indeed. These golden "faux" fries will satisfy any cravings you have for the other kind.*

SERVES 4

**4 russet-type baking potatoes (about 8 ounces each)**
**Salt**

Preheat oven to 475 degrees F. Line a baking sheet with parchment paper and lightly spray with nonstick spray. Or use a nonstick baking sheet lightly sprayed with nonstick spray (see Tip, page 251).

Peel potatoes, if desired. (You can leave the skins on.) Cut potatoes lengthwise into finger-like pieces about ½ inch thick. Arrange potatoes on prepared baking sheet in a single layer, not touching. Sprinkle with salt. Bake until golden, about 25 minutes.

Serving size: ¼ of the "fries"
Calories: 177
Fat: 0.11 g
Cholesterol: 0 mg
Carbohydrate: 40.4 g
Protein: 4.6 g
Sodium: 16.0 mg (with no salt added)

**TIP**

Look for rolls of parchment paper in your supermarket wherever the wax paper is stocked. It's great for lining baking sheets because foods tend not to stick to it. However, with these moist potato slices, it's a good idea to spray the parchment lightly for insurance.

# HOMEMADE CHUNKY APPLESAUCE

*You can flavor this basic applesauce however you like: with a little vanilla, cinnamon, ginger, or cardamom. It's also quite tasty just as it is. Double the recipe if you like and enjoy the extra for breakfast over the next several days.*

SERVES 4

**4 apples, preferably Rome Beauty, Golden Delicious, Granny Smith, or Gala**

**½ cup frozen apple juice concentrate**

Peel, quarter, and core the apples. Cut into ¾-inch dice. Put apples, apple juice concentrate, and ½ cup water in a large saucepan. Bring to a simmer over moderate heat, cover, and adjust heat to maintain a gentle simmer. Cook until apples are tender, about 6 minutes. Transfer mixture to a food processor and pulse to achieve desired consistency. Serve warm or cold.

*Serving size: ½ cup*
*Calories: 131*
*Fat: 0.5 g*
*Cholesterol: 0 mg*
*Carbohydrate: 33.4 g*
*Protein: 0.3 g*
*Sodium: 2.2 mg*

> **TIP**
>
> Apple varieties vary in their moisture content. If your sauce looks too wet, cook it with the lid off for a few minutes to evaporate excess moisture; if it looks too dry, add a few spoonsful of water.

"CASUAL DINNER WITH FRIENDS"
**Sweet Potato Soup with Lime**
**Rice-Stuffed Bell Peppers**
**Black Bean Sauce**
Steamed Swiss Chard
**Carrot Cake with Cream Cheese Frosting**

If only for the sake of American health, it's a good thing the elaborate dinner parties of the 1980s are now passé. Typically multicourse meals of rich French food with fat-laden sauces, these dinners were as hard on the cook as on the heart. Today, people want to entertain more simply and healthfully, and they enjoy serving guests food with more ethnic flavor. This menu fits that bill and is just one among many menus in this book that you could proudly serve to company. You may be eating a very low-fat vegetarian diet, but you can still entertain—and please—guests who aren't.

The timing: Make the cake in the morning or several hours ahead, but don't frost it yet. About an hour and a half before dinnertime, frost the cake and make the soup. Stuff and bake the peppers. While they are baking, make the black bean sauce and prepare the chard for steaming. Reheat the soup and serve it as a first course. Steam the chard just before you are ready to serve the second course.

## SWEET POTATO SOUP WITH LIME

*Thanks to a squeeze of lime at the end and an optional cilantro garnish, this easy soup has a Latin stamp. If you prefer, season it with dried thyme instead of lime and serve with a small dollop of nonfat sour cream.*

FROM ELIZABETH KAPSTEIN, CHEF
*Dr. Ornish Program for Reversing Heart Disease at Beth Israel Medical Center, New York, New York*
MAKES 12 CUPS

1⅓ cups thinly sliced leeks, white part only
Approximately 3½ cups Vegetable Broth (page 18), or more as needed
4 pounds sweet potatoes, peeled and cut into ½-inch cubes
Juice of 2 limes
Salt and pepper
¼ cup chopped cilantro (optional)

Put leeks and ½ cup vegetable broth in a large pot. Bring to a simmer over moderately high heat and cook 1 minute. Add sweet potatoes and cook 4 minutes more. Add 6 cups water, reduce heat to medium, and cook until sweet potatoes are soft, about 25 minutes. Transfer mixture to a food processor or blender and blend until smooth, adding as much of the additional vegetable broth as you need to make a soup consistency. Return to pot and stir in lime juice, salt, and pepper to taste. Reheat. Serve in warm bowls, garnishing each serving with a little chopped cilantro, if desired.

*Serving size: 1½ cups*
*Calories: 156*
*Fat: 0.52 g*
*Cholesterol: 0 mg*
*Carbohydrate: 34.4 g*
*Protein: 2.4 g*
*Sodium: 66.0 mg (with no salt added)*

| TIP |
| :---: |
| **Six Easy Ways to Eat More Fiber** |

1. Substitute fresh unpeeled fruit for fruit juice at breakfast.

2. Add some grated carrots or some chopped broccoli florets to a green salad.

3. Make vegetable soup heartier by adding whole wheat pasta or whole grains, such as brown rice, wild rice, or bulgur.

4. Add cannellini beans or chickpeas to your favorite tomato sauce for pasta.

5. Make a quick bean dip for raw vegetables by blending canned beans with garlic, herbs, or spices.

6. Switch breakfast cereals. (All-Bran with Extra Fiber has 15 grams of soluble fiber, compared to 0.3 gram for Rice Krispies.)

See page 70 for more ideas on adding fiber to your diet.

## RICE-STUFFED BELL PEPPERS

*These rice-stuffed peppers look beautiful cut in half and arranged on a pool of black bean sauce.*

### SERVES 8

8 large bell peppers, preferably red
2½ cups Vegetable Broth, homemade (page 18) or store-bought
½ teaspoon salt
¼ teaspoon black pepper
1 cup diced mushrooms
½ cup finely diced onion
½ cup finely diced celery
2 cups basmati rice
½ cup canned diced tomatoes
1 teaspoon cumin seed
1 cup green peas, fresh or frozen

Make "caps" for each pepper by slicing about ⅓ inch off the top of each one. Set the caps aside. Carefully remove the seeds and white ribs inside each pepper. Boil the peppers in a large pot of salted water until tender, 5 to 7 minutes. Drain and plunge into ice water to stop the cooking. When cool, drain again and pat dry.

Bring the broth to a simmer in a large saucepan. Add salt, pepper, mushrooms, onion, and celery. Simmer until vegetables are tender, about 5 minutes. Add rice, tomatoes, and cumin. Return to a simmer, cover, reduce heat to lowest setting, and cook 18 minutes. Uncover and put peas on top; do not stir in. Cover pot again, remove from heat, and let stand 7 minutes to allow peas to cook through. Transfer mixture to a large bowl and fluff with a fork.

Preheat oven to 425 degrees F. Divide the stuffing evenly among the peppers; you should have about 1 cup stuffing for each pepper. Top with lids. Arrange them in a 9 by 13-inch baking dish; if they don't want to "stand," lay them gently on their sides. Bake, uncovered, for 20 minutes, or until peppers are hot throughout. Serve with Black Bean Sauce (see below).

*Serving size: 1 stuffed pepper*
*Calories: 229*
*Fat: 0.65 g*
*Cholesterol: 0 mg*
*Carbohydrate: 50.2 g*
*Protein: 5.8 g*
*Sodium: 45.0 mg*

> **TIP**
>
> The stuffing alone makes a delicious rice pilaf. On a busy evening, serve the pilaf with a spinach salad and some canned black bean soup.

## BLACK BEAN SAUCE

*You will probably find a lot of uses for this chunky black bean sauce. Serve it over flour tortillas stuffed with stir-fried vegetables, or as an accompaniment to Spicy Mexican Rice (page 190) and a steamed green vegetable. If you prefer a smooth sauce, you can blend it in the food processor or blender, thinning as needed with water or vegetable broth.*

MAKES 3 CUPS

½ cup diced onion
1 teaspoon minced garlic
1 (15-ounce) can black beans
1 (15-ounce) can tomato sauce
½ teaspoon ground cumin
1 teaspoon ground coriander
1 teaspoon chili powder
Salt and pepper

In a saucepan, combine onion, garlic, and ¼ cup water. Bring to a simmer and simmer until liquid evaporates and onion is transparent, 3 to 5 minutes. Stir in black beans with their liquid, tomato sauce, cumin, coriander, and chili powder. Simmer, covered, until flavors are blended, 15 to 20 minutes. Stir occasionally to prevent sticking; thin, if needed, with a little water. Season to taste with salt and pepper.

*Serving size: about ⅓ cup*
*Calories: 66*
*Fat: 0.4 g*
*Cholesterol: 0 mg*
*Carbohydrate: 12.8 g*
*Protein: 3.8 g*
*Sodium: 208.7 mg (with no salt added)*

| TIP |
|---|
| Dishes made with beans often taste better the second day, perhaps because the beans have had time to absorb all the seasonings. Whenever you make a bean dish, consider doubling the recipe and enjoying it over the next day or two. |

## CARROT CAKE WITH CREAM CHEESE FROSTING

*Where's all the oil that makes carrot cake moist? In this version, it's replaced with crushed pineapple and carrot puree (use jarred baby food with no added fat) to make a low-fat cake as appealing as the original. Top it with cream cheese frosting and serve it for birthdays or dinner parties.*

MAKES ONE 9-INCH CAKE • SERVES 12

Cake:
2 cups grated peeled carrots
½ cup sugar
1 (4-ounce) can crushed pineapple with juice

1 (4-ounce) jar carrot puree

½ cup egg whites (from approximately 4 large eggs) or liquid egg
   substitute

2 teaspoons vanilla extract

¼ teaspoon salt

1¼ cups sifted cake flour

1¼ cups oat bran

2 teaspoons baking soda

1½ teaspoons cinnamon

*Frosting:*

8 ounces nonfat cream cheese, softened

¼ cup sugar

Preheat oven to 425 degrees F. Prepare a 9-inch pie pan, nonstick or lightly sprayed with nonstick spray (see Tip, page 251). In a large bowl, whisk carrots, sugar, pineapple, carrot puree, egg whites, vanilla, and salt until well blended.

In another bowl, stir together flour, oat bran, baking soda, and cinnamon. Add dry ingredients to liquid ingredients; fold in gently.

Pour batter into prepared pan. Bake until lightly browned and firm to the touch, about 30 minutes. Cool in pan, then unmold and frost.

To make frosting: Beat cream cheese and sugar with a stiff whisk, a hand-held mixer, or a wooden spoon until smooth and creamy. Spread evenly over cake surface.

*Serving size: ¹⁄₁₂ of the cake*
*Calories: 118*
*Fat: 0.9 g*
*Cholesterol: 0 mg*
*Carbohydrate: 26.7 g*
*Protein: 4.9 g*
*Sodium: 101.3 mg*

---

**TIP**

Carrots are one of the best sources of beta-carotene, which is converted to vitamin A in the body. Beta-carotene belongs to a family of substances known as carotenoids, plant pigments which are thought to protect against cancer through their action as antioxidants. And you don't have to eat carrots raw to get the benefits. In fact, cooked carrots are higher in vitamin A than raw carrots. Carrots are also a good source of soluble fiber, vitamin C, and calcium.

"A Thanksgiving Groaning Board"
Relish Tray: **Deviled Eggs,** Pickled Cherry Peppers, Baby Carrots, Celery Hearts
**Autumn Vegetables in a Squash**
White and Wild Rice Pilaf
**Glazed Holiday Yams**
**Old-Fashioned Bread Dressing**
**Brandied Cranberry Relish**
Watercress and Beet Salad
**Apple Cranberry Cake**

What a feast! This Thanksgiving menu is missing nothing in the way of variety, color, taste, and bounty. Recruit some kitchen helpers, then relax and enjoy the process of cooking for family and friends.

The timing: As always, Thanksgiving dinner is a major organizational feat and timing challenge. Enlist helpers to do some of the chores, like peeling yams or stuffing hard-cooked egg whites. And before you start, you might want to make a timetable so you don't forget to cook a dish! Here's a suggested rough timetable: make the cranberry relish a day ahead. Make the deviled egg filling and the hard-cooked egg whites a day ahead, but fill them just before serving. Make the apple cranberry cake several hours ahead. Wash and dry the watercress, wrap in paper towels, and refrigerate. Drain canned sliced or julienned beets. Toss them with a favorite nonfat dressing and chill. Trim the baby carrots and celery hearts, cover with water, and chill an hour or two to crisp them.

Prepare the bread stuffing but don't bake it yet. Put all the ingredients for the autumn vegetable stew in the pot but don't cook it yet. Put all the ingredients for the glazed yams in the pot but don't cook them yet. Bake the kabocha squash.

When guests arrive, fill the deviled eggs and set out the relish platter—including store-bought pickled cherry peppers—so everyone can nibble while you finish cooking. When the kabocha squash come out of the oven, raise the temperature to 400 degrees F. and put the bread dressing in. Start the rice pilaf at the same time. (Buy a convenient packaged blend, if you like.) Five minutes later, begin cooking the yams and the autumn vegetables. Slice off the top of the kabochas and remove the strings and seeds. Toss together the watercress and the dressed beets. Put the braised autumn vegetables in the squash and all the other dishes in appropriate serving bowls. Time to eat!

# DEVILED EGGS

*This recipe makes enough filling for 24 egg halves. Or fill 16 halves (for eight people) and save the remainder for a sandwich the next day. You may find yourself making this creamy spread throughout the year, to enjoy as a sandwich filling on rye bread with lettuce and tomato.*

MAKES 16 STUFFED EGG HALVES WITH LEFTOVER FILLING

8 whole eggs
1 (15-ounce) can chickpeas (garbanzo beans)
¼ cup chopped parsley
4 teaspoons whole grain mustard
½ teaspoon grated lemon zest
½ teaspoon minced garlic
⅛ teaspoon black pepper
1 tablespoon minced red onion
1 tablespoon minced capers
Paprika

Place eggs in a saucepan. Cover with hot water. Bring to a boil over high heat, adjust heat to maintain a simmer, and cook 12 minutes. Drain and cool in cold water. Peel eggs, then cut in half lengthwise. Remove the yolks and discard. Gently wash the whites to remove traces of yolk. Pat dry.

Drain garbanzo beans, reserving ⅓ cup liquid. In a food processor or blender, puree beans, parsley, mustard, lemon zest, garlic, and pepper until smooth. Transfer to a bowl and stir in red onion and capers. Taste and adjust seasoning.

Fill egg halves with about a tablespoon of filling. Sprinkle lightly with paprika.

*Serving size: 2 deviled eggs*
*Calories: 35*
*Fat: 0.2 g*
*Cholesterol: 0 mg*
*Carbohydrate: 3.7 g*
*Protein: 4.3 g*
*Sodium: 34.5 g*

## TIP

Learn to make maximum use of "free foods," the flavor-packed ingredients that jazz up dishes without adding appreciable fat or calories. They are your culinary arsenal, battling blandness and fending off boredom. Some of them aren't inexpensive, but have you checked the price of red meat lately? Treat yourself.

*Some useful free foods:*

capers

catsup

herbs, fresh and dried

horseradish

hot sauce

Liquid Smoke

mustards: Dijon, whole grain, or herb-flavored

pickles: dill pickles, pickled peppers, and other pickled vegetables

salsa

soy sauce

spices

taco sauce

vinegars: balsamic, tarragon, cider, rice, sherry, red and white wine, raspberry

If you are salt-sensitive, rinse the capers, choose low-sodium soy sauce, and skip the pickles. Also, be aware of the high sugar content of most catsup.

# Autumn Vegetables in a Squash

*This quick braise of colorful fall vegetables is made in a single pot, then spooned into the cavities of two cooked winter squash for a festive presentation. Guests help themselves to some of the vegetables as well as some of the sweet squash. Ask your produce manager for a kabocha squash, a particularly sweet-fleshed, forest-green autumn squash that comes in large sizes. If you can't find two large kabochas, then buy four acorn squash and serve each guest a half-squash filled with these glistening fall vegetables. A Halloween-type pumpkin is not a good choice because the flesh is not very tasty.*

SERVES 8

2 kabocha squash, 4½ to 5 pounds each
Salt to taste plus 1 teaspoon
Black pepper to taste plus ½ teaspoon
4 cups small brussels sprouts
4 cups carrots, in large dice, or 2 cups whole baby carrots
2 cups peeled shallots, halved if large, or 2 cups peeled baby onions
2 cups diced turnips in large dice
2 cups diced parsnips in large dice
12 garlic cloves, peeled and left whole, or halved if large
2 cups Vegetable Broth, homemade (page 18) or store-bought
2 tablespoons sugar
1½ teaspoons dried thyme

Preheat oven to 375 degrees F. Spray squash skin lightly with non-stick spray (see Tip, page 251). Bake kabocha squash whole until a knife slips in easily, about 45 minutes. Let rest 15 minutes, then cut a thick slice off the stem end to make a "cap"; if using acorn squash, cut them in half through the stem end. If desired, make the cuts in a zigzag pattern to give a sawtooth edge to both the squash top and bottom. Remove the seeds and stringy parts in the seed cavity. Season the cavities with salt and pepper. Set aside.

Trim ends of brussels sprouts; remove the tough outer leaves. Cut an "X" in the bottom of each sprout so heat penetrates better.

Combine brussels sprouts and all remaining ingredients, including 1 teaspoon salt and ½ teaspoon pepper, in a large pot. Bring to a boil over high heat. Reduce heat to moderate and simmer, uncovered, stirring occasionally, until liquid reduces to a glaze and vegetables are tender, about 20 minutes.

Divide vegetables between the squash cavities. Pass the squash at the table.

*Serving size: 1¼ cups*
*Calories: 164*
*Fat: 0.6 g*
*Cholesterol: 0 mg*
*Carbohydrate: 39.7 g*
*Protein: 4.8 g*
*Sodium: 350.0 mg*

**TIP**

They aren't everyone's favorite vegetable, but brussels sprouts have a lot to recommend them. When they're small and fresh and not overcooked, they have a mild, almost sweet flavor that may surprise people who have only had them at their worst. What's more, they are a rich vein of phytochemicals, the plant chemicals that scientists are investigating as possible cancer inhibitors. Like other members of the cabbage family, brussels sprouts contain sulforaphane, a phytochemical that appears to protect lab animals against breast cancer. They are also exceptionally high in vitamin C.

## GLAZED HOLIDAY YAMS

*You don't have to give up this Thanksgiving favorite: brown sugar, corn syrup, and orange juice make such a delicious, fat-free glaze for tender yams that you may toss out your old recipe.*

### SERVES 8

2 pounds yams or sweet potatoes, peeled and cut into 1½-inch chunks
1 cup orange juice
½ cup light corn syrup
2 tablespoons brown sugar
½ teaspoon salt
¼ teaspoon black pepper
½ teaspoon cinnamon

Put all ingredients in a 4-quart nonstick pot with ½ cup water. Cover and cook 5 minutes over moderately high heat. Uncover and cook, stirring occasionally, until liquid has reduced to a glaze and potatoes are tender, about 15 minutes.

Serving size: 1 cup
Calories: 170
Fat: 0.2 g
Cholesterol: 0 mg
Carbohydrate: 41.6 g
Protein: 1.4 g
Sodium: 166.0 mg

**TIP**

Fresh sweet potatoes are a nutritional gold mine with, ounce for ounce, even more beta-carotene than carrots and more vitamin C than tomatoes. They also deliver 100 percent of the RDA for vitamin E in a 3½-ounce serving. What most Americans and many markets call a yam is actually a sweet potato with a moist, dark orange flesh. True yams belong to another family and are more starchy than sweet.

## OLD-FASHIONED BREAD DRESSING

*There may not be a turkey on your Thanksgiving table, but there can be a wonderful bread dressing. This low-fat version, fragrant with herbs and chunky with vegetables, may become part of your year-round repertoire. On another occasion, serve it with a green salad and tomato soup.*

### SERVES 8

2 cups quartered mushrooms
1½ cups diced onion
1 cup diced green bell pepper
¾ cup diced celery
¼ cup raisins
2¼ cups Vegetable Broth, homemade (page 18) or store-bought
2 cups unpeeled diced apple
1 pound stale whole wheat bread, in ½-inch cubes (about 8 cups)
½ cup egg whites (from approximately 4 large eggs) or liquid egg substitute
½ cup minced parsley
½ teaspoon dried thyme
1 tablespoon chopped fresh sage
½ teaspoon salt
¼ teaspoon black pepper

Preheat oven to 400 degrees F. Prepare a 9 by 13-inch baking dish, either nonstick or lightly sprayed with nonstick spray (see Tip, page 251).

In a large nonstick pot, combine mushrooms, onion, bell pepper, celery, and raisins. Add ¼ cup vegetable broth. Bring to a simmer over high heat, cover, and cook 1 minute.

Uncover and add apple. Simmer until liquid evaporates, about 3 more minutes.

Put bread cubes in a large bowl. In another bowl, whisk egg whites lightly just to break them up. Stir in remaining 2 cups vegetable broth, parsley, thyme, sage, salt, and pepper. Pour egg white mixture over bread. Add sautéed vegetables and blend well.

Put stuffing into prepared dish. Pack it firmly with a spatula. Cover with aluminum foil and bake 20 minutes. Uncover and bake an additional 5 minutes to crisp the top.

*Serving size: 1 cup*
*Calories: 301*
*Fat: 2.6 g*
*Cholesterol: 0 mg*
*Carbohydrate: 61.2 g*
*Protein: 10.0 g*
*Sodium: 466.0 mg*

> ### TIP
>
> When whole wheat is milled to make white flour, 60 to 90 percent of vitamins $B_6$ and E, folate, and other nutrients are lost. That's because the bran and tiny germ, removed during milling, contain a disproportionate amount of the vitamins, minerals, and fiber. Thiamin, niacin, riboflavin, and iron are added back when white flour is enriched, but still, refined flour is just a shadow of its former, highly nutritious self. It has only 7 percent of the fiber, 40 percent of the calcium, and none of the lysine, an essential amino acid, that was in the whole wheat berry. And if the refined flour is bleached to whiten it, the rest of its modest amount of vitamin E is lost. For that reason, unbleached flour is a better choice than bleached, but whole wheat flour and whole wheat products are the best choice of all.

## BRANDIED CRANBERRY RELISH

*What's a Thanksgiving table without it? Double the recipe if you have cranberry relish fans at your table.*

### MAKES 1½ CUPS

3 cups fresh or frozen cranberries
1 cup frozen apple juice concentrate
2 tablespoons sugar
1 tablespoon brandy (optional)

Combine all ingredients in a saucepan and bring to a boil. Simmer until cranberries pop and begin to form a sauce, about 5 to 8 minutes. Cool. Chill if desired.

*Serving size: 3 tablespoons*
*Calories: 90*
*Fat: 0.2 g*
*Cholesterol: 0 mg*
*Carbohydrate: 22.1 g*
*Protein: 0.3 g*
*Sodium: 9.3 mg*

> **TIP**
>
> Fresh cranberries appear in the market just before Thanksgiving and tend to disappear shortly thereafter. (That's because most of the cranberry crop is juiced or canned.) If you like them, buy a few extra bags and freeze them so you can make this easy sauce all year. A small spoonful of cranberry sauce would be delicious in the hollow of a poached pear or peach half.

## APPLE CRANBERRY CAKE

*Studded with moist bits of fresh apple, raisins, and tangy cranberries, this elegant cake may remind you of a white fruitcake. Rising high in the pan with a pretty browned top, it makes a festive end to a holiday meal.*

MAKES ONE 10-INCH ROUND TO SERVE 12

1 cup unbleached all-purpose flour
1 cup oat bran
1 tablespoon baking soda
1 teaspoon cinnamon
2 cups plain nonfat yogurt
½ cup maple syrup
1 teaspoon grated lemon zest
2 tablespoons vanilla extract
½ cup raisins
1 cup cranberries
2 cups bread crumbs from stale fat-free bread (See Tip, page 231)
1 cup egg whites (from approximately 8 large eggs)
¼ teaspoon salt
¼ cup sugar
2 cups diced, cored, unpeeled apple

Preheat oven to 375 degrees F. Prepare a 10-inch round cake pan, either nonstick or lightly sprayed with nonstick spray (see Tip, page 251).

In a bowl, stir together flour, oat bran, baking soda, and cinnamon until well blended.

In a large bowl, whisk together yogurt, maple syrup, lemon zest, and vanilla. Stir in raisins, cranberries, and bread crumbs.

In a large bowl, whisk egg whites, salt, and sugar to soft peaks.

Add flour mixture to yogurt mixture, stirring just to blend. Do not overwork. Gently fold in egg whites, then apples, taking care not to overwork the batter. Transfer to prepared pan. Bake until firm to the touch and lightly browned, about 45 minutes. Cool in pan before unmolding.

*Serving size: 1/12 of the cake*
*Calories: 235*
*Fat: 1.4 g*
*Cholesterol: 0 mg*
*Carbohydrate: 50.6 mg*
*Protein: 8.7 g*
*Sodium: 219.0 mg*

| TIP |
| --- |
| To make bread crumbs, put stale bread in a food processor fitted with the steel blade and process until bread is reduced to crumbs. |

# WINTER

**Spicy Arkansas Chili**
Steamed Basmati Rice
Assorted Chili Fixings
Basket of Crackers
**Mixed Citrus Compote with Cinnamon Yogurt Sauce**

**Confetti Rice Pilaf with Split Peas**
Steamed Sweet Potatoes
**Spinach and Cucumber Raita**
Whole Wheat Pita Bread
**Winter Fruit Platter with Raspberry Sorbet**

**Stuffed Cabbage with Lentils and Brown Rice**
**Steamed Red Potatoes and Baby Peas**
Sour Cream with Fresh Chives
Pumpernickel Bread or Rye Bread
Crisp Green Apple Wedges

**Penne Pasta with White Bean and Sun-Dried Tomato Sauce**
**Wilted Spinach with Garlic and Lemon**
Crusty Italian Bread
**Pears Poached in Red Wine**

**Potato Pancakes with Warm Applesauce**
**Beet and Cabbage Borscht with Sour Cream**
Warm Rye Bread
**Sliced Oranges in Spiced Syrup**

**White and Wild Rice Salad with Baby Artichoke Hearts**
**White Bean Soup with Winter Greens**
Whole Grain Toast
Fresh Orange Sections

**Hearty Barley-Lentil Soup**
Toasted Whole Wheat Bagels
**Spinach and Mushroom Salad with Buttermilk Dressing**
**Baked Bananas with Orange Sauce**
🍅

**Baked Sweet Potatoes with Thyme**
**Braised Cabbage with Onions and Caraway**
Steamed Wild Rice with Petite Peas
Whole Wheat Rolls
**Warm Apple Crisp**
🍅

**Dr. Crawford's Haystacks**
Fresh Tomato Salsa (page 192)
**Steamed Chayote with Red Onion and Lime**
Baked Tortilla Chips or Fat-Free Flour Tortillas
**Spiced Pumpkin Bars**
🍅

"CHRISTMAS DINNER"
**Consommé with Vegetable Brunoise**
**Herbed Mushroom Risotto**
**Braised Brussels Sprouts and Chestnuts**
**Glazed Acorn Squash with Orange and Ginger**
**Brandied Pear Bread Pudding**
🍅

"NEW YEAR'S DAY BUFFET"
**Hoppin' John**
**Nell's Southern Eggplant Dressing**
**Collard Greens with Tomatoes, Onions, and Peppers**
**John's Gingerbread**
Applesauce (page 217)
🍅

What good timing: just when the weather turns cold and full-bodied dishes start to have more appeal, the fruits and vegetables with the heartiest character are ready to harvest. Root vegetables like rutabagas and parsnips and sturdy greens such as collards and kale make winter meals satisfying and varied. Soup always sounds tempting when it's cold outside, but the soups in this chapter are likely to tempt you even when it's not. Try the chunky Beet and Cabbage Borscht drizzled with sour cream (page 251), the Tuscan-style White Bean Soup with Winter Greens (page 255), a toe-warming Hearty Barley-Lentil Soup (page 257), or an elegant Consommé with Vegetable Brunoise (page 268). You'll also find recipes for such cold-weather favorites as stuffed cabbage, spicy chili, and potato pancakes with applesauce. Apples, oranges, pears, and bananas star in old-fashioned winter desserts, like Warm Apple Crisp (page 262), Baked Bananas with Orange Sauce (page 259), and Brandied Pear Bread Pudding (page 273).

In winter look for:

bananas
Belgian endive
broccoli
broccoli rabe
cabbage, green and red
cardoon
celery root
collard greens
escarole
fennel
grapefruit
kale

kiwi fruit
mustard greens
oranges
parsnips
pomegranates
rutabagas
tangerines
turnips
wild mushrooms

**Spicy Arkansas Chili**
Steamed Basmati Rice
Assorted Chili Fixings
Basket of Crackers
**Mixed Citrus Compote with Cinnamon Yogurt Sauce**

☼

Serve this meaty-tasting "bowl of red" over fluffy steamed rice and set out a variety of chili fixings (or "fixin's" as it's said in Little Rock). Some accompaniment ideas: pickled jalapeño rings; minced red or green onion; pickled okra; pickled baby corn; grated nonfat cheese or sour cream; fresh carrot, celery, and jicama sticks; and cherry peppers. Fill a basket with favorite nonfat crackers or make a batch of corn bread (page 183) if you have the time. After the spicy chili, pass a bowl of cooling citrus compote and a pitcher of cinnamon yogurt sauce.

The timing: Prepare the citrus compote and yogurt sauce and chill. Make the chili. While it's simmering, steam the rice and set out relishes and crackers.

## SPICY ARKANSAS CHILI

*What makes this an Arkansas chili? Chef Martin Mongiello, its creator, says it needs to be made with bottled Arkansas spring water, but you'll probably find that's not strictly necessary. He also suggests serving it with Arkansas-grown basmati rice, the aromatic long-grain rice that's prized in India. But even chef Mongiello would probably agree that his hearty chili will taste just fine with whatever rice you have on hand.*

FROM CHEF MARTIN C. J. MONGIELLO:
SERVES 4

10 (2.5-ounce) Boca Burger "No Fat Original" patties (see Tip,
  page 178)
1 cup diced onion
1 cup diced green bell pepper
1 garlic clove, minced
2 tablespoons chili powder
1 tablespoon ground cumin

1 cup canned ground tomatoes, or diced tomatoes diced finer by hand
¼ cup tomato salsa (no added fat)
Salt

Cook Boca Burgers according to package directions. Chop coarsely.

In a nonstick pot, combine onion, bell pepper, garlic, chili powder, and cumin. Add ¼ cup water, bring to a simmer, and simmer until vegetables are soft and water evaporates, about 5 minutes. Add tomatoes, salsa, chopped Boca Burgers, and 2 cups water. Bring to a simmer, cover, and adjust heat to maintain a slow simmer. Cook until chili is thick and flavorful, about 20 minutes. Season to taste with salt.

*Serving size: 2 cups*
*Calories: 247*
*Fat: 0.3 g*
*Cholesterol: 0*
*Carbohydrate: 30.6 g*
*Protein: 31.3 g*
*Sodium: 534.7 mg (with no salt added)*

> **TIP**
>
> This tasty basic chili could accommodate the seasonings and ingredients you like best. Add a minced jalapeño chile if you like, or some dried oregano, frozen corn, or pinto beans. Use vegetable broth in place of water for an even more flavorful chili. Make a double batch and enjoy the leftovers as "sloppy Joes" in a bun the next day.

## MIXED CITRUS COMPOTE WITH CINNAMON YOGURT SAUCE

*This compote will be refreshing and appealing with navel oranges and pink grapefruit alone, but it will be all the prettier if you can find citrus of different colors, such as blood oranges, white grapefruit, and ruby grapefruit.*

### SERVES 4

6 navel oranges, or a combination of navel and blood oranges
2 grapefruit, preferably 1 white and 1 ruby
½ cup nonfat plain yogurt
1½ teaspoons brown sugar
Dash ground cinnamon

Grate enough of one orange to make 1 tablespoon zest (orange part only).

*Everyday Cooking with Dr. Dean Ornish*

Cut the ends off the oranges and set the oranges on one end. With a sharp knife, cut from top to bottom all the way around the oranges to remove the peel and all the white pith. Holding the oranges over a bowl to catch the juices, loosen the segments by cutting between the fruit and the membrane with a small knife. Lift out each segment in one piece. Transfer to the bowl. Repeat the peeling and sectioning procedure with the grapefruit, removing any seeds. Gently toss together orange and grapefruit segments and any accumulated juices. Stir in 2½ teaspoons of the orange zest.

In a small bowl, combine remaining ½ teaspoon orange zest, yogurt, brown sugar, and cinnamon. Stir in 1½ teaspoons citrus juice from the fruit bowl. To serve, put about ¾ cup of citrus segments in each of four bowls. Top each serving with 2 tablespoons of yogurt sauce.

---

**TIP**

Serve this orange- and cinnamon-spiced yogurt sauce with sliced pineapple, bananas, mangoes, or fresh summer fruit, such as the Summer Fruit Salad on page 170.

---

*Serving size: ¾ cup fruit, 2 table spoons sauce*
*Calories: 160*
*Fat: 0.4 g*
*Cholesterol: 0.5 mg*
*Carbohydrate: 38.4 g*
*Protein: 4.8 g*
*Sodium: 24.0 mg*

**Confetti Rice Pilaf with Split Peas**
Steamed Sweet Potatoes
**Spinach and Cucumber Raita**
Whole Wheat Pita Bread
**Winter Fruit Platter with Raspberry Sorbet**

So many Indians are vegetarians that the cuisine offers lots of inspiration. The cumin-scented pilaf in this menu—a combination of rice and legumes—is an Indian idea, as is the soothing raita, a yogurt salad that's meant to be spooned over rice or used as a dipping sauce for bread. Add cubed and steamed sweet potatoes for color and a beta-carotene boost, and complete the meal with a platter of beautifully sliced and arranged winter fruits paired with store-bought sorbet.

---

The timing: Trim and slice the fruits and refrigerate. (Don't peel the banana until just before serving.) Make the rice pilaf. While it cooks, prepare the raita. About 10 minutes before you are ready to eat, slice and steam the sweet potatoes.

## CONFETTI RICE PILAF WITH SPLIT PEAS

*This is a particularly pretty pilaf, the rice flecked with confetti-like bits of yellow, orange, and green. Cumin seed gives it a subtle Indian fragrance and flavor.*

SERVES 4

1 cup diced onion
½ cup diced carrots
½ cup diced celery
½ cup yellow or green split peas
1 cup long-grain rice, preferably basmati
1 teaspoon cumin seed
1 bay leaf
½ teaspoon salt
¼ teaspoon pepper

Combine all ingredients in a 3-quart saucepan with 3 cups water. Bring to a simmer over high heat. Cover, reduce heat to lowest setting, and simmer 25 minutes. Let stand 5 minutes, covered; transfer to a serving bowl and fluff with a fork. Remove the bay leaf before serving.

*Serving size: 1½ cups*
*Calories: 278*
*Fat: 1.5 g*
*Cholesterol: 0 mg*
*Carbohydrate: 55.9 g*
*Protein: 10.4 g*
*Sodium: 130.0 mg*

> **TIP**
> Toasting brings out the flavor of many dry spices. To enhance this pilaf, toast the cumin seed first in a small dry skillet over low heat, shaking the skillet often, until cumin darkens slightly and begins to smell fragrant. Then add to pilaf as directed above.

# SPINACH AND CUCUMBER RAITA

*Raita is a creamy yogurt-based salad that Indians serve as a cooling accompaniment to spicy dishes. Enjoy it with Confetti Rice Pilaf with Split Peas (page 240), or with other steamed grains; as a dressing for greens or sliced tomatoes; or as a dip for pita bread or fresh vegetables. It will keep in the refrigerator for a couple of days.*

## SERVES 4

1 small cucumber
½ cup squeezed dry, thawed, frozen chopped spinach
1 cup plain nonfat yogurt
1 garlic clove, minced
1 tablespoon chopped fresh cilantro, mint, or parsley
½ teaspoon grated lemon zest
Salt and pepper

Peel cucumber, halve it lengthwise, and scrape out seeds with a small spoon. Cut cucumber in ¼-inch dice. You should have about 1 cup.

In a bowl, combine cucumber, spinach, yogurt, garlic, cilantro, and lemon zest. Season to taste with salt and pepper.

*Serving size: ½ cup*
*Calories: 36*
*Fat: 0.15 g*
*Cholesterol: 1.0 mg*
*Carbohydrate: 5.2 g*
*Protein: 3.6 g*
*Sodium: 49.0 mg (with no salt added)*

> **TIP**
>
> Of course you can make this raita with fresh spinach. Start with one 12-ounce bunch of fresh spinach, stems removed; blanch the washed leaves in a large pot of salted water over high heat just until they wilt, about 1 minute. Drain in a sieve and cool under cold running water. Squeeze dry, then chop. You should have about ½ cup.

# WINTER FRUIT PLATTER WITH RASPBERRY SORBET

*A platter of sliced fresh fruit arranged in mounds of contrasting color makes an appetizing sight at the end of a meal. All the fruit except the banana can be cut ahead of time; cut the banana just before serving to prevent browning. Many markets carry imported mangoes year-round; if you can't find one, substitute a fruit that will contrast with the others in color and texture, such as an orange. Cut off the ends, cut away the peel and white pith, then slice into rounds or sections.*

SERVES 4

¼ small pineapple
2 kiwi fruit
1 mango
1 banana
1 cup store-bought raspberry sorbet, no sugar added
Mint sprigs

Remove pineapple core. Carefully slice the flesh away from the rind, leaving the flesh in one piece, then cut the flesh into ½-inch-thick slices. Set aside.

Cut the kiwi in half lengthwise. With a soupspoon, scoop the kiwi flesh away from the skin in one piece. Cut each half in thirds lengthwise. Set aside.

To peel the mango, cradle it in one hand and, with a small sharp knife, peel the side that's facing up. Carefully slice the flesh away from the pit in lengthwise slices. Turn the mango over and peel and slice the other side.

On a large serving platter, arrange the pineapple, kiwi, and mango attractively in separate mounds. Leave room for the banana. Cover with plastic wrap and refrigerate until ready to serve, then peel the banana, slice it thickly, and add it to the platter.

To serve, put ¼ cup raspberry sorbet on each of four chilled dessert plates. Garnish with a sprig of mint. Pass the fruit at the table so diners can serve themselves.

*Serving size: 1 cup fruit, ¼ cup
    sorbet*
*Calories: 128*
*Fat: 0.5 g*
*Cholesterol: 0 mg*
*Carbohydrate: 23.0 g*
*Protein: 1.5 g*
*Sodium: 33.0 mg*

### TIP

A mango puree makes an excellent sauce for almost any fresh fruit. To make it, peel, slice, and dice a ripe mango, then push the fruit through a sieve with a wooden spoon. Add a pinch of sugar, if necessary, and a squeeze of lemon or lime. Serve with sliced bananas, raspberries, peaches, blackberries, or pineapple. How do you know when a mango is ripe? Smell it. It should have an alluring tropical perfume.

*Everyday Cooking with Dr. Dean Ornish*

**Stuffed Cabbage with Lentils and Brown Rice**
**Steamed Red Potatoes and Baby Peas**
Sour Cream with Fresh Chives
Pumpernickel Bread or Rye Bread
Crisp Green Apple Wedges
☙

T oday we know that humble cooking can be more healthful than
haute cuisine. We know that when prosperity invites us to adopt
a diet of thick steaks and sugary desserts, it is doing us no favors. We
are better off eating stuffed cabbage, especially if it's filled with a savory
mixture of nutritious brown rice, lentils, and caraway. Paired with red
potatoes steamed with peas and topped with a dollop of sour cream,
stuffed cabbage delivers the warmth and simple goodness of a home-
cooked meal.

The timing: Prepare and bake the stuffed cabbage first. While it's
baking, steam the potatoes and peas. Slice the apples into thick wedges
just before you are ready for dessert.

## STUFFED CABBAGE WITH LENTILS AND BROWN RICE

*Slice into these plump, tomato-sauced cabbage rolls and you'll find a savory
filling of lentils, rice, and caraway. A dollop of sour cream on top brings all
the flavors together. Blanch the cabbage leaves and prepare the stuffing a few
hours ahead, if you like; you can even fill the rolls ahead and bake them just
before serving.*

FROM KATHERINE CHEPENUK OF DEVON, PENNSYLVANIA:
*Katherine and Max Chepenuk are parents of Melanie Elliott, R.N., who is
on staff at our Preventive Medicine Research Institute in Sausalito. Melanie
remembers growing up with this old family recipe, then made with beef,
lamb, or turkey. "I think it tastes even better now," says Melanie, "and it
still is my comfort food, reminding me of home."*
SERVES 4

**Stuffing:**
3 cups Vegetable Broth, homemade (page 18) or store-bought
1 cup diced onion

½ cup diced carrot
½ cup diced celery
½ cup lentils
1 teaspoon minced garlic
1 teaspoon caraway seed
½ teaspoon salt
¼ teaspoon black pepper
1 cup basmati rice
1 large head cabbage (about 2½ pounds)
1½ cups nonfat Marinara Sauce, homemade (page 92) or store-bought

*Sour Cream with Fresh Chives:*
½ cup nonfat sour cream mixed with 1 tablespoon minced fresh chives or
  parsley

Bring vegetable broth to a simmer in a large saucepan. Add onion, carrot, celery, lentils, garlic, caraway seed, salt, and pepper. Simmer 5 minutes. Add rice, stir with a fork, and return to a simmer; cover and reduce heat to lowest setting. Cook 20 minutes. Remove from heat and let stand 5 minutes.

Preheat oven to 425 degrees F.

Cut out and remove the cabbage core. Bring a large pot of salted water to a boil over high heat. Add cabbage and simmer, turning the head occasionally with tongs so it cooks evenly. After about 12 minutes, the outer leaves should begin to peel away from the head. Carefully remove them with tongs to a bowl of ice water to stop the cooking. You will need twelve large pretty leaves for stuffing. Reserve the remaining cabbage for another use, such as soup.

Drain the twelve blanched leaves and pat them dry. Spread them out on a work surface. Put a scant 1/2 cup stuffing on the bottom third of each leaf. Roll the bottom of the leaf over the filling, fold the sides in, then continue rolling to enclose the filling neatly. Arrange rolls in a baking dish just large enough to hold them in one layer. Top with marinara sauce, spreading it evenly over the rolls. Bake until rolls are hot throughout, about 15 minutes. Serve with sour cream with fresh chives.

*Everyday Cooking with Dr. Dean Ornish*

Serving size: 3 cabbage rolls
Calories: 228
Fat: 1.3 g
Cholesterol: 0 mg
Carbohydrate: 45.5 g
Protein: 11.3 g
Sodium: 895.0 mg

**TIP**

The filling for these cabbage rolls is a variation of the Confetti Rice Pilaf with Split Peas (page 240). It is so delicious on its own that you may be tempted to forget about stuffing the cabbage with it. For a faster dinner, serve the pilaf "unstuffed" alongside steamed shredded cabbage with paprika and nonfat sour cream.

## STEAMED RED POTATOES AND BABY PEAS

*For even cooking, choose a skillet large enough to hold all the potato quarters in one layer. And of course you can use fresh peas in season. They will take 5 to 8 minutes to cook, depending on size, so add them to the potatoes at the appropriate time.*

### SERVES 4

½ cup Vegetable Broth, homemade (page 18) or store-bought
1 pound small red-skinned potatoes, quartered
1 cup frozen petite green peas
2 green onions, minced
2 tablespoons chopped fresh dill
Salt and pepper

Put broth in a medium skillet and bring to a boil over high heat. Add potato quarters, cover, and reduce heat to low. Cook until potatoes are tender when pierced, 12 to 14 minutes. Scatter the peas over the potatoes, cover, and cook until peas are heated through, about 2 more minutes. Uncover; if there is still broth remaining in the skillet, boil, uncovered, until it evaporates. Gently stir in green onions and dill. Season to taste with salt and pepper.

Serving size: ¾ cup
Calories: 99

**TIP**

In summer, you may be able to find more unusual potatoes, such as Yellow Finns, Bintjes, fingerlings, or Yukon Golds. This simple recipe would show off these flavorful varieties. For all potatoes, the skin is a good source of fiber so it's best to leave it on.

Fat: 0.9 g
Cholesterol: 0 mg
Carbohydrate: 21.3 g
Protein: 3.5 g
Sodium: 6.0 mg (with no salt added)

**Penne Pasta with White Bean and Sun-Dried Tomato Sauce**
**Wilted Spinach with Garlic and Lemon**
Crusty Italian Bread
**Pears Poached in Red Wine**

Italians have long known that pasta and beans are a harmonious duo. They put them together in soups, stews, and rustic pasta dishes, consciously or unconsciously creating a highly nutritious and balanced meal. Pairing whole wheat pasta and white beans yields a high-fiber dish and a tasty marriage besides. Serve wilted spinach as a separate course so you can appreciate its pure, intense flavor, then conclude with pears bathed in spiced red wine.

The timing: Prepare the pears and chill. Make the pasta sauce. While the sauce is simmering, prepare the ingredients for the wilted spinach but don't cook it yet. Start boiling the pasta when the sauce is almost done. When the pasta is about half-done, start the spinach.

## PENNE PASTA WITH WHITE BEAN AND SUN-DRIED TOMATO SAUCE

*If you can't find penne, use another short, stubby pasta such as rigatoni, fusilli (spirals), or large elbow macaroni. This hearty sauce, thinned with vegetable broth, would make an excellent bean soup.*

SERVES 4

1 cup sliced onions
1 teaspoon minced garlic
1 cup Vegetable Broth, or more if needed, homemade (page 18) or store-bought
2 (15-ounce) cans white cannellini beans, or 3 cups home-cooked cannellini, beans with 1½ cups liquid

1 cup sun-dried tomatoes (not oil-packed), quartered

1 teaspoon dried thyme, or 2 teaspoons minced fresh thyme

1 teaspoon dried basil, or 1 tablespoon fresh basil in chiffonade
   (page 211)

Salt and pepper

1 pound whole wheat penne pasta

2 tablespoons chopped parsley

Combine onions, garlic, and ¼ cup broth in a large pot. Simmer over moderately high heat until onions are soft, about 5 minutes. Stir in beans with their liquid, sun-dried tomatoes, thyme, basil, and remaining ¾ cup broth. Bring to a simmer and cook, uncovered, over moderate heat, stirring often, until flavors are well blended, 15 to 20 minutes. Thin, if desired, with additional vegetable broth. Season to taste with salt and pepper. Keep warm.

Bring a large pot of salted water to a boil over high heat. Add pasta and boil until al dente, about 12 minutes. Drain and transfer to a warm bowl. Add sauce and toss to coat. Serve on warm plates, topping each portion with ½ tablespoon chopped parsley.

*Serving size: 2 cups pasta,*
   *1 cup sauce*
*Calories: 454*
*Fat: 1.7 g*
*Cholesterol: 0 mg*
*Carbohydrate: 88.5 g*
*Protein: 22.0 g*
*Sodium: 312.0 mg (with no salt*
   *added)*

| TIP |
|-----|
| Buy dried herbs and spices in small quantities, as they quickly lose intensity upon exposure to air. Keep them in airtight containers in a cool, dark place (*not* next to or over the stove) and replace them when they have lost their punch. |

## WILTED SPINACH WITH GARLIC AND LEMON

*If you cook spinach over high heat, it quickly wilts into a soft heap of deep green, highly nutritious leaves. Season it with sautéed garlic and pass lemon wedges to make an easy side dish you can serve all year round.*

SERVES 4

¼ cup Vegetable Broth, homemade (page 18) or store-bought
2 garlic cloves, minced
1 pound washed and dried spinach leaves, thick stems removed
Salt and pepper
Lemon wedges

Bring the broth to a simmer in a small skillet over moderate heat. Add garlic and cook, stirring, until softened, 1 to 2 minutes.

Set a large, deep skillet, pot, or Dutch oven (see Tip below) over high heat for 1 minute. Add half the spinach leaves, then stir constantly with a wooden spoon until the leaves begin to wilt, about 1 minute. Add the remaining spinach and cook, stirring constantly, until all the leaves are wilted, about 2 to 3 minutes longer. Add the garlic and any broth in the skillet and stir to combine. Season to taste with salt and pepper. Transfer to a serving bowl. Pass lemon wedges.

*Serving size: ½ cup*
*Calories: 21*
*Fat: 0.2 g*
*Cholesterol: 0 mg*
*Carbohydrate: 3.3 g*
*Protein: 2.7 g*
*Sodium: 63.0 mg (with no salt added)*

> **TIP**
>
> Buying washed and dried spinach, available bagged in most supermarkets, is a big time-saver. If you buy unwashed spinach and wash it yourself, be sure to dry the leaves thoroughly in a salad spinner or your cooked spinach will be afloat in liquid. It's probably best not to use a nonstick pan for this dish, because you must preheat the empty pan over high heat; prolonged exposure to high heat can damage the coatings on some pans.

## PEARS POACHED IN RED WINE

*These rosy pear halves keep well in their poaching liquid, so it's smart to make enough for more than one meal. Serve ½ pear to each diner with some of the spiced wine sauce, and save the rest to enjoy over the next few days.*

SERVES 8

2 cups dry red wine
¼ cup sugar

¼ cup orange juice concentrate

1 tablespoon lemon juice

2 cinnamon sticks

1 teaspoon vanilla extract

4 Anjou or Bosc pears, peeled, halved, and cored

In a large saucepan, combine wine, sugar, orange juice concentrate, lemon juice, cinnamon, vanilla, and 1 cup water. Bring to a simmer, adjust heat to maintain a gentle simmer, and cook 5 minutes to blend flavors. Add pear halves. Simmer gently, uncovered, until just tender when pierced, about 8 minutes. Cool in liquid, then chill.

Serve each pear half in a small bowl with 3 tablespoons of the flavorful poaching liquid.

*Serving size: 1 pear, 3 tablespoons*
  *sauce*
*Calories: 93*
*Fat: 0.1 g*
*Cholesterol: 0 mg*
*Carbohydrate: 13.7 g*
*Protein: 0.4 g*
*Sodium: 4.0 mg*

> **TIP**
>
> **Peel pears just before poaching to prevent browning. Use a melon baller to remove the cores easily.**

---

**Potato Pancakes with Warm Applesauce**
**Beet and Cabbage Borscht with Sour Cream**
Warm Rye Bread
**Sliced Oranges in Spiced Syrup**

On a cold night, a rib-sticking soup can be more inviting than the most elaborate meal. For a sure chill-chaser, make a pot of beet and cabbage borscht, a dish that has sustained countless people through bitter Russian winters. Precede it with a stack of potato pancakes hot from the skillet, served with a spoonful of warm applesauce. Fresh fruit makes an appealing conclusion: serve orange wedges if you're short on time; if not, slice the oranges and marinate them in a gently spiced syrup.

The timing: Make the dessert and chill. Make the borscht and set

---

aside. Lastly, prepare the pancake batter, warm the applesauce, and make the pancakes.

## POTATO PANCAKES WITH WARM APPLESAUCE

*Crisp and golden-brown, these savory pancakes are a Chanukah tradition. But they are worth making throughout the year—to serve with soup, as in this menu; with a vegetable stew; or for Sunday brunch. Parboiling (blanching) the potatoes first keeps them from turning brown and helps the pancakes cook faster.*

MAKES 16 PANCAKES TO SERVE 4

4 russet-type baking potatoes
¾ cup egg whites (from approximately 6 large eggs) or liquid egg
   substitute
¼ cup grated onion
2 tablespoons chopped parsley
Pinch ground nutmeg
Salt and pepper
1 cup applesauce, homemade (page 217) or store-bought
1 teaspoon minced fresh thyme, or ground cinnamon to taste

Bring a large pot of salted water to a boil over high heat. Peel potatoes, then blanch them whole in the boiling water for 2 minutes. Set aside to air-dry for 10 minutes, then grate by hand or in a food processor using the coarse grating attachment. In a bowl, combine grated potatoes, egg whites, onion, parsley, and nutmeg. Season to taste with salt and pepper.

Spray a large nonstick skillet lightly with cooking spray (see Tip page 251). Set over moderate heat. When skillet is hot, make pancakes, using ⅓ cup batter for each pancake. Cook until golden-brown and done throughout, about 4 minutes per side. Transfer to a warm platter.

Combine applesauce and thyme. Heat gently in a small saucepan or in a microwave until hot. Serve with potato pancakes.

*Serving size: 4 pancakes*
*Calories: 174*
*Fat: 0.2 g*
*Cholesterol: 0 mg*
*Carbohydrate: 17.6 g*
*Protein: 8.6 g*
*Sodium: 92.0 mg*

> **TIP**
>
> Cooking sprays are not innocent when it comes to fat. They are made primarily of vegetable oils, and if you are not careful when spraying, you can add a significant amount of fat to your foods. Choose a nonstick spray made of canola oil and spray lightly. A one-third-of-a-second spray delivers more than ¼ gram of fat. So if you've been heavy on the trigger, lighten up.

## Beet and Cabbage Borscht with Sour Cream

*Canned beets make quick work of this satisfying soup, but of course you can cook and slice your own fresh beets. They should be in matchsticklike pieces.*

### Serves 4

2 cups thinly sliced green cabbage
½ cup diced leeks, white part only
½ cup diced carrots
½ cup diced onion
½ cup diced celery
2 cups Vegetable Broth, homemade (page 18) or store-bought
2 (15-ounce) cans julienne beets, or 3 cups cooked fresh beets, in matchsticks (page 79)
2 tablespoons tomato paste
¼ teaspoon caraway seed
2 teaspoons red wine vinegar
Salt and pepper
¼ cup nonfat sour cream
1½ teaspoons minced fresh chives or dill

Put cabbage, leeks, carrots, onions, and celery in a large pot with ¼ cup vegetable broth. Bring to a simmer and simmer until vegetables are softened, about 5 minutes. Stir in shredded beets with their liquid, remaining 1¾ cups vegetable broth, tomato paste, and caraway. Simmer, covered, for 10 minutes. Stir in vinegar. Season to taste with salt and pepper. Remove from heat and whisk in sour cream and chives. Serve in warm bowls.

*Serving size: 1½ cups*
*Calories: 87*
*Fat: 0.4 g*
*Cholesterol: 0 mg*
*Carbohydrate: 40.0 g*
*Protein: 4.1 g*
*Sodium: 117.0 mg (with no salt added)*

**TIP**

It's not always easy to season a dish so it pleases all the palates at the table. So diners can season their food to taste, set your table with a pepper mill and a bowl of lemon and/or lime wedges. You may want to add a pretty glass cruet or two of vinegar, perhaps a wine or herb vinegar and a balsamic vinegar. These table accessories can make even a simple meal look appetizing.

## SLICED ORANGES IN SPICED SYRUP

*Fresh orange juice infused with an aromatic spiced syrup makes an exotic sauce for sliced oranges. Don't be put off by the quantity of spices used; the result is subtle and light.*

### SERVES 4

½ teaspoon whole black peppercorns
20 whole cloves
8 cardamom pods
2 cinnamon sticks
2 tablespoons plus 2 teaspoons sugar
1 tablespoon plus 1 teaspoon lemon juice
1 teaspoon cornstarch
1 cup orange juice
2 large navel oranges

In a 10-inch skillet or other wide pan, combine peppercorns, cloves, cardamom, cinnamon, sugar, lemon juice, cornstarch, and 2 cups water. Whisk to dissolve the cornstarch. Bring to a boil over high heat and simmer until almost all the liquid has evaporated and big bubbles begin to appear on the skillet bottom, about 10 minutes. Remove from heat and add orange juice. Scrape the sides of the skillet with a rubber spatula. Cover and let mixture infuse 20 minutes or until cold. Strain through a sieve.

Cut the ends off the oranges and set the oranges on one end. With a sharp knife, cut from top to bottom all the way around the orange to remove the peel and all the white pith. Slice oranges into rounds about ¼ inch thick.

To serve, put orange slices in four dessert bowls. Top each serving with ¼ cup of the spiced orange syrup.

*Serving size: ½ orange, ¼ cup syrup*
*Calories: 83*
*Fat: 0.2 g*
*Cholesterol: 0 mg*
*Carbohydrate: 20.1 g*
*Protein: 1.0 g*
*Sodium: 0.6 mg*

> **TIP**
>
> A lot of chefs are steeping herbs in liquids to make "infusions" that add flavor to dishes without adding fat. You can infuse a liquid with spices, as in this recipe, or with herbs. Try infusing a light syrup or fruit juice with fresh mint, lemon verbena, or lavender; or infusing a savory broth with rosemary or thyme.

### White and Wild Rice Salad with Baby Artichoke Hearts
### White Bean Soup with Winter Greens
Whole Grain Toast
Fresh Orange Sections

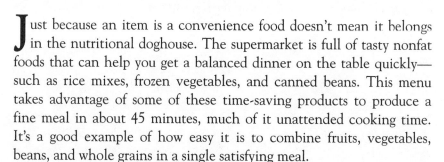

Just because an item is a convenience food doesn't mean it belongs in the nutritional doghouse. The supermarket is full of tasty nonfat foods that can help you get a balanced dinner on the table quickly— such as rice mixes, frozen vegetables, and canned beans. This menu takes advantage of some of these time-saving products to produce a fine meal in about 45 minutes, much of it unattended cooking time. It's a good example of how easy it is to combine fruits, vegetables, beans, and whole grains in a single satisfying meal.

The timing: Make the rice salad first, even several hours ahead. While the rice is cooking, start the soup.

# White and Wild Rice Salad with Baby Artichoke Hearts

*Pack this pretty rice salad on your next picnic. It travels easily, and making it several hours ahead doesn't harm it at all.*

### Serves 4

1 (9-ounce) package frozen artichoke hearts, thawed
1 (4.3-ounce) package long-grain and wild rice mix
Salt to taste, plus ½ teaspoon
¼ cup diced roasted red pepper
1½ teaspoons minced fresh tarragon
¼ cup bottled nonfat Italian salad dressing
Pepper

Slice the artichoke hearts lengthwise into pieces about ½ inch wide. In a medium saucepan, combine artichokes, rice mix (omit the seasoning packet and butter or margarine called for on the box), salt, and 1⅔ cups water. Bring to a boil over high heat, stir with a fork, then cover, reduce the heat to lowest setting, and cook until the water is absorbed and rice is tender, about 30 minutes. Transfer to a bowl and let cool to room temperature, fluffing the rice occasionally with a fork.

Add red pepper, tarragon, and dressing and stir with a fork to blend. Season to taste with salt and pepper.

*Serving size: 1¾ cups*
*Calories: 278*
*Fat: 0.8 g*
*Cholesterol: 0 mg*
*Carbohydrate: 60.0 g*
*Protein: 8.0 g*
*Sodium: 598.0 mg*

> **TIP**
>
> Some of the popular packaged rice blends contain a separate seasoning packet that contributes a hefty amount of sodium to the finished dish. It's better to discard the seasoning packet and season the rice with favorite fresh or dried herbs.

*Everyday Cooking with Dr. Dean Ornish*

# WHITE BEAN SOUP WITH WINTER GREENS

*Lemon zest stirred in at the last minute gives this soup a fresh, lively flavor. You could vary the recipe by making it with cooked red or black beans; by adding some chopped tomato; or by stirring in some small pasta, such as elbows or shells.*

*You can make this soup a couple of hours ahead, but don't add the kale and lemon zest until you are ready to reheat it.*

SERVES 4

1 bunch fresh kale or chard (10 to 12 ounces)
3 cups Vegetable Broth, homemade (page 18) or store-bought
1 russet-type baking potato, peeled, in ¼ -inch dice
½ medium yellow onion, chopped
2 teaspoons minced garlic
1 bay leaf
2 (15-ounce) cans navy beans or cannellini beans, or 4 cups home-
   cooked beans with 1½ cups liquid
Salt and pepper
1 teaspoon grated lemon zest

Remove and discard tough kale ribs. Bring a large pot of salted water to a boil over high heat. Add kale leaves and boil 2 minutes. Drain in a sieve or colander. Refresh under cold running water. Drain again well. Chop coarsely.

In a medium pot, combine broth, potatoes, onion, garlic, and bay leaf. Bring to a simmer, cover, and adjust heat to maintain a simmer. Cook until potatoes are just tender, about 10 minutes. Add beans and their liquid. Cook, covered, over low heat, until potatoes are soft and flavors are well blended, about 15 minutes.

Add chopped kale and simmer 1 minute, uncovered. Season to taste with salt and pepper. Remove the bay leaf. If you would like the soup a little thinner, add water as needed. Stir in lemon zest and serve.

Serving size: 1¾ cups

Calories: 303

Fat: 1.0 g

Cholesterol: 0 mg

Carbohydrate: 58.0 g

Protein: 17.5 g

Sodium: 499.0 mg (with no salt
added, using canned broth and
beans)

> **TIP**
>
> One cup of cooked kale contains 179 mg of calcium, about 25 percent of the RDA. A frost-hardy plant, it's usually available in winter when other leafy greens may be scarce. You can steam the leaves (remove the tough ribs) in a steamer basket in a covered pot over boiling water until they are limp; or boil them in a large quantity of salted water; or chop them raw and sauté them in a little vegetable broth. Season with sliced garlic, soy sauce, or chopped onion, or stir chopped cooked kale into bean dishes or soups.

## Hearty Barley-Lentil Soup
Toasted Whole Wheat Bagels
### Spinach and Mushroom Salad with Buttermilk Dressing
### Baked Bananas with Orange Sauce

A mong the first foods cultivated, barley and lentils have been sustaining civilizations for thousands of years. Today they are among those "peasant foods" gaining new respect because of their nutritional power. Both are high in fiber, minerals, and complex carbohydrates. Together they make a complete protein and an invigorating soup. Add a fresh spinach salad with a creamy dressing that will probably become a fixture in your refrigerator, and finish with warm baked bananas.

The timing: Prepare the soup first. While the soup is simmering, make the salad dressing, prepare the other salad ingredients, and assemble the bananas in their foil packets. Toast the bagels just before you are ready to serve the soup, and put the bananas in the oven partway through dinner.

# HEARTY BARLEY-LENTIL SOUP

*Packed with vegetables, beans, and grains, this sturdy soup is truly a meal in a bowl. You can make it ahead but it will thicken as it rests; thin it as needed with stock or water when you reheat it.*

FROM FRANK AND JUDY SEBRON OF OMAHA, NEBRASKA:
*Frank and Judy Sebron are participants in the Ornish program at Immanuel Medical Center/The Heart Institute in Omaha, Nebraska. Frank has been with the program since it began in October 1993, and has done well. "The best Christmas present we had were the results of Frank's PET scan," says Judy. "Frank had not cooked in thirty-three years. Now he makes food that tastes really good." Meat-and-potatoes eaters, the Sebrons say it was initially hard giving up those foods. "But when you feel so good and actually see the results, it is worth it," adds Judy. Another of Frank's accomplishments: twenty-five-mile bike rides.*

SERVES 4

5 cups Vegetable Broth, or more if needed, homemade (page 18) or
   store-bought
1 cup canned ground tomatoes, or diced tomatoes diced finer by hand
1 cup diced onion
1 cup diced celery
1 cup diced potato
¾ cup dried lentils
½ cup diced carrot
½ cup diced green beans
½ cup pearl barley
1 cup diced zucchini
½ cup dried elbow macaroni
Salt and pepper

In a large soup pot, combine 5 cups vegetable broth, tomatoes, onion, celery, potato, lentils, carrots, green beans, and barley. Bring to a simmer over moderate heat. Cover, adjust heat to maintain a slow simmer, and cook 30 minutes. Add zucchini and macaroni. Cook, uncovered, until macaroni is done, about 15 minutes. Add additional broth if soup is too thick. Season with salt and pepper.

Serving size: 2¾ cups
Calories: 290
Fat: 1.25 g
Cholesterol: 0 mg
Carbohydrate: 62.2 g
Protein: 10.0 g
Sodium: 165.5 mg (with no salt
    added)

<table>
<tr><td>TIP</td></tr>
<tr><td>Use this recipe as a blueprint that you can modify as you like. In place of carrots and green beans, you could substitute rutabagas and chard. Use split peas instead of lentils, brown rice in place of barley, cabbage in place of zucchini. Just make sure the items you substitute cook in about the same time as the item you're replacing.</td></tr>
</table>

## SPINACH AND MUSHROOM SALAD WITH BUTTERMILK DRESSING

*This recipe makes more dressing than you need. Leftover dressing will keep in the refrigerator, tightly covered, for 3 to 4 days. Use on other salads or on steamed artichokes, asparagus, broccoli, or cauliflower.*

SERVES 4

**Buttermilk Dressing:**
½ cup nonfat plain yogurt
¼ cup nonfat mayonnaise
¼ cup nonfat sour cream
2 tablespoons lemon juice
½ teaspoon minced garlic
Salt and pepper

4 cups cleaned spinach leaves, stems removed
¼ pound mushrooms, sliced ¼ inch thick
½ cup halved cherry tomatoes

Make buttermilk dressing: Combine yogurt, mayonnaise, sour cream, lemon juice, and garlic in a bowl and whisk to blend. Season to taste with salt and pepper.

Put spinach leaves, mushrooms, and halved tomatoes in a large salad bowl. Add half the dressing and toss well to coat leaves evenly. Serve immediately.

*Serving size: 1 cup spinach, ½ cup dressing*
*Calories: 37*
*Fat: 0.2 g*
*Cholesterol: 0.2 mg*
*Carbohydrate: 5.7 g*
*Protein: 3.2 g*
*Sodium: 68.0 mg*

> **TIP**
>
> Some markets carry packaged fresh spinach leaves already washed and dried, or cleaned baby spinach leaves sold by the pound. They're more expensive than fresh spinach in bunches, but less work. Or check the salad bar in your supermarket to see if you can buy fresh cleaned spinach leaves by the pound. You will need about ⅓ pound for this recipe.

## BAKED BANANAS WITH ORANGE SAUCE

*An aluminum foil packet traps all the flavor inside when you bake ripe bananas. They turn soft and creamy, and they absorb a lot of the aromatic orange and rum mixture in the packet. Let each diner unfold his or her package to experience the appetizing aroma that's released. The bananas cook so quickly that you can put them in to bake partway through dinner.*

### SERVES 4

1 tablespoon orange juice concentrate
1 teaspoon sugar
½ teaspoon vanilla extract
1 teaspoon rum
4 ripe bananas, peeled
2 cinnamon sticks, halved (optional)

Preheat oven to 450 degrees F.

In a small bowl, whisk together orange juice concentrate, sugar, vanilla, rum, and 2 tablespoons water.

Make aluminum foil packages for the bananas: Assemble four 12 by 15-inch sheets of foil. Fold each sheet in half along the 12-inch side. Working from each short side, fold about ½ inch in toward the center two or three times to seal the edge. Stand the package on its spine and prop it open like a boat. Put a banana and a half cinnamon stick in each package. Spoon one quarter of the orange juice mixture into each package. Fold foil over along the top to seal. Set packets on a baking sheet and bake 15 minutes.

Serving size: 1 banana
Calories: 118
Fat: 0.55 g
Cholesterol: 0 mg
Carbohydrate: 29.5 g
Protein: 1.2 g
Sodium: 93.0 mg

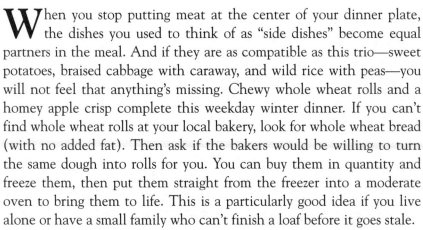

> **TIP**
>
> Ripe bananas can also be broiled for a quick dessert. Halve them lengthwise and place them under a preheated broiler, several inches from the heat, until they are hot throughout and browned.

**Baked Sweet Potatoes with Thyme**
**Braised Cabbage with Onions and Caraway**
Steamed Wild Rice with Petite Peas
Whole Wheat Rolls
**Warm Apple Crisp**

When you stop putting meat at the center of your dinner plate, the dishes you used to think of as "side dishes" become equal partners in the meal. And if they are as compatible as this trio—sweet potatoes, braised cabbage with caraway, and wild rice with peas—you will not feel that anything's missing. Chewy whole wheat rolls and a homey apple crisp complete this weekday winter dinner. If you can't find whole wheat rolls at your local bakery, look for whole wheat bread (with no added fat). Then ask if the bakers would be willing to turn the same dough into rolls for you. You can buy them in quantity and freeze them, then put them straight from the freezer into a moderate oven to bring them to life. This is a particularly good idea if you live alone or have a small family who can't finish a loaf before it goes stale.

The timing: Start the wild rice first (see page 46), adding frozen petite peas, thawed, during the final minute or two, just to heat them through. Put the sweet potatoes in to bake. While they are baking, braise the cabbage. While the cabbage is simmering, assemble the crisp. Put the crisp in the oven when you sit down to dinner.

## BAKED SWEET POTATOES WITH THYME

*Sweet potatoes hold their shape when peeled, cubed, and baked in a covered casserole—a pleasant change from whole roast sweet potatoes. Be sure to* buy the variety with light brown skin and golden flesh. Garnet yams—the ones with dark reddish-brown skin and deep orange flesh—become soft and mushy baked this way.

SERVES 4

4 sweet potatoes (about 8 ounces each)
⅓ cup Vegetable Broth, homemade (page 18) or store-bought
¼ teaspoon salt
¼ teaspoon dried thyme
Black pepper

Preheat oven to 375 degrees F. Peel sweet potatoes and cut into 1-inch cubes. In a 1½-quart baking dish, toss the sweet potatoes with the broth, salt, thyme, and pepper to taste. Cover and bake until the potatoes are tender when pierced, 35 to 40 minutes.

*Serving size: 1 sweet potato*
*Calories: 118*
*Fat: 0.1 g*
*Cholesterol: 0 mg*
*Carbohydrate: 27.7 g*
*Protein: 2.0 g*
*Sodium: 612.0 mg*

> **TIP**
>
> Sweet potatoes have four times the U.S. Recommended Dietary Allowance for beta-carotene, a "pre-vitamin" that the body converts to vitamin A. Researchers are continuing to look closely at the role beta-carotene, an antioxidant, may play in cancer prevention. Sweet potatoes also have significant amounts of vitamin $B_6$, vitamin C, and fiber—and even more fiber when eaten with the skin.

## BRAISED CABBAGE WITH ONIONS AND CARAWAY

*The caraway gives this tender cabbage a subtle German accent. You will probably think of lots of ways to use it: Pile it on a soyburger or soy hot dog; toss it with hot pasta; or make a nonfat Alsatian choucroute by serving it with steamed red potatoes and carrots, soy hot dogs, and a variety of mustards. On another evening, serve it with Roasted Carrots, Parsnips, and Beets (page 116) and Steamed Bulgur with Lemon Zest (page 96).*

SERVES 4

½ medium green cabbage (about ¾ pound)
1 onion, halved and sliced
¼ cup cider vinegar
1 tablespoon brown sugar
1 bay leaf
1 teaspoon caraway seed
Salt and pepper
2 tablespoons minced fresh parsley

Cut the cabbage half into three or four wedges. Remove the core from each wedge. Slice each wedge into fine shreds. Put the cabbage in a large saucepan with onion, cider vinegar, brown sugar, bay leaf, caraway seed, and ¼ cup water. Cover and bring to a simmer over moderate heat. Cook, stirring two or three times, until cabbage is wilted and tender, 15 to 20 minutes. If liquid evaporates before cabbage is tender, add a few tablespoons more water.

Season to taste with salt and pepper. Remove bay leaf. Add parsley and toss to combine. Transfer to a serving bowl.

*Serving size: ¾ cup*
*Calories: 162*
*Fat: 0.8 g*
*Cholesterol: 0 mg*
*Carbohydrate: 37.6 g*
*Protein: 5.2 g*
*Sodium: 57.9 mg (with no salt added)*

> **TIP**
>
> You can make this same recipe with red cabbage, if you like. For a change of pace, add some grated cooked beets about 5 minutes before the red cabbage is done. They add a lovely sweetness and complementary flavor.

## WARM APPLE CRISP

*Crunchy on top, soft and bubbly underneath, a fruit crisp is one of those old-fashioned American desserts that everyone loves. Fortunately, you don't need fat to make a pleasingly textured topping, as this recipe shows.*

MAKES ONE 9-INCH ROUND

6 apples, preferably Rome Beauty or Golden Delicious
2 tablespoons apple juice concentrate
1 tablespoon plus 2 teaspoons sugar

1 tablespoon cornstarch
2 teaspoons lemon juice
½ teaspoon cinnamon

*Crisp Topping:*
⅔ cup rolled oats
⅓ cup Grape-Nuts cereal
1 tablespoon peach jam

Preheat oven to 375 degrees F. Peel, core, and quarter the apples. Cut them into ½-inch pieces. In a large saucepan, combine apples, apple juice concentrate, sugar, cornstarch, lemon juice, cinnamon, and 2 cups water. Bring to a simmer over moderate heat, adjust heat to maintain a simmer and cook 15 minutes. The syrup should thicken slightly and fall below the level of the apples.

Make crisp topping: Combine oats (set aside 1 tablespoon), Grape-Nuts, and jam in a food processor and process until jam is evenly distributed and mixture has a streusel-like feel. Transfer to a bowl and stir in the reserved 1 tablespoon rolled oats.

Transfer the apples to a 9-inch pie pan. Spread the crisp topping evenly over the apples, pressing it lightly into place. Bake until apples are bubbly and topping is lightly browned, about 25 minutes.

*Serving size:* ⅙ *of the crisp*
*Calories: 198*
*Fat: 1.7 g*
*Cholesterol: 0 mg*
*Carbohydrate: 44.5 g*
*Protein: 3.8 g*
*Sodium: 34.8 mg*

---

**TIP**

Other fruits make delicious crisps. In season, try peaches, nectarines, plums, berries, strawberry/rhubarb, apricots, or peaches mixed with berries.

---

**Dr. Crawford's Haystacks**
Fresh Tomato Salsa (page 192)
**Steamed Chayote with Red Onion and Lime**
Baked Tortilla Chips or Fat-Free Flour Tortillas
**Spiced Pumpkin Bars**

From the recipes they submitted for this book, it's apparent that Mexican and Tex-Mex foods are real favorites with Reversal Diet participants. Fortunately, it's easy to adapt these foods to Reversal Diet guidelines thanks to relatively new nonfat products like baked tortilla chips, flour tortillas, vegetarian refried beans, and cheese. This menu puts some of those items to use in a quick and healthful Mexican meal that would otherwise be high in fat. Add store-bought salsa (no fat added) or make your own (page 192). If you can't find chayote, substitute zucchini, which will cook more quickly.

The timing: Make the pumpkin bars first. Then steam the chayote squash. While it's steaming, prepare the haystacks.

## DR. CRAWFORD'S HAYSTACKS

*This guaranteed child-pleaser includes all the foods that make a burrito so delicious—hot rice, refried beans, cheese, lettuce, everything but the tortilla. Stack the ingredients in a mound like a haystack, then dip in with fat-free chips. Or make your own burritos by spooning the filling into fat-free flour tortillas. Dinner doesn't get any easier.*

FROM C. W. CRAWFORD, M.D., OF GREEN BAY, WISCONSIN:
*Dr. Crawford is a retired physician who has attended the Ornish retreat in California. He has been a vegetarian all his life but with a diet that included high-fat items. "I didn't think I could stick to the Reversal Diet, but I have been very pleased," says the doctor. "Your palate adjusts easily. I just bought a gas grill and there isn't anything much better than a trip to the farmers' market and then grilling outside." Between farmers' market trips, Dr. Crawford runs three miles a day, five days a week.*
SERVES 4

1½ cups chopped green bell pepper
¼ cup Vegetable Broth, homemade (page 18) or store-bought
1 (16-ounce) can fat-free vegetarian refried beans
2 cups cooked brown rice (instant is okay)
1 head romaine lettuce, shredded
1 cup grated nonfat Cheddar cheese
2 cups chopped fresh tomatoes

1 cup thinly sliced green onions
Pickled jalapeño rings (optional)

In a skillet, combine bell pepper and broth and simmer over moderately high heat until pepper is soft and liquid evaporates, about 5 minutes.

Heat beans in a small saucepan with 2 tablespoons water, stirring often, or put in a microwave-safe bowl, cover with plastic, and heat in microwave until hot, about 4 minutes. Keep warm.

To assemble Haystacks, spread the hot beans on a large serving platter or on four individual plates. Top with rice, then with green pepper, lettuce, cheese, tomato, and green onions. Serve immediately, passing the jalapeño rings at the table, if desired.

*Serving size: ½ cup rice, ½ cup beans, ¼ head romaine, 1 ounce cheese, ½ cup tomatoes, ½ cup onions*
*Calories: 196*
*Fat: 0.5 g*
*Cholesterol: 4.0 mg*
*Carbohydrate: 30.0 g*
*Protein: 45.0 g*
*Sodium: 894.0 mg*

---

**TIP**

Iceberg lettuce may be the favorite green in American salad bowls, but it is virtually a nutritional washout. Other salad greens—such as romaine, green or red leaf, butter lettuce, arugula (sometimes called rocket or roquette), chicory, and watercress—have much more vitamin C and beta-carotene. Arugula, in particular, is a real nutrition powerhouse, delivering high levels of beta-carotene, vitamin C, and calcium.

In general, the darker the leaf, the more nutrients it packs. (The pale Belgian endive, for example, ranks right down there with iceberg.) Just replacing the iceberg in your sandwiches and salads with any of these darker leafy greens will put you ahead nutritionally.

---

## STEAMED CHAYOTE WITH RED ONION AND LIME

*Appreciated by Latin American cooks and in Louisiana (where it's called mirliton), chayote is a pale green, pear-shaped squash that tastes something like a cross between zucchini and cucumber. It's easy to cook and quite low in calories, so you might want to try it if you never have. This recipe gives you basic directions for steaming. On another occasion, you could toss the steamed chayote with cooked corn kernels and diced red pepper and serve it with brown rice, wild rice, or quinoa.*

SERVES 4

---

1½ pounds chayote squash
½ cup diced red onion
3 tablespoons fresh lime juice
1 tablespoon chopped fresh oregano or ½ teaspoon dried oregano
Salt and pepper

Cut about ¼ inch off the narrow end of each chayote. Peel the chayote with a vegetable peeler. Halve lengthwise. Using a teaspoon or a knife, scoop out or cut out the pit in each half. Cut each half lengthwise into four slices, then cut crosswise into ½-inch pieces.

Put diced squash in a steamer set over boiling water. Cover and steam until chayote is almost tender, about 15 minutes. Scatter onion over the chayote. Cover and steam until chayote is tender when pierced, about 5 more minutes. Transfer to a serving bowl. Add lime juice, oregano, and salt and pepper to taste. Toss gently.

*Serving size: ¾ cup*
*Calories: 42*
*Fat: 0.2 mg*
*Cholesterol: 0 mg*
*Carbohydrate: 9.3 g*
*Protein: 1.9 g*
*Sodium: 6.7 mg (with no salt added)*

> **TIP**
>
> In New Orleans, cooks love to stuff chayote halves with savory mixtures. Here's one idea: Halve and pit chayotes. Steam the halves until just tender. Scoop out some of the flesh, leaving a shell to hold the stuffing. Dice the flesh and add it to seasoned nonfat bread crumbs along with cooked onions and red bell pepper. Stuff the shells and bake in a moderate oven until hot throughout.

## SPICED PUMPKIN BARS

*Fragrant with "pumpkin pie" spices, these cakelike bar cookies would be welcome in a lunch box or picnic basket. Or pass a platter of pumpkin bars as the finale to a holiday meal, paired with hot herb tea.*

FROM VIVIAN GREGORY OF OMAHA, NEBRASKA:
*Vivian and Robert Gregory participate in the Ornish program at Immanuel Medical Center/The Heart Institute in Omaha, Nebraska. Both have lost about twenty pounds and report having more energy and feeling better. Vivian says they have had no trouble giving up meat but did have a little*

*trouble planning meals until she stopped thinking of dinner as meat-plus-sides.*

SERVES 24

1 cup egg whites (from approximately 8 large eggs) or liquid egg
    substitute
1 cup unsweetened applesauce
1½ cups granulated sugar
2 cups canned unsweetened pumpkin (see Tip below)
2 cups unbleached all-purpose flour
1 tablespoon baking powder
1 teaspoon baking soda
½ teaspoon salt
2 teaspoons ground cinnamon
½ teaspoon ground ginger
¼ teaspoon ground nutmeg
¼ teaspoon ground cloves
Confectioners' sugar, sifted

Preheat oven to 375 degrees F. Lightly spray a 12 by 18 by 1-inch pan with nonstick spray (see Tip, page 251).

In a large bowl, whisk together egg whites, applesauce, sugar, and pumpkin.

Sift or stir together the flour, baking powder, baking soda, salt, and spices. Gently fold dry ingredients into pumpkin mixture; do not overwork. Spread mixture evenly in prepared pan. Bake until firm to the touch and lightly browned, 20 to 25 minutes. Cool, then slice into 24 bars. Dust lightly with confectioners' sugar just before serving.

*Serving size: 1 bar*
*Calories: 102*
*Fat: 0.1 g*
*Cholesterol: 0 mg*
*Carbohydrate: 23.0 g*
*Protein: 2.4 g*
*Sodium: 68.0 mg*

---

**TIP**

Be sure to buy unsweetened pumpkin and not prepared pumpkin pie filling. If you have it, you can substitute 1 tablespoon pumpkin pie spice for the cinnamon, ginger, nutmeg, and cloves listed above.

---

"CHRISTMAS DINNER"
**Consommé with Vegetable Brunoise**
**Herbed Mushroom Risotto**
**Braised Brussels Sprouts and Chestnuts**
**Glazed Acorn Squash with Orange and Ginger**
**Brandied Pear Bread Pudding**

Even on a very low-fat vegetarian diet, you can celebrate holidays with special foods, such as Italian porcini (dried mushrooms) and chestnuts. These two add little fat to dishes, but they make a meal into a special occasion. As this menu suggests, the Reversal Diet shouldn't keep you from maintaining the enjoyable rituals that go along with the end-of-year holidays. You can adapt your own recipes or adopt this entire low-fat menu as your new tradition. Serve the consommé in delicate china cups or bowls if you have them, and follow with the trio of vegetable dishes on your prettiest plates.

The timing: Make the consommé several hours ahead but don't add the vegetable brunoise until just before serving. Make the bread pudding several hours ahead and chill, or make a couple of hours ahead and leave at room temperature. Soak the dried mushrooms for the risotto. Assemble the squash and seasonings in their baking dish but do not bake yet. Trim the brussels sprouts. About 40 minutes before dinner, put the squash in to bake. Reheat the consommé with the vegetable brunoise and serve it as a first course. After the soup, start the risotto and brussels sprouts simultaneously. They should be done about the same time.

## CONSOMMÉ WITH VEGETABLE BRUNOISE

*A classic consommé is a foundation dish that every French cooking student must master. The goal is a crystal-clear broth in which to float small pasta shapes or a tiny dice of vegetables (a brunoise). Egg whites do the work of clarifying: they bind with the solid particles and float to the top of the broth, leaving a clear liquid underneath. Strained, the clarified broth makes an elegant start to a holiday meal.*

SERVES 8

*Consommé:*

2 quarts tomato juice

2 quarts V-8 juice

3 cups egg whites (from approximately 2 dozen large eggs)

2 cups diced onion

2 garlic cloves, minced

*Vegetable Garnish:*

1 cup diced carrots

1 cup frozen green peas

1 cup diced leeks, white part only

2 tablespoons minced parsley or chives

Put tomato juice and V-8 juice in a large pot. In a bowl, whisk together egg whites, onion, and garlic just to break up the whites. Add them to the pot, whisking. Bring mixture to a boil over moderate heat, stirring occasionally. Adjust heat to maintain a simmer and cook, uncovered, for 20 minutes. Strain mixture through a sieve lined with a double thickness of cheesecloth, or with paper towels or a coffee filter. The consommé should be crystal-clear.

Return consommé to a clean saucepan. Taste and adjust seasoning. Bring to a boil over moderately high heat. Add carrots, peas, and leeks. Simmer 2 minutes. Serve in bowls, garnishing each portion with a little minced parsley.

*Serving size: 1 cup*

*Calories: 30*

*Fat: 0 g*

*Cholesterol: 0 mg*

*Carbohydrate: 1.3 g*

*Protein: 0.1 g*

*Sodium: 300.0 mg*

> **TIP**
>
> Like vegetable broth, consommé freezes well. Freeze it in small containers and reheat it for a mid morning or mid afternoon pick-me-up. Few things are more soothing than a cup of hot consommé on a cold winter day.

# HERBED MUSHROOM RISOTTO

*Dried porcini mushrooms add a rich, earthy flavor to many Italian dishes, such as this creamy risotto. They are not inexpensive, but they are worth the splurge for a holiday or special occasion. Look for them in Italian markets or specialty food stores. On another occasion, you can make a more frugal version of this dish using 2 cups sliced fresh mushrooms in place of the porcini. Of course you won't need to soak the fresh mushrooms.*

SERVES 8

2 cups dried porcini mushrooms
2 cups hot water
2 ½ quarts Vegetable Broth, homemade (page 18) or store-bought
1 cup diced Roasted Onions (page 22)
2 garlic cloves, minced
3 cups Arborio rice
¼ cup minced parsley
¼ cup minced chives or green onions
Salt and pepper

Break any large porcini into smaller pieces, then put porcini in a small bowl and cover with 2 cups hot water. Let soak 10 minutes, then carefully lift the porcini out of the water with a slotted spoon so that any dirt or sand remains behind. Strain the soaking liquid through a coffee filter or a sieve lined with cheesecloth. Put the strained liquid in a saucepan with the 2½ quarts vegetable broth and bring to a simmer; adjust heat to keep liquid barely simmering.

In a saucepan, combine onions, garlic, porcini, rice, and 6 cups hot broth. Bring mixture to a simmer over moderately high heat, adjust heat to maintain a simmer, and cook, stirring occasionally, until most of the liquid has been absorbed, about 10 minutes. Add more hot broth 1 cup at a time, stirring often and waiting until rice has absorbed most of the liquid before adding more. After 12 to 14 more minutes, the rice should be just tender, and it should have absorbed about 11 cups total liquid. Add a little more liquid if rice seems underdone or mixture seems dry. Risotto should be creamy, but not soupy. Remove from heat and stir in parsley and chives. Season with salt and pepper. Serve immediately.

Serving size: 1⅛ cups
Calories: 336
Fat: 0.9 g
Cholesterol: 0 mg
Carbohydrate: 73.7 g
Protein: 8.0 g
Sodium: 5.7 mg (with no salt added)

> **TIP**
>
> Dried porcini are a wonderful flavor enhancer to have on hand. Just a few of these intense mushrooms, softened in water and chopped, can add depth and richness to a tomato sauce, a bean soup, or a rice pilaf. They will keep indefinitely in a tightly covered glass jar in the pantry.

## BRAISED BRUSSELS SPROUTS AND CHESTNUTS

*It may surprise you to know that chestnuts—unlike other nuts—contain virtually no fat and fit into the Reversal Diet guidelines. So you can enjoy them in this classic holiday dish, where they add a sweet counterpoint to brussels sprouts. Fresh chestnuts, harvested in autumn, aren't widely available and are time-consuming to peel. For convenience, look for peeled and vacuum-packed chestnuts with no added liquid. They are an excellent, albeit expensive, product. If you can't find them or prefer not to buy them, you can braise the brussels sprouts without them; the sprouts are perfectly delicious on their own.*

### SERVES 8

2 pounds fresh brussels sprouts
1 cup Vegetable Broth, homemade (page 18) or store-bought
½ teaspoon dried thyme
1 pound peeled chestnuts, vacuum-packed without liquid
Salt and pepper

Wash the brussels sprouts and remove any blemished outer leaves. Halve each sprout through the stem end.

In a large skillet, combine the halved sprouts with the broth and thyme. Bring to a boil over high heat, then cover and reduce the heat to maintain a simmer. Simmer until the sprouts are tender when pierced, 15 to 17 minutes. Add the chestnuts and stir gently until heated through, 2 to 3 minutes. Season with salt and pepper to taste.

Serving size: ¾ cup
Calories: 135
Fat: 0.8 g
Cholesterol: 0 mg
Carbohydrate: 2.8 g
Protein: 30.0 g
Sodium: 15.3 mg (with no salt added)

## GLAZED ACORN SQUASH WITH ORANGE AND GINGER

*Orange juice, orange marmalade, and fresh ginger make a delicious glaze for baked acorn squash halves. The mixture seeps into the flesh as it bakes, enhancing the squash's delicate sweet flavor.*

### SERVES 8

4 acorn squash, halved and seeded
Salt and pepper
½ cup orange juice
½ cup sugar-free orange marmalade
2 teaspoons grated fresh ginger

Preheat oven to 425 degrees F. Season acorn halves with salt and pepper. Cut a slice off the rounded side of each half so that they can sit in a baking dish without wobbling. Place halves in a large baking dish or two smaller dishes. Whisk together orange juice, marmalade, and ginger. Put one quarter of the mixture in each acorn half and spread it evenly around the cavity and on the squash rims. Cover dish tightly with aluminum foil or a lid and bake 30 minutes. Uncover, baste squash rims with any accumulated juices, and bake, uncovered, until squash is lightly glazed, about 10 minutes.

Serving size: ½ of one squash
Calories: 77
Fat: 0.1 g
Cholesterol: 0 mg

*Carbohydrate: 34.9 g*
*Protein: 1.1 g*
*Sodium: 4.0 mg (with no salt added)*

## BRANDIED PEAR BREAD PUDDING

*Moist and custardlike, this delicate bread pudding makes an elegant finale to a holiday meal. In other seasons, try replacing the pears with fresh plums, apricots, or berries. A 1-pound loaf of bread should yield the 8 cups cubes you need.*

MAKES ONE 10-INCH ROUND • SERVES 12

8 cups 1-inch cubes stale nine-grain bread
¾ cup sugar
¼ cup brandy
4 cups diced peeled pears
½ cup raisins
1 cup egg whites (from approximately 8 large eggs) or liquid egg
   substitute
¼ teaspoon salt
1½ cups nonfat milk
½ cup nonfat sour cream
1 tablespoon vanilla extract
1 teaspoon cinnamon

Preheat oven to 425 degrees F. Prepare a 10-inch round baking pan, either nonstick or lightly sprayed with cooking spray (see Tip, page 251). Put bread cubes in a large bowl. Put sugar and brandy in a 10-inch skillet and bring to a simmer over moderately high heat. Add pears and simmer 3 minutes. Pour contents of skillet over bread and add raisins. Toss to blend.

In a large bowl, lightly beat egg whites and salt, just to break up the whites. Whisk in milk, sour cream, vanilla, and cinnamon. Pour over bread mixture. Mix well. Transfer to prepared pan. Smooth the surface evenly with a spatula. Bake until firm and golden, 30 to 35 minutes. Let cool in pan. Serve at room temperature or chilled.

*Serving size: ¹⁄12 of the cake*
*Calories: 223*
*Fat: 1.2 g*
*Cholesterol: 0.35 mg*
*Carbohydrate: 47.0 g*
*Protein: 7.5 g*
*Sodium: 316.0 mg*

---

**TIP**

Pears oxidize and darken quickly after peeling, so it's best to peel and dice them just before you need them. If you want to do them a little while ahead, however, you can put them in a bowl of water acidulated with the juice of ½ lemon. The acidulated water will keep them from darkening. Drain and pat them dry before continuing.

---

### "NEW YEAR'S DAY BUFFET"
### Hoppin' John
### Nell's Southern Eggplant Dressing
### Collard Greens with Tomatoes, Onions, and Peppers
### John's Gingerbread
Applesauce (page 217)

Invite friends over to watch the bowl games or just to visit, and welcome them with a Southern feast: seasoned black-eyed peas mixed with rice, a rib-sticking eggplant and corn bread dressing, flavor-rich collard greens stewed with tomatoes, onions, and green peppers, and warm wedges of old-fashioned gingerbread with applesauce. Offer several types of bottled hot sauce for guests to use at their discretion on the Hoppin' John and collard greens. If you thought good Southern cooking depended on pork fat for flavor, this tasty food will change your mind.

The timing: Make the corn bread for the eggplant dressing a day or two ahead. If you prefer, you can make the Hoppin' John a day ahead (see Tip, page 275). Make the applesauce and gingerbread several hours ahead. Prepare the collard greens and set aside; they reheat well. If you have not made the Hoppin' John ahead, prepare it now. Mix and bake the eggplant dressing. Just before serving, reheat the collard greens and, if necessary, the Hoppin' John.

# HOPPIN' JOHN

*It's a widely known fact: eating black-eyed peas on New Year's Day brings luck throughout the year. That's why this tasty combination of black-eyed peas and rice turns up on many Southern tables on the first of January.*

SERVES 8

1 (20-ounce) bag frozen black-eyed peas
1 onion, chopped
1 cup chopped celery
2 garlic cloves, minced
3¾ cups Vegetable Broth, homemade (page 18) or store-bought
1 bay leaf
1½ teaspoons salt
½ teaspoon pepper
2¾ cups instant brown rice
1 red bell pepper, seeds and ribs removed, finely diced
Liquid hot pepper sauce or hot pepper vinegar (optional)

In a large saucepan or Dutch oven, combine peas, onion, celery, garlic, broth, bay leaf, salt, and pepper. Bring to a boil over high heat, then reduce the heat, cover, and simmer gently 30 minutes.

Uncover, add rice, and stir to combine. When liquid returns to a boil, cover and simmer 5 minutes. Remove from heat and let rest, covered, for 10 minutes. Remove the bay leaf.

Just before serving, add the bell pepper and stir with a fork to fluff the mixture. Taste and adjust seasoning with salt and pepper. Transfer to a serving bowl. Serve, if desired, with hot pepper sauce or hot pepper vinegar.

*Serving size: 1 cup*
*Calories: 318*
*Fat: 2.2 g*
*Cholesterol: 0 mg*
*Carbohydrate: 66.3 g*
*Protein: 9.0 g*
*Sodium: 748.0 mg*

> **TIP**
>
> You can make Hoppin' John a few hours ahead, as it reheats well. If it seems a little dry, add a few tablespoons vegetable broth or water when reheating.

# NELL'S SOUTHERN EGGPLANT DRESSING

*Nell's peppery version of a traditional Southern corn bread dressing is moister than most bread stuffings and will hold together when spooned into a dish. Be sure to make a double recipe of Perfect Fat-Free Corn Bread (page 183) one or two days ahead.*

FROM NELL STEENBURGEN OF LITTLE ROCK, ARKANSAS:
*Nell is actress Mary Steenburgen's mom. She has attended two Ornish retreats in California and says she has felt great ever since. Nell actually needed to gain a little weight and has done so without eating fat.*

SERVES 8

1 cup diced onion
1 cup diced celery
½ cup diced green bell pepper
1 cup Vegetable Broth (page 18) or water
2 large eggplants, peeled, cut into large chunks
1 (10-ounce) can Ro-Tel chopped tomatoes with chiles (see Tip,
    page 277)
4 egg whites
1 teaspoon dried sage
1 teaspoon pepper
4 cups crumbled Perfect Fat-Free Corn Bread (page 183), 1 to 2 days old

Preheat oven to 425 degrees F. Prepare a 13 by 9-inch baking dish, either nonstick or lightly sprayed with nonstick spray (see Tip, page 251).

In a medium skillet, combine onion, celery, bell pepper, and broth. Bring to a simmer over moderate heat and cook until vegetables are softened, about 10 minutes. Put eggplant in a large saucepan or Dutch oven and add water to barely cover, about 2 cups. Cover and bring to a simmer over high heat. Reduce heat and simmer until eggplant is tender, 10 to 12 minutes. Remove from heat, drain, and mash the eggplant with a fork or potato masher.

In a large bowl, combine the onion mixture, mashed eggplant, tomatoes, egg whites, sage, and pepper. Mix well. Stir in the crumbled corn bread. Transfer mixture to prepared pan.

Bake until the sides are lightly browned and the center springs back when touched, about 30 minutes.

Serving size: 1 cup
Calories: 170
Fat: 0.6 g
Cholesterol: 0.5 mg
Carbohydrate: 35.5 g
Protein: 6.3 g
Sodium: 209.0 mg

> **TIP**
>
> If you shy away from spicy food, substitute regular canned diced tomatoes for the Ro-Tel tomatoes.

## COLLARD GREENS WITH TOMATOES, ONIONS, AND PEPPERS

*You might make a double batch of these greens while you're at it; they reheat well. With the extra, you could make a quick soup by adding cooked rice, diced potatoes, or canned chickpeas and some vegetable broth.*

FROM ELIZABETH KAPSTEIN, CHEF
*Dr. Ornish Program for Reversing Heart Disease at Beth Israel Medical Center, New York, New York*
SERVES 8

2 bunches collard greens or kale (10 to 12 ounces each)
2 small green bell peppers, seeds and ribs removed, in ¼-inch-wide strips
1 cup diced onion
2 garlic cloves, minced
3 cups canned diced tomato
1 teaspoon balsamic vinegar
Salt and pepper

Remove tough ribs and stems from greens and discard. Bring a large pot of salted water to a boil over high heat. Add collard leaves and boil until tender, about 5 minutes. Drain, refresh under cold running water, and drain again well. Chop coarsely.

In a large skillet, combine bell peppers, onion, garlic, and ½ cup water. Bring to a simmer and simmer until water evaporates and onion is softened, about 5 minutes. Add tomato and simmer 10 minutes. Stir in chopped collards and cook 1 minute. Add vinegar and season to taste with salt and pepper.

Serving size: ¾ cup
Calories: 27
Fat: 0.3 g
Cholesterol: 0 mg
Carbohydrate: 5.0 g
Protein: 2.1 g
Sodium: 36.0 mg (with no salt
    added)

> **TIP**
>
> Store greens such as collards in the refrigerator crisper in perforated plastic bags. The bag keeps moisture in, while the perforations allow air to circulate and postpone decay. Always remove any bands around the greens before storing to allow them to breathe better and prevent decay at the band site.

## JOHN'S GINGERBREAD

*San Francisco food writer John Phillip Carroll created this spicy, moist gingerbread.*

MAKES ONE 9-INCH ROUND OR 8-INCH SQUARE

⅔ cup nonfat sour cream
⅓ cup unsweetened applesauce
⅓ cup liquid egg substitute
3 tablespoons brown sugar
2 tablespoons molasses
¾ cup whole wheat flour
¾ cup unbleached all-purpose flour
1 tablespoon plus 1 teaspoon ground ginger
1 teaspoon cinnamon
½ teaspoon ground cloves
1 teaspoon baking soda
1 teaspoon baking powder
½ teaspoon salt

Preheat oven to 350 degrees F. Prepare a 9-inch round or 8-inch square cake pan, either nonstick or lightly sprayed with nonstick spray (see Tip, page 251). In a medium bowl, combine sour cream, applesauce, egg substitute, brown sugar, and molasses. Stir until smooth and well blended.

In another medium bowl, stir together whole wheat flour, all-purpose flour, ginger, cinnamon, cloves, baking soda, baking powder, and salt. Sift them onto a sheet of wax paper. Add dry ingredients to the sour cream mixture and stir just until blended; do not overmix. A few lumps are okay.

Spread the batter evenly in prepared pan. Bake until the gingerbread has risen to the top of the pan and a toothpick inserted in the center comes out clean, about 25 minutes. Cool 30 minutes before cutting into wedges or squares.

*Serving size: ⅛ of the gingerbread*
*Calories: 122*
*Fat: 0.3 g*
*Cholesterol: 0 mg*
*Carbohydrate: 26.4 g*
*Protein: 4.2 g*
*Sodium: 182.0 mg*

> **TIP**
>
> This gingerbread keeps well at room temperature for a couple of days. For a weekend brunch treat, enjoy a slice or square of it with fresh raspberries or sliced mango.

# BREAKFAST

Hashed Browns

Waffles

Wholesome Pancakes

Artichoke Frittata

French Toast

Pumpkin Bread

Irish Soda Bread

Strawberry-Banana Smoothie

Maple Granola

Raisin-Bran Muffins

Most people would love to wake up and have a leisurely breakfast every day of the week. Unfortunately for our bodies, most of us don't. We tend to rush on weekday mornings and reserve relaxed breakfasts for weekends. A good breakfast improves mental and physical performance and should not be skipped.

Breakfast on the Reversal Diet is easy and will probably be the meal with the fewest changes for you. Unless, of course, you were eating the traditional heart-stopping breakfast of high-fat, high-cholesterol animal foods. Focus on getting a jump start in the morning from whole grain cereals, breads, nonfat dairy products or soy milk, and fresh fruit. Or, if you prefer, from scrambled egg whites with tofu, whole grain pancakes (page 287), wholesome quick breads (pages 290–293), hearty bran muffins (page 294), flour tortillas filled with scrambled egg whites and salsa, Waffles (page 286) topped with fresh fruit, or a quickly made fruit smoothie (page 293) with a toasted whole wheat bagel. Or spoon some berries over nonfat cottage cheese and add a bowl of homemade granola (page 294). Some Ornish program participants enjoy dinner leftovers for breakfast: cold pasta; reheated leftover brown rice with nonfat milk, and fresh fruit; even reheated soup.

Whatever you choose, try to have foods from at least three groups on the Reversal Diet Pyramid (page 298). Better to have fresh fruit than fruit juice, since juices are a concentrated source of calories without the fiber benefits of fresh fruit.

Creating a good breakfast is the easy part. Making time for it may be harder. Here are some suggestions to help you swing it:

- Set the table the night before with placemats, napkins, silverware, plates, and any nonperishable foods.
- Make cooked cereals the night before. Chill in the refrigerator. Microwave the next morning.

- Make ahead and freeze muffins or waffles for quick reheating or toasting.
- Create your own breakfast blender smoothies from soy milk, nonfat milk, nonfat yogurt, or tofu with fresh fruits.
- Mix a variety of whole grain cereals to create your own designer blend. Take to work, if you must, along with nonfat bran muffins, fresh fruit, and an aseptic container of soy milk.


## ABOUT GRAIN COFFEES AND CAFFEINE-FREE TEAS

It's easier to kick the caffeine habit if you can replace your treasured coffee or tea with another soothing, warm beverage. Grain coffees and herbal teas fill the niche for many Ornish program participants.

Grain coffees are made from roasted barley or other grains and look similar to instant coffee granules. Some have flavorings added, such as chicory or dried fig. These warming beverages provide the satisfaction of a hot cup of coffee without the caffeine. (Even decaffeinated coffees and teas have some caffeine.)

Among the most popular brands are Cafix, Bambu, Coffree, Pero, Kaffree Roma, and Postum. Some, such as Bambu and Kaffree Roma, are offered in individual packages that are useful when you travel or dine out. Most come in resealable jars, although you may also find them in bulk in some stores. Mainstream markets carry these products, but a natural food store in your area will probably have the best selection.

When buying herb and spice teas, read labels carefully to make sure what you are buying contains no caffeine, tea, or other stimulants. Look for non-tea ingredients such as chamomile flowers, peppermint leaves, rose hips, spices, hibiscus flowers, and orange peel. Celestial Seasonings and Stash make a great array of these soothing, caffeine-free teas, although both also produce some herb teas with caffeine. Scrutinize the label, or make your own. Fresh peppermint tea is an aromatic treat and simple to make. Fill a teapot with a bunch of fresh peppermint from the garden or grocer. Add boiling water and steep until tea reaches the strength you like.

# HASHED BROWNS

*This breakfast favorite is usually loaded with fat. Here's how to make "fried" potatoes virtually fat-free.*

### SERVES 4

**2 russet-type baking potatoes**
**Salt and pepper**

Bring a large pot of salted water to a boil over high heat. Peel potatoes, then blanch them whole in the boiling water for 2 minutes. Set aside to air-dry for 10 minutes, then grate by hand or in a food processor using the coarse grating attachment. Season grated potatoes to taste with salt and pepper.

Spray a 10-inch nonstick skillet lightly with cooking spray (see Tip, page 251). Set over moderate heat. When skillet is hot, add potatoes, spreading them out so they cover the bottom evenly. Press down on the potatoes with a rubber spatula to form a cake. Cook until potatoes are browned on the bottom, about 6 minutes, then turn with a spatula. Press down again and cook until potatoes are done throughout, about 6 more minutes. Transfer to a cutting board and cut into four wedges.

*Serving size: 1 wedge*
*Calories: 44*
*Fat: 0.1 g*
*Cholesterol: 0 mg*
*Carbohydrate: 60.0 g*
*Protein: 1.2 g*
*Sodium: 7.0 mg (with no salt added)*

> **TIP**
>
> These crisp potato wedges aren't just breakfast fare. Serve them for dinner with steamed or stir-fried seasonal vegetables or with spicy black beans and a green salad.

# WAFFLES

*Enjoy these light and airy waffles on Sunday morning with fresh seasonal fruit.*

FROM RICHARD AXELROD OF WILMETTE, ILLINOIS:
*When Richard "maxed out" his last treadmill stress test, his physician said, "I'm not sure what you are doing, but it's working." Richard travels a lot but cooks on the weekend, making soups, casseroles, and his excellent waffles. His reply upon hearing his recipe made it into this book: "My mom will be proud."*

SERVES 4

1 cup unbleached all-purpose flour
1¼ teaspoons baking powder
Pinch salt
1 cup nonfat milk
3 egg whites
2 tablespoons plus 2 teaspoons unsweetened applesauce
½ teaspoon vanilla extract

Preheat a waffle iron, either nonstick or lightly sprayed with nonstick spray (see Tip, page 251).

In a medium bowl, stir together flour, baking powder, and salt. In another bowl, combine milk, 2 egg whites, applesauce, and vanilla. Whisk to blend.

In a small bowl, beat remaining egg white to firm peaks.

Add milk mixture to dry ingredients and stir to blend. Gently fold in beaten egg white.

Bake waffles immediately according to the directions for your waffle iron. Serve piping hot.

> **TIP**
>
> If you have a large lunch, consider having "breakfast" for dinner: some fruit and a waffle, for example, or a bowl of cereal and fruit with nonfat milk, or a fruit smoothie and some whole wheat toast.

*Serving size: 1 waffle*
*Calories: 102*
*Fat: 0.2 g*
*Cholesterol: 0.7 mg*
*Carbohydrate: 18.6 g*
*Protein: 5.3 g*
*Sodium: 48.0 mg*

> **TIP**
>
> Freeze any leftover waffles as soon as they are cool. Reheat in a toaster. They aren't quite as good as when freshly made, but they're a nice alternative to toast on a busy weekday morning.

# WHOLESOME PANCAKES

*Whole wheat flour gives these pancakes a wholesome, nutty taste, but it doesn't weigh them down; they are as light as can be. Serve them on weekend mornings with a shower of fresh fruit or a light brushing of maple syrup.*

FROM GUY COUTANCHE OF THUNDER BAY, ONTARIO, CANADA: *Guy and Joan Coutanche have attended the Ornish retreat in California. Within a short time, Guy's stress test showed enough improvement to motivate him to stay with the program. The couple says their biggest challenge in sticking with the guidelines has been on the road. Their advice: rent a place with a kitchenette and stock the pantry.*

MAKES 18 PANCAKES TO SERVE 6

½ cup quick-cooking (not instant) rolled oats
2½ cups nonfat milk
1 cup unbleached all-purpose flour
¾ cup whole wheat flour
2 tablespoons sugar
1 tablespoon baking powder
½ teaspoon salt
½ teaspoon cinnamon
3 egg whites
1 teaspoon vanilla extract

Preheat an electric griddle or a nonstick frying pan or griddle over moderate heat.

In a medium bowl, combine oats and milk. Stir to blend and set aside.

In a large bowl, combine unbleached flour, whole wheat flour, sugar, baking powder, salt, and cinnamon. Stir to blend well.

Add egg whites and vanilla to oat mixture; stir to combine. Add wet ingredients to flour mixture and stir just until all ingredients are moistened. Do not overmix.

Make pancakes, using ¼ cup batter for each pancake. Turn when bubbles begin to pop on the surface and underside is browned; continue cooking until second side is brown. Serve hot.

*Serving size: 3 pancakes*
*Calories: 237*
*Fat: 1.5 g*
*Cholesterol: 1.8 mg*
*Carbohydrate: 44.5 g*
*Protein: 11.6 g*
*Sodium: 276.0 mg*

> **TIP**
>
> Oatmeal is a good source of the soluble fiber that can help lower cholesterol levels. And cholesterol levels are strongly correlated with heart disease risk. That's why it's smart to start your day with a bowl of oatmeal and some high-fiber fruit, or to slip oatmeal into recipes where it's not usually found, such as in these tasty pancakes.

## Artichoke Frittata

*Treat yourself to a leisurely weekend breakfast or brunch featuring a warm Italian frittata. Add steamed potatoes, whole grain toast, and fresh fruit to make the kind of morning meal that keeps you going for hours. In place of artichokes, try roasted peppers, sliced mushrooms, or diced boiled potatoes. A frittata also makes a lovely light supper.*

### SERVES 4

2 cups liquid egg substitute
¼ cup minced parsley
¼ cup chopped fresh basil
1 tablespoon unbleached all-purpose flour
½ teaspoon salt
¼ teaspoon pepper
One (10-ounce) package frozen artichoke hearts, thawed and quartered
¾ cup Roasted Onions (page 22)
¼ cup sun-dried tomatoes (not oil-packed), quartered

Preheat oven to 400 degrees F. Spray an 8-inch pie pan lightly with nonstick spray (see Tip, page 251). Whisk together egg substitute, parsley, basil, flour, salt, and pepper. Sprinkle artichokes, onions, and sun-dried tomatoes evenly over the bottom of the prepared pie pan. Pour in egg mixture. Bake until center feels firm, 25 to 30 minutes.

*Serving size: ¼ of one fritatta*
*Calories: 128*

*Fat: 0.27 g*
*Cholesterol: 0 mg*
*Carbohydrate: 15.5 g*
*Protein: 16.9 g*
*Sodium: 511.0 mg*

## SUNDAY MORNING SPECIAL

It's a lot easier to get out of bed on Sunday morning when you can look forward to a generous and relaxed breakfast. Here's a recipe for Sunday mornings at the home of Ornish program participants Joanne Shipe and Robert Riegel in Birdsboro, Pennsylvania:

**Eggs:** In a nonstick frying pan, sauté fresh mushrooms, green pepper, onion, and jalapeño chile. Add Egg Beaters or whisked egg whites and cook until firm. Garnish with freshly snipped chives or parsley.

**Potatoes:** Preheat broiler. Thinly slice unpeeled red potatoes. Lightly spray a baking sheet with cooking oil. Place potatoes on baking sheet in a single layer. Sprinkle with store-bought seasoning mix or cayenne pepper. Broil until potatoes are browned and crisp.

**Oranges:** Mix ½ cup orange juice and 1 teaspoon fresh or dried mint. Cut away peel and white pith of one orange. Cut orange into skinless sections. Add to juice.

**Toast:** Use fresh whole grain bread from a local bakery. Toast and serve with favorite fruit spreads.

# FRENCH TOAST

*Serve hot from the skillet with fresh seasonal fruit—such as sliced peaches or berries—or unsweetened applesauce.*

## SERVES 4

1 cup nonfat milk
½ cup liquid egg substitute
1 tablespoon maple syrup
1 tablespoon sugar
1 teaspoon vanilla
½ teaspoon cinnamon
8 day-old slices whole grain bread

Whisk together milk, egg substitute, maple syrup, sugar, vanilla, and cinnamon. Over moderate heat, preheat a nonstick skillet sprayed lightly with vegetable cooking spray (see Tip, page 251). Dip bread in batter one slice at a time and let soak for about 10 seconds. Cook on each side until golden, about 2 minutes per side.

*Serving size: 2 slices*
*Calories: 188*
*Fat: 1.6 g*
*Cholesterol: 2.5 mg*
*Carbohydrate: 35.0 g*
*Protein: 10.0 g*
*Sodium: 31.0 mg*

> **TIP**
>
> Read the label carefully when buying egg substitutes. Some brands contain oil. Look for a brand that's made with egg whites, with no added fat.

# PUMPKIN BREAD

*Start your day with a slice or two of this spiced pumpkin bread, some fresh fruit, and a pot of soothing herb tea.*

FROM EVELYNE JOHNSON, NEW YORK, NEW YORK:
*Evelyne and Bud Johnson have attended the Ornish retreat in California. Evelyne is a master at cooking without salt and has written several cook-*

*books. They entertain frequently and say they have no trouble creating deli-*
*cious company meals. The pumpkin bread is a favorite.*

MAKES ONE 9-INCH LOAF • SERVES 12

1 cup unbleached all-purpose flour
1 cup whole wheat flour
2 teaspoons baking powder
1 teaspoon baking soda
1 teaspoon cinnamon
Pinch ground nutmeg
¾ cup canned unsweetened pumpkin
4 egg whites or ½ cup liquid egg substitute
¼ cup nonfat milk
¼ cup mashed ripe banana
¼ cup honey
½ cup raisins

Preheat oven to 350 degrees F. Prepare a 9-inch loaf pan, either non-stick or lightly sprayed with nonstick spray (see Tip, page 251).

In a large bowl, stir together unbleached flour, whole wheat flour, baking powder, baking soda, cinnamon, and nutmeg.

In another bowl, stir together pumpkin, egg whites, milk, banana, and honey. Add wet ingredients to dry and stir just until combined. Do not overmix. Stir in raisins.

Transfer batter to prepared pan and bake until a toothpick inserted in the center comes out clean, 45 to 50 minutes. Remove from pan and cool before slicing.

*Serving size: ¹⁄12 of loaf*
*Calories: 127*
*Fat: 0.4 g*
*Cholesterol: 0.9 mg*
*Carbohydrate: 28.0 g*
*Protein: 4.0 g*
*Sodium: 76.0 mg*

**TIP**

A wire whisk works well for combining dry ingredients.

**TIP**

For a prettier rounded surface, use the back of a spoon to make a shallow trough down the center of the batter before baking. This helps keep the rising cake from peaking and cracking.

# IRISH SODA BREAD

*Enjoy a warm slice or two of this currant bread for breakfast with a pot of herb tea. It takes only 45 minutes to make from start to finish, so you can stir it up on a leisurely weekend morning. Like many quick breads, it is best when fresh. You may want to freeze the second loaf as soon as it's cool if you don't plan to serve it that day or the next. Even day-old soda bread should be warmed or toasted.*

FROM PAULA MORIARTY, CHEF/OWNER,
NAPOLI RESTAURANT & BAKERY, EUGENE, OREGON:
*Paula trained at the Culinary Institute of America in Hyde Park, New York, and now specializes in low-fat cooking. She encourages people who want to minimize dietary fat to explore different ethnic cuisines, many of which lend themselves to healthy cooking. She also advises new vegetarians to stop trying to create meals that resemble the ones they used to eat, with meat and two side dishes. "Get away from that notion," says Paula. "Don't try to imitate meat."*
MAKES TWO 8-INCH ROUND LOAVES • SERVES 8

1 cup currants
2 cups unbleached all-purpose flour
2 cups whole wheat flour
1 tablespoon baking powder
2 teaspoons baking soda
¾ teaspoon caraway seed
¼ teaspoon salt
1 cup nonfat yogurt
1 cup nonfat milk

Preheat oven to 375 degrees F.

In a small bowl, soak currants for 5 minutes in enough hot water to cover. Drain.

In a large bowl, stir together all-purpose flour, whole wheat flour, baking powder, baking soda, caraway seed, and salt. Add currants and stir to combine.

In another bowl, whisk yogurt and milk until smooth. Add wet ingredients to dry ingredients and stir just until blended. Divide dough in half. With floured hands, transfer each half to a nonstick baking sheet and shape into a slightly flattened round about 8 inches across.

*Everyday Cooking with Dr. Dean Ornish*

Cut an "X" in the top of each loaf. Bake until the loaves sound hollow when tapped on the bottom, 30 to 35 minutes. Serve warm.

*Serving size: ¼ of one loaf*
*Calories: 293*
*Fat: 1.0 g*
*Cholesterol: 1.0 mg*
*Carbohydrate: 62.0 g*
*Protein: 10.0 g*
*Sodium: 114.0 mg*

> **TIP**
>
> Serve warm soda bread for dinner with Creamy Split Pea Soup (page 86) or Beet and Cabbage Borscht with Sour Cream (page 251) or enjoy it for lunch with a salad. It also makes an appealing mid-morning or mid-afternoon snack: spread it lightly with nonfat cream cheese and top with a sliced peach, banana, or pear.

## STRAWBERRY-BANANA SMOOTHIE

*So many smoothie recipes call for a lot of sugar or highly sweetened frozen yogurt, additions that aren't needed if you start with ripe fruit. Use this smoothie as a model for others made with other fruit, such as peaches, berries, or mangoes. Using a frozen banana (freeze it in chunks) makes a thicker smoothie.*

SERVES 2

1 medium banana, in chunks
1 cup sliced strawberries
1 cup nonfat milk
1 tablespoon wheat germ
1 teaspoon vanilla

Combine all ingredients in blender or food processor and blend until smooth. Divide between two glasses.

*Serving size: 1¼ cups*
*Calories: 144*
*Fat: 1.4 g*
*Cholesterol: 2.2 mg*
*Carbohydrate: 7.3 g*
*Protein: 28.0 g*
*Sodium: 64.0 mg*

> **TIP**
>
> If you have access in autumn to Hachiya persimmons (the heart-shaped ones, not the squat Fuyu variety), you can freeze them whole and enjoy them in smoothies all year. To make a persimmon smoothie, thaw the fruit just enough to be able to quarter it. Remove the stem. Puree persimmon quarters in a food processor or blender with a little vanilla extract and enough nonfat milk to achieve desired consistency.

# Maple Granola

*There's no easier breakfast than a bowl of this crunchy granola topped with a cup of nonfat milk and some sliced fruit. Make a double or triple batch and keep in an airtight container, where it will stay fresh and crisp for at least a week.*

## MAKES 4 CUPS

¼ cup maple syrup
1 teaspoon vanilla extract
2 cups rolled oats
2 cups puffed corn
2 cups puffed brown rice
½ cup wheat germ

Preheat oven to 400 degrees F. In a large bowl, stir together maple syrup and vanilla. Add remaining ingredients and toss to coat. Spread mixture evenly on a baking sheet. Bake 10 minutes.

*Serving size: 1 cup*
*Calories: 392*
*Fat: 5.9 g (naturally occurring fat)*
*Cholesterol: 0 mg*
*Carbohydrate: 70.4 g*
*Protein: 16.2 g*
*Sodium: 3.9 mg*

> **TIP**
>
> You may wonder how 6½ cups of grains becomes only 4 cups of granola. That's because the fine wheat germ and rolled oats slip down into the spaces between the two puffed grains. Wheat germ is a great source of protein and essential fatty acids. Since it is high in fat, enjoy it in small quantities.

# Raisin-Bran Muffins

*The thought of these honey-brown muffins on the breakfast table would make it a lot easier to get up in the morning. If you're usually rushed on weekday mornings, mix the dry ingredients and wet ingredients the night before. (Refrigerate the wet ingredients.) Preheat the oven while you take your morning shower, then mix and bake the muffins. They'll be ready to eat in 20 minutes.*

## MAKES 12 MUFFINS

1 cup wheat bran
1 cup unbleached all-purpose flour
1½ teaspoons baking soda
1 teaspoon baking powder
½ teaspoon salt
⅓ cup liquid egg substitute or 3 egg whites
¾ cup nonfat plain yogurt
⅓ cup unsweetened applesauce
¼ cup brown sugar
2 tablespoons molasses
½ cup raisins

Preheat oven to 400 degrees F. Spray a standard muffin pan lightly with nonstick spray (see Tip, page 251).

In a medium bowl, combine bran, flour, baking soda, baking powder, and salt. Stir to blend well.

In another bowl, combine egg substitute, yogurt, applesauce, brown sugar, molasses, and raisins. Whisk until smooth and well blended. Add to dry ingredients and stir with a fork just until batter is blended; do not overmix.

Spoon about ¼ cup batter into each muffin cup, filling the cup almost full. Bake until the muffins spring back when touched lightly and a toothpick inserted in a muffin comes out clean, about 15 minutes. Cool in the pan 5 minutes, then remove and serve warm.

*Serving size: 1 muffin*
*Calories: 101*
*Fat: 0.3 g*
*Cholesterol: 0.2 mg*
*Carbohydrate: 22.8 g*
*Protein: 3.6 g*
*Sodium: 158.0 mg*

---

**TIP**

A standard muffin pan has 12 cups, each with a ⅓-cup capacity and a 2½-inch diameter. You can, of course, use miniature muffin pans for this recipe, although the muffins will bake faster.

---

# Your Everyday Choices

by Helen Roe, M.S., R.D.
Director, Nutrition Services
Preventive Medicine Research Institute

LIFE CHOICES

*What choice before me I conspire*
*to bind old habits to my heart*
*and fear the shedding of desires*
*that long control my tempted state.*

*I see the brightness near the crest*
*the bright lit star that leads my soul*
*with eyes upward I choose the best*
*and let new habits guard my gate.*

—Patrick L. Burns, Upland, California

This excerpt from Patrick's poem speaks of the new habits he had to embrace when he began the Life Choice program. Like others in the program, Patrick found that it was much simpler to make the changes than he first thought. He felt so much better so quickly that the changes were easy for him to maintain.

Although the guidelines for the Reversal Diet are basically simple— consume a variety of whole grains, fresh fruits, and vegetables, some nonfat dairy, and avoid high-fat foods, such as animal products, nuts, seeds, avocados, and oils—what helped Patrick was having more information, more choices.

For those of you who, like Patrick, want more information, here are more choices. Choices you can make when you are deciding how to plan your meals, how to evaluate your daily eating plan, how to dine out, how to read labels, how to select snack foods, and more. More life choices.

## THE REVERSAL DIET

The Reversal Diet, also called the Life Choice diet, is an optimal diet for most people. It is a low-fat vegetarian diet developed by Dean Ornish, M.D., and has been reviewed by several nationally recognized nutrition experts. The Reversal Diet in combination with stress management, exercise, and psychosocial support has been shown to be effective in improving blood flow to the heart.

Vegetarian diets are viewed as desirable and nutritionally adequate by the American Dietetic Association and other health associations. Nevertheless, it is prudent to obtain medical approval before beginning the Reversal Diet—as you should for any significant change to your diet—and to see your physician at regular intervals to assure that the diet is safe for you. Each person initiating the Reversal Diet has a different medical history and different nutritional needs. If at any time you are not feeling well or experience rapid weight loss (more than one to two pounds per week after the initial two weeks on the diet) or are seriously underweight, contact your physician. Your physician may order tests to assess your nutritional status and may make dietary recommendations.

## THE REVERSAL DIET PYRAMID:
## A GUIDE TO DAILY FOOD CHOICES

If you eat enough calories from a variety of foods, a very low-fat, vegetarian diet can provide you optimal nutrition. The major exceptions include children, burn patients, postsurgical patients, and pregnant women. To be certain you receive the nutrition you need, choose your foods according to the Reversal Diet Pyramid.

This Reversal Diet Pyramid is visually like the food pyramid that the

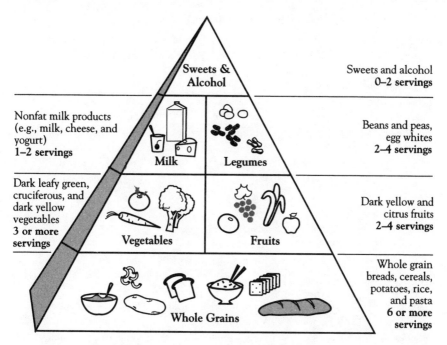

The pyramid contains the following sections:

Sweets & Alcohol — Sweets and alcohol 0–2 servings

Nonfat milk products (e.g., milk, cheese, and yogurt) 1–2 servings — Milk

Legumes — Beans and peas, egg whites 2–4 servings

Dark leafy green, cruciferous, and dark yellow vegetables 3 or more servings — Vegetables

Fruits — Dark yellow and citrus fruits 2–4 servings

Whole Grains — Whole grain breads, cereals, potatoes, rice, and pasta 6 or more servings

*(Source: Modified and derived from: U.S. Department of Agriculture: Eating Right Food Pyramid, 1992, U.S. Government Printing Office.)*

U.S. Government developed to recommend dietary patterns to all Americans. However, there are great differences between these two pyramids. The greatest difference is that the one developed by government agencies recommends a diet that does not reverse or arrest heart disease. In fact, that diet has been documented in many studies as contributing to heart disease getting worse. Eating according to the Reversal Diet Pyramid provides both adequate nutrition and meets the nutritional guidelines to support heart disease regression. Each food group is rich in slightly different nutrients.

The Reversal Diet Pyramid omits foods high in fat, saturated fat, cholesterol, and caffeine and encourages whole grains, dark leafy green and cruciferous vegetables, fresh fruits, beans, and peas, and nonfat dairy products. Nonfat sweets, wine, beer, and liquor provide minimal nutrition and are limited in amounts.

# THE REVERSAL DIET

| FOOD GROUP | SERVINGS | MAJOR NUTRIENTS | SERVING SIZES |
|---|---|---|---|
| **Whole Grains:** | | | |
| cereals, pasta, | 6+ | Complex Carbohydrates | 1 slice bread |
| potatoes, corn, | | Fiber | ½ cup rice, pasta, cooked |
| rice, breads | | Protein | cereal, corn, potatoes |
| | | Thiamin | ½ bagel |
| | | Riboflavin | 1 ounce dry cereal |
| | | Iron | 1 small baked potato |
| | | Niacin | |
| | | Folate | |
| | | Magnesium | |
| | | Zinc | |
| | | Essential Fatty Acids* | |
| **Vegetables:** | | | |
| dark leafy green, | 3+ | Vitamin A | ½ cup raw or cooked |
| yellow, and | | Vitamin C | vegetables |
| cruciferous | | Fiber | 1 cup leafy vegetables |
| | | Folate | |
| | | Magnesium | |
| | | Calcium | |
| | | Essential Fatty Acids* | |
| **Fruits** | 2 to 4 | Vitamin C | ½ cup cooked fruit |
| | | Fiber | ½ cup juice |
| | | Potassium | 1 whole piece fruit |
| | | | ¼ cup dried fruit |
| | | | 1 melon wedge |
| **Nonfat Dairy:** | | | |
| nonfat milk, | 1 to 2 | Protein | 1 cup milk |
| yogurt, cottage | | Calcium | 1 ounce cheese |
| cheese, cheese | | Riboflavin | 1 cup yogurt |
| | | Potassium | ½ cup cottage cheese |
| | | Zinc | |
| | | Vitamin A | |
| | | Vitamin $B_{12}$ | |
| | | Vitamin D | |
| **Beans and Peas;** | | | |
| **Egg Whites:** | | | |
| soy milk, tofu, meat | 2 to 4 | Protein | ½ cup cooked beans or peas |
| substitutes (tempeh, | | Niacin | 1 cup soy milk |
| soy burgers, soy hot | | Iron | 1½ ounces tofu |

| FOOD GROUP | SERVINGS | MAJOR NUTRIENTS | SERVING SIZES |
|---|---|---|---|
| dogs, deli slices) | | Vitamin B$_6$<br>Zinc<br>Essential Fatty Acids* | 2½ ounces meat substitute |
| *Nonfat Sweets* | 0 to 2 | none | 1 serving as listed on<br>    package<br>2 teaspoons jam, jelly,<br>    sugar, syrup |
| *Alcohol* | 0 to 1 | none | 4 ounces wine,<br>1½ ounces hard liquor,<br>12 ounces beer |

*Whole grains, dark leafy green vegetables, and some beans, including soybean products (not nonfat), supply essential fatty acids.*

---

## CHOICES GALORE

These are just a few of the many foods you can enjoy on the Reversal Diet.

> *I teach my participants the Reversal Diet is about abundance, not about deprivation. They begin to look at food in a different way, focusing on the vast array of foods available to them, instead of focusing on the few foods they will be giving up.*
> —Diane Sorensen, R.D., L.D.,
> Dr. Ornish Program for Reversing
> Heart Disease, Mercy Hospital
> Medical Center/Iowa Heart Center,
> Des Moines, Iowa

### NONFAT MILK PRODUCTS

**1 to 2 servings per day**
nonfat buttermilk
nonfat cheese

nonfat cottage cheese
nonfat cream cheese
nonfat milk

nonfat sour cream
nonfat yogurt

### LEGUMES

**2 to 4 servings per day**
adzuki beans
black beans
black-eyed peas
brown beans
chickpeas
Great Northern beans

kidney beans
lentils
mung beans
navy beans
peas
pinto beans

red Mexican beans
split peas
soybeans
soy milk
textured soy products
tofu

## VEGETABLES

### 3 or more servings per day

| | | |
|---|---|---|
| artichokes | eggplant | red leaf lettuce |
| asparagus | escarole | romaine lettuce |
| bamboo shoots | garlic | rutabagas |
| beets | Jerusalem artichoke | scallions |
| broccoli | kale | shallots |
| brussels sprouts | leeks | sorrel |
| cabbage | mushrooms | spinach |
| carrots | mustard greens | sprouts |
| cauliflower | okra | squash |
| celery | onions | turnips and turnip greens |
| chard | parsley | watercress |
| chili peppers | potatoes | zucchini |
| collards | pumpkin | |
| cucumbers | radishes | |

## FRESH FRUITS

### 2 to 4 servings per day

| | | |
|---|---|---|
| apples | figs | pineapple |
| apricots | grapefruit | plums |
| bananas | grapes | pomegranates |
| blackberries | guava | prunes |
| blueberries | honeydew melon | raisins |
| cantaloupe | kiwi | raspberries |
| casaba melon | kumquats | strawberries |
| cherries | lemons | tangelos |
| cranberries | papayas | tangerines |
| currants | peaches | tomatoes |
| dates | pears | watermelon |

## WHOLE GRAINS

### 6 or more servings per day

| | | |
|---|---|---|
| amaranth | millet | triticale |
| barley | oats | wheat |
| brown rice | quinoa | whole grain bread |
| buckwheat | potatoes | whole grain cereal |
| bulgur | rye | whole wheat pasta |
| corn | sweet potatoes | yams |

## EVALUATING YOUR DIET

At our week-long retreats in California and at our hospital-based programs, the nutritionists introduce participants to the Reversal Diet guidelines and explain how to plan meals to include all the food groups. Many people find it helpful to keep a diary of what they eat, categorized according to food group. Then they can quickly see what changes, if any, they want to make. You may want to try keeping a food diary while you are learning this new way of eating. After a while, thinking in terms of the food groups will be second nature.

> *Keeping a food diary has been helpful for participants. It really shows them how they are eating, and what changes they need to make. I suggest they keep it on their refrigerator as a reminder of how to plan their meals.*
> —Katie Sparks, R.D., Dr. Ornish Program for Reversing Heart Disease, North Broward Hospital District/Broward General Hospital, Fort Lauderdale, Florida.

Write down everything you eat or drink, including water, for one day. Be specific about the kind of food and how much you consume. Afterward, calculate how many servings you had in each food group. Compare the number of servings you had with the recommendations. Decide what changes, if any, you will make in your diet. (See sample meal plan on page 308.)

## GUIDELINES FOR DINING OUT

At first glance, you might think it's almost impossible to adhere to the Reversal Diet when you travel or dine out. But that's not the case. Many Ornish program participants are successful businesspeople who eat in restaurants and on airplanes constantly and have found approaches that work. To help you feel more comfortable dining out, here are a few guidelines:

1. *Frequent the same restaurants.* Develop a few restaurants where the staff knows you and is willing either to prepare something special for you or to modify a menu item to meet your needs.

2. *Call ahead.* Speak to the manager or person in charge and explain your eating plan to them. You might say, "I am following a very low-fat diet. Could you suggest something your chef might prepare that would not have red meat, fish, chicken, or any added fats or oils, including cheese and nuts?" It is best not to call during a busy time. Try early morning or mid-afternoon so you miss the lunch rush. You will probably get better service and more of the chef's attention if you make your reservation at off-peak dining times. To make it as easy as possible for the kitchen to accommodate you, ask the reservationist to recommend a time for you to dine.

3. *Make friends with your waiter.* If you can't call ahead, enlist the assistance of your server. Explain your dietary requirements and ask for a recommendation or ask your server to check with the chef. You still have to make the final decision on what you order. Don't hesitate to ask questions about how the food is prepared: Is it sautéed in oil? Is it steamed? Does it come with the dressing on it? Is it sprinkled with cheese? Is it already prepared or made to order? Will the chef be able to make this without fat?

If all else fails, consider making your own menu item. For instance, ask for steamed rice with the vegetables of the day—steamed, of course; or ask for a baked potato without the usual toppings, but with steamed broccoli instead; ask your server if the chef might make pasta sauced with fresh chopped tomatoes, onions, basil, and steamed vegetables. At a sandwich shop, ask if the kitchen could make you a vegetable sandwich on whole grain bread with mustard, and with no cheese, avocado, or mayonnaise. You may be surprised at how creative the chef can be. Or like Jack Nicholson in the movie *Five Easy Pieces*, order the chicken, lettuce, and tomato sandwich on whole wheat and ask them to hold the chicken!

> *Eating out is one of the biggest challenges our participants have in the Des Moines area. I am working with restaurant chefs to teach them about the guidelines of the Reversal Diet. Hopefully, someday it will be common for restaurants to offer Ornish food without having to be coaxed.*
>
> —Mandy Corliss, R.D., L.D.,
> Dr. Ornish Program for Reversing
> Heart Disease, Mercy Hospital Medical
> Center/Iowa Heart Center,
> Des Moines, Iowa

Learn to be assertive in asking for what you want. A restaurant staff wants to please you, so don't hesitate to ask. Of course, being considerate and grateful helps.

You may find that taking certain food items to restaurants helps you follow the Reversal Diet. Some participants take their own nonfat salad dressings. (For example, Weight Watchers makes a ranch dressing packaged in individual serving sizes.) Research participant Conrad Knudsen says, "I ask for egg-free pasta at restaurants. If they do not have it, I take a package out of my jacket and ask if the chef would mind cooking it for me. They have never refused."

Seasoned travelers and research participants Werner and Eva

Hebenstreit have no trouble following the Reversal Diet away from home. "First of all, I know my health depends upon it," says Werner. "Traveling is no excuse for not following the guidelines. We go nowhere without taking a few basic items with us." Their list may include: herb teas and grain coffee, nonfat crackers, nonfat salad dressing, fresh fruit, bagels, rice cakes, soup cups, water, ramen noodles, nonfat dry milk, and raw vegetables like carrots and zucchini. "We take leftovers from home for the first day of travel," says Werner. "Lentils, rice, pasta salads, and bean salads travel pretty well. That way, we aren't dependent on airline food."

> *You can eat anywhere as long as you tell them exactly what you want and how to prepare it. If it comes out wrong, send it back. We need to teach them about our diet. Chefs are usually more than willing to accommodate.*
>
> —Charlie Spehl, participant,
> Dr. Ornish Program for
> Reversing Heart Disease,
> Richland Memorial Hospital,
> Columbia, South Carolina.

Last year, Werner and Eva traveled to Italy, Switzerland, and Austria. "It is better if you stay a week in one place," says Werner. "That way the staff gets to know you and is willing to take care of your special needs. We present a list of foods to avoid to the manager and chef at the hotel. We put this list in an envelope and enclose a small gratuity. They always are pleased to help us."

John Cardozo, another research participant, offers this advice: "When Phyllis and I travel, we stay in a place with a kitchen. That way we can do most of our own cooking. Sometimes we 'house exchange.' It feels more like being a part of the place we are visiting, and it helps us manage our meals better."

Airlines offer vegetarian meals, with or without dairy products, but they are rarely low-fat. It's better to order a fruit plate. Of course, it's best to bring your own food. If your flight changes, tell the flight attendants about your special meal requirements. Sometimes, if they have extra food trays, they can combine items from the leftover trays to make a special tray for you. Breakfast is usually no problem: ask for cereal, fruit, and nonfat milk. Check the airport food vendors between flights. You may find a vendor offering plain baked potatoes or a salad bar. Take these on the plane with you instead of depending upon a suitable airline meal. Be sure to drink a lot of water when you fly to prevent dehydration.

# Commonly Asked Questions About the Reversal Diet

These questions are frequently asked by participants in the Ornish program.

*Can I overeat on this diet?*
Yes. After all, there are few limits on the number of servings of foods on the Reversal Diet. However, it is unlikely that you will. To check that you are not overeating, follow your body's natural demand for food. Eat when you are hungry. Stop eating when you feel satisfied, not full. Be aware of the amount of nonfat sweets you are eating. Nonfat doesn't mean noncalorie. Most nonfat sweets are loaded with some form of sugar and provide excess calories which are converted to fat in your body. Also, weigh yourself once a week. Compare your weight change to the goals your physician or registered dietitian have set for you. Not gaining weight is the objective established for most normal weight people. Slow weight loss is indicated for most overweight people.

> *I tell my participants it is possible to overeat, but they will usually feel satisfied before having too many calories. Unless they are eating too many processed foods, including nonfat sweets, which can be high in sugar and low in fiber.*
> —Caitlin Hosmer, M.S., R.D., Dr. Ornish Program for Reversing Heart Disease, Beth Israel Hospital, Boston, Massachusetts.

*What size is a serving?*
A "serving" does not refer to the amount you serve yourself but rather to the amounts of food within a food group that are nutritionally equivalent. For example, a tortilla, a pancake, a half-cup of rice, and a slice of bread are each one serving of grains. This method helps determine the nutrition in foods that are more or less than a typical serving. For example, a huge green salad may be three cups of lettuce, or three "servings." Using the idea of "servings" helps you evaluate and plan your diet without a computer.

## Serving Sizes

½ **cup:** whole grains, fruits, cooked vegetables, raw vegetables, cooked beans and peas, tofu, gluten, cottage cheese

**1:** piece of fruit, slice of bread, tortilla

**1 cup:** milk, soy milk, yogurt, soup, raw leafy vegetables

**1 ounce:** cheese, dry cereal

**2 teaspoons:** jams, jellies, sugars, syrups

**1 serving:** as listed on packaged sweets

*What's a typical day's menu?*

The following sample menu fits the Reversal Diet guidelines and includes the recommended number of servings from the Reversal Diet Pyramid.

This menu is just a sample and should be tailored to fit your own food preferences by making substitutions within the same food group. It supplies approximately 2,000 calories in the form of 8 percent fat, 19 percent protein, and 77 percent carbohydrate. If it is too much food for you, cut down the portion sizes instead of cutting out the food group. Similarly, if you need more calories, follow the basic menu and add more servings or additional foods from the same group. This menu is based on whole foods instead of processed foods and is nutritionally adequate in nutrients including protein, complex carbohydrates, essential fatty acids, fiber, vitamins and minerals, and supplies phytochemicals and antioxidants. Six small meals including whole grain breads, cereals, and starchy vegetables are provided to keep your blood sugar stable, supplying you with a constant source of energy. Whole grain breads, cereals, and pastas are encouraged. If you simply cannot get these products, you may add ¼ cup wheat germ and ¼ cup wheat bran during the day to supply the fiber and essential nutrients missing in the refined foods. You may use soy milk if you choose not to have dairy products.

*How do I know what commercial products are okay?*

The Reversal Diet encourages whole foods and discourages processed foods. However, using some processed foods can be okay. But how do you know which ones fit into the guidelines?

Read the labels. Most prepared or processed foods are combinations of many foods and sometimes sources of fat are hard to recognize. Fortunately, the new labeling law has made it easier to discern the fat content. Finding prepared foods that fit the Reversal Diet can be simple if you follow these guidelines:

Look at the Nutrition Facts section on the product. Find the total

# The Reversal Diet Food Diary and Evaluation Form
## Sample Meal Plan
### NUMBER OF SERVINGS

| Time | Food | Amount | Whole Grains | Vegetables | Fresh Fruits | Beans & Peas | Nonfat Dairy | Alcohol & Sweets |
|---|---|---|---|---|---|---|---|---|
| 6 A.M. | Shredded Wheat | 1 cup | 2 | | | | | |
| | nonfat milk | 1 cup | | | | | 1 | |
| | whole wheat toast | 1 slice | 1 | | | | | |
| | jam | 2 teaspoons | | | | | | 1 |
| | banana | ½ | | | ½ | | | |
| | grain coffee | free | | | | | | |
| 10 A.M. | rye crackers | 4 | 1 | | | | | |
| | fresh orange | 1 | | | 1 | | | |
| 12:30 P.M. | black beans | 1 cup | | | | 2 | | |
| | brown rice | ½ cup | 1 | | | | | |
| | firm tofu | ½ cup | | | | 1 | | |
| | fresh tomato salsa | ½ cup | | 1 | | | | |
| | fresh spinach salad | 1 cup | | 1 | | | | |
| | nonfat Italian dressing | free | | | | | | |
| | whole wheat roll | 1 small | 1 | | | | | |

NUMBER OF SERVINGS

| Time | Food | Amount | Whole Grains | Vegetables | Fresh Fruits | Beans & Peas | Nonfat Dairy | Alcohol & Sweets |
|---|---|---|---|---|---|---|---|---|
| 3:30 P.M. | rye crackers | 4 | 1 | | | | | |
| | raw carrots | ½ cup | | 1 | | | | |
| | fresh apple | 1 | | | 1 | | | |
| 7 P.M. | whole wheat pasta | 1 ½ cup | 3 | | | | | |
| | fresh tomato sauce with zucchini | 1 cup | | 2 | | | | |
| | steamed broccoli | ½ cup | | 1 | | | | |
| | romaine lettuce salad | 1 cup | | 1 | | | | |
| | nonfat dressing | free | | | | | | |
| | whole grain bread | 2 slices | 2 | 1 | | | | |
| 10 P.M. | nonfat yogurt | 1 cup | | | | | 1 | |
| | fresh berries | ½ cup | | | 1 | | | |
| Total number of servings | | | 12 | 7 | 4 | 3 | 2 | 1 |
| Recommended servings | | | 6+ | 3+ | 2 to 4 | 2 to 4 | 1 to 2 | 0 to 2 |

fat. The food should contain no more than 3 grams of fat per serving.

Read the list of ingredients. The food should not include added fats.

Below are two labels for vegetarian burgers. Read the list of ingredients for yourself. Remember that the product should not include any foods with added fat (page 311). Double-check your evaluation by noticing the total grams of fat per serving and the serving size. Be sure the serving size is realistic and not a gross underestimation of the amount you typically consume.

The ingredients list below appears on the packaging for a vegetarian burger that *does not* meet the Reversal Diet guidelines:

Ingredients: mushrooms, brown rice, onions, rolled oats, part skim milk mozzarella, cottage cheese curd, egg white, Cheddar cheese, bulgur wheat, natural seasonings and spices, olive oil, tapioca starch, vegetable gum.

(The serving size is one burger and the total fat per serving is 2.5 grams.)

It has fewer than 3 grams of fat per serving. Why doesn't it meet the guidelines?

Look at the ingredients again. The source of this fat is mozzarella cheese, cottage cheese, Cheddar cheese, and olive oil. These are added fats. For this reason, this product does not meet the guidelines.

The ingredients list below describes a vegetarian burger that *does* meet the Reversal Diet guidelines:

Ingredients: soy protein, purified water, potato starch, soy fiber, dehydrated onion, natural flavors, spices, carrageenan, fresh garlic, natural malt extract.

(The serving size is one burger and the total grams of fat is zero.)

This product meets the guidelines because the total fat is zero, and there is no added fat.

What if the label indicates that the food contains fat even though fat is not listed in the ingredients?

Almost all foods contain fat called "naturally occurring." Even an apple has fat. So does broccoli. Corn and whole wheat have fat. These foods provide the essential fatty acids in your diet. For instance, the Nutrition Facts on the label of whole wheat bread may state it contains fat, although there is no added fat in the ingredient list. These fats are a natural component of the whole wheat. Foods with naturally occurring fats fit Reversal Diet guidelines as long as they do not have more than 3 grams of fat per serving. Foods with added fats are not on the diet. (See below—"How do I know if the food has added fat?")

What if there is added fat in the food but it is mainly monounsaturated?

Skip it. Even canola and olive oils contain some saturated fat. The people who adhere strictly to the Reversal Diet as well as to the stress management, group support, and exercise components of the program do best. Often when people compromise in adhering to the program, they slide down a slippery slope toward a lifestyle that makes heart disease worse, not better.

*How do I know if the food has added fat?*
Many terms are used to describe added fat. Here are some common ones:

beef fat
butter
canola oil
chocolate
coconut oil
corn oil
cream
diglycerides
hydrogenated oils
lard
lecithin
margarine
mayonnaise
monoglycerides
nut oils

olive oil

palm kernel oil

palm oil

partially hydrogenated oils

part skim milk

peanut oil

rapeseed oil

safflower oil

sesame seed oil

shortening

soybean oil

sunflower seed oil

vegetable oils

walnut oil

whole milk solids

Many participants in the Ornish program enjoy the "Life Choice" line of frozen foods. Although they contain canola oil, the amount of oil is so small that these foods are acceptable on the Reversal Diet.

*Do "fat-free" food products fit the Reversal Diet guidelines?*
"Fat-free" doesn't necessarily mean fat-free; nor does low fat definitely mean low fat. The Food and Drug Administration (FDA) has established the following guidelines:

**Fat Free**   ½ (0.50) gram of fat or less per serving
½ (0.50) gram of saturated fat or less per serving

**Low Fat**   3 grams of fat or less per serving
1 gram of saturated fat or less per serving

**Reduced Fat**   25 percent  less total fat (and saturated fat) per serving
than a similar standard food product

Fat-free products can have up to ½ gram of fat per serving and still be labeled fat-free. Check the label to identify sources of fat (page 311). If the product does contain fat in the ingredient list and if you have several servings a day of these fat-free products, you can be eating a significant amount of fat. These fat-free products, particularly the snack foods, contribute few nutrients and most of them contain high amounts of sugar. Often they replace other foods that offer better nutrition.

It is much better to look for an alternative snack ("Snack Foods," page 320). If you must have fat-free cakes and cookies, limit them to two servings per day (servings according to the package label).

Also note: some deli meats, such as turkey slices, may be low enough in fat to be labeled fat-free, but they still have some fat and cholesterol just as any animal product does. So avoid them.

*Since soy products are high in fat, how much can I have?*
Soybean products have no cholesterol and supply essential fatty acids and are an exception to the guideline of no more than 3 grams of fat per serving. However, use good judgment. Eating too much of any one food is not a good idea. If you want to eat soybean products, a good rule of thumb is: stay within ½ cup soybeans, 4 ounces tofu, or 2 cups soy milk per day. Soy milk—the rich, creamy product of soybeans ground with water—is an excellent cholesterol-free alternative to cow's milk. It is available plain and flavored, in a range of fat contents. Choose plain soy milk in aseptic (unrefrigerated) containers.

*Is it possible to get too little fat on the Reversal Diet?*
Yes, but it is extremely difficult to get too little fat if you follow the Reversal Diet guidelines and the Reversal Diet Pyramid. Even though the Reversal Diet does not include high-fat foods or added fats, you will get naturally occurring fats from whole grains, beans, including soy products, fruits, and vegetables. These supply the two essential fatty acids you need. You don't need much of these two fatty acids, and there is no benefit to eating more.

Essential fatty acids regulate vital functions of the body. The two you need are linoleic acid, which supplies omega-6 fatty acids; and alpha-linolenic acid, which supplies omega-3 fatty acids. You also need a certain balance or ratio of these two fatty acids in your diet (too much omega-6 in relation to omega-3 can do more harm than good). However, it is easy to meet your requirements for both essential fatty acids in the recommended ratio if you follow the Reversal Diet Pyramid. The omega-3 fatty acids will come from the dark leafy green vegetables, some beans, and peas, including soybeans and soybean products. The omega-6 fatty acids will be supplied by whole grains. And since the Reversal Diet limits rich sources of omega-6 fatty acids (fats and oils), eating according to the pyramid will provide the proper balance of essential fatty acids.

## Will I get enough calcium on the Reversal Diet?

The fact is that once you've reached adulthood, you probably don't need the calcium in milk to strengthen your bones or prevent osteoporosis. The Chinese provide an interesting example: they consume almost no dairy products and about half the calcium of Americans, but they have little osteoporosis. They get most of their calcium from vegetables.

> *Some of the women in the Ornish program ask this question. I tell them to check with their physician, but if they follow the Reversal guidelines, they should get all the calcium they need.*
>
> —Mary Hyer, R.D., CNSD, Mt. Diablo Medical Center/Heart Health Center, Concord, California.

Although dietary calcium does help to build peak bone mass in youngsters and teens, high calcium intake in adulthood seems to have little to do with strong bones. More important is to prevent the calcium *loss* that affects bone mass. Studies suggest that you can minimize urinary calcium loss by avoiding animal protein, caffeine, tobacco, and a sedentary lifestyle.

Our adult bodies do need calcium, but the amount remains debatable. The RDA for adults recently increased to 800 milligrams, but the World Health Organization recommends 400 to 500 milligrams a day. Some experts believe that a higher calcium intake does not prevent osteoporosis.

The Reversal Diet allows the equivalent of 2 cups of nonfat dairy products a day, but it's possible to achieve adequate calcium levels from plant sources alone. We can get much of it in green vegetables (particularly dark, leafy greens), dried beans, and peas. What's more, these plant sources deliver their calcium packaged with fiber, antioxidants, complex carbohydrates, and little or no fat. The Reversal Diet encourages consumption of dark leafy greens, beans, and peas and is low in the animal protein that provokes calcium loss.

## Will I get enough protein on the Reversal Diet?

Americans tend to be overly concerned about getting enough protein. In fact, meat eaters tend to get too much. Eating too much protein, especially animal protein, can increase your risk of cancer, diabetes, and heart disease. And because there is a connection between protein intake and calcium loss, excess protein may lead to osteoporosis.

On the Reversal Diet, you get all the protein you need without the health risks associated with a high animal-protein diet.

> *When I first explain the Reversal Diet, some of our participants ask if they will be getting enough protein without eating meat. I assure them it is actually hard not to get enough protein, as long as they eat enough calories from a variety of foods.*
>
> —Laurie Jones, R.D., Dr. Ornish Program for Reversing Heart Disease, Beth Israel Medical Center, New York.

*Where do I get protein on the Reversal Diet?*
The body's protein requirement is about 50 grams per day for women and about 60 grams per day for men. High-protein food sources on the Reversal Diet are beans and peas, including soy milk and tofu; egg whites; and nonfat dairy products. Other vegetables, whole grains, and cereals are good sources of protein. Even if you don't have milk or egg whites, you can still get all the protein you need.

*Because it's a vegetarian diet, do I need to worry about combining proteins?*
For years, nutritionists warned vegetarians to combine complementary proteins at every meal or risk protein deficiency. If you had corn for dinner, for example, you were supposed to pair it with legumes, which contain the essential amino acids in which corn is deficient. We now know that we can be much more relaxed about it.

A little background: amino acids are the building blocks of protein. We need them to build and maintain body tissue and to perform other essential body functions. Our bodies produce all but nine of the amino acids we require. These nine essential amino acids have to come from the foods we eat. Nutritionists once thought that animal products were the only source of "complete" protein, containing all these essential amino acids. Now we recognize that some plant foods do indeed contain all of them, although some of the amino acids are not present in sufficient quantity. So you may have to just eat a little more of them. (The soybean is the only plant food with enough of all the essential amino acids to be considered a complete protein.)

The good news is, our bodies have more time than we thought to find a complement for an incomplete protein. If you have corn for din-

---

*Your Everyday Choices*

ner, which is low in the essential amino acid lysine, you do need to find the lysine somewhere else. But you don't have to do it at that meal. A portion of legumes—which are high in lysine—in the next day or two will do the job. If you follow Reversal Diet guidelines and eat a varied diet that includes daily portions of beans, whole grains, fruits, and vegetables, you should have no trouble getting enough of all the essential amino acids.

*Why isn't fish on the Reversal Diet?*
Although fish can be low in fat, it is an animal product and does contain cholesterol. A 3-ounce serving has from 40 to 70 milligrams of cholesterol. (A typical restaurant portion is 6 to 8 ounces.) Three ounces of boiled shrimp have about 166 milligrams of cholesterol. Some are touting the benefits of certain fish because they contain omega-3 fatty acids, but you can get these essential fatty acids from dark leafy greens, soybeans, and soybean products (such as tofu) without the harmful cholesterol.

*What is the difference between simple and complex carbohydrates?*
Carbohydrates provide the main source of energy for the body. Simple carbohydrates are referred to as sugars; complex carbohydrates are referred to as starches. The Reversal Diet emphasizes complex carbohydrates (whole grains, breads, cereals, pastas, beans) and limits simple carbohydrates (fruits, fruit juices, sugar, sugar products, jams, jellies, and syrups).

Complex carbohydrates provide protein, vitamins, minerals, fiber, and, in the case of whole grains, essential fatty acids. The starches have a complex structure of many sugars. When digested, these sugars are broken down and used for energy. Since this happens slowly, they supply a constant source of energy and help you maintain a steady blood sugar level.

Simple carbohydrates consist of one or two sugars and are either refined or naturally occurring. Refined sugar (table sugar)

> *I tell my diabetic participants that the Reversal Diet will fit into their overall care, but that it is important for them to check with their physician about any dietary changes they make.*
> —Carol Throckmorton, R.D., L.D., C.D.E., Dr. Ornish Program for Reversing Heart Disease, Mercy Hospital Medical Center/Iowa Heart Center, Des Moines, Iowa.

*Everyday Cooking with Dr. Dean Ornish*

contributes few nutrients to your eating plan. The naturally occurring sugars found in fruits, vegetables, and dairy products provide vitamins, minerals, and, in some cases, fiber. When you eat foods high in simple carbohydrates, your blood sugar rises quickly, your pancreas secretes insulin to drive the blood sugar into your cells, then you have lower blood sugar than what you started with, leaving you tired and sluggish. That's why simple carbohydrates are limited on the Reversal Diet.

If you are diabetic, insulin-resistant, or have high triglycerides, controlling your intake of simple carbohydrates is especially important. If you have these conditions, the Reversal Diet will fit into your overall care, but it is important to check with your physician about any dietary changes you make.

### Should I use honey instead of table sugar?

Honey, raw sugar, and brown sugar provide no more nutritional benefits than table sugar. Tablespoon for tablespoon, the calories, nutrients, and sweetening power are virtually the same. Honey contains fructose, which the body metabolizes a little differently than table sugar (glucose), but fructose ends up as glucose in the body. When the body absorbs glucose, it doesn't care whether it came from table sugar, honey, or any other carbohydrate.

### What if I have a sweet tooth?

Satisfy it with fresh fruit, whole grain bread, spiced herbal tea, or non-fat dairy products, such as yogurt. Carrots have one of the highest sugar contents of all vegetables and will satisfy your need to munch.

Avoid commercial baked goods and frozen desserts even if they are labeled "fat-free." They contribute little or nothing to your overall good nutrition. Even if they are fat-free, they are not calorie-free. In fact, most are very high in refined sugar and calories. Excess calories, whether from fat or sugar, will be stored as body fat.

### What are antioxidants?

When people talk about antioxidants, they are usually referring to vitamins C and E and beta-carotene, from which vitamin A is formed. Recent studies suggest that these antioxidants combat cell-damaging molecules in the body called free radicals. Free radicals are a normal by-product of metabolism. We also produce them in response to triggers such as sunlight, air pollution, and tobacco smoke. Researchers believe the antioxidant vitamins protect us against cell damage by neutralizing these free radicals or preventing their formation. When they do their work, antioxidants are protecting us against a number of chronic diseases, including cancer and heart disease. The Reversal Diet contains foods that are rich sources of antioxidants, and eating according to the guidelines will supply you with adequate amounts of antioxidants.

## Foods High in Antioxidants

*High in Vitamin C*
  broccoli
  brussels sprouts
  cabbage
  cantaloupe
  cauliflower
  citrus fruits and juices: orange, grapefruit, lemon
  collards
  kiwi
  peppers, green or red
  raspberries
  snow peas
  strawberries
  sweet potatoes
  tomatoes
  watermelon

*High in Beta-Carotene*
  broccoli
  dark leafy green vegetables: collards, kale, spinach
  deep orange or yellow vegetables: carrots, sweet potatoes, winter
    squash
  deep orange or yellow fruits: cantaloupe, peaches, mangoes

*High in Vitamin E*
  broccoli
  cooked leafy greens: collards, kale, spinach, cabbage

*Everyday Cooking with Dr. Dean Ornish*

corn

fortified cereals

green peas

oatmeal

wheat germ

(*Source: U.S. Department of Agriculture, Human Nutrition Information Service, Agriculture Handbook, Number 8–16. Revised December 1986.*)

*I have a hearty appetite and I really enjoy the foods on the Reversal Diet. But I get hungry a few hours after eating. What can I do?*

It is not uncommon for people who follow the Reversal Diet to feel hungry between meals. Since the diet includes many high-fiber foods, you may quickly feel full at meals before you have eaten a large volume of food. This is one of the benefits of the eating plan— you feel full before you eat too many calories—but also a challenge for people who can't eat enough at one meal to tide them over until the next.

The solution for some people is to eat small, frequent meals or snacks, perhaps five to six a day. These small meals do more than just appease hunger.

When you eat a small meal, your digestive system has to work less to handle the smaller load. This helps your heart, which has to pump less blood to the stomach and intestines. You actually feel more energized after eating rather than feeling sluggish.

Smaller, more frequent meals can help regulate your blood sugar levels. This is especially important if you are diabetic or insulin-resistant. When your blood sugar levels are better regulated, you don't have the energy peaks and lows associated with eating large amounts of food.

And if you need to lose weight, smaller, more frequent meals or snacks can actually help you. Most of us overeat when we get too hungry. And we don't make good food choices when we are ravenous. You may be able to manage your appetite better by having small, frequent meals so you never get overly hungry.

Plan regular times to eat your small meals or snacks. Consider three to four hours between each small meal. A typical schedule might be: breakfast, mid-morning snack, lunch, mid-afternoon snack, dinner, bedtime snack. See the sample meal plan on page 308.

# Snack Foods:
## What to Eat When Hunger Strikes

It's between meals and you're so hungry you can't think of anything but food. Do you hang tough and vow to make it until dinnertime? Not good. You may then be so hungry, you overeat. Instead, have a snack.

Snacking, or eating between meals, has an undeservedly bad reputation. A mid-morning, mid-afternoon, or bedtime snack can help you moderate your blood sugar and your weight. But a fat-laden bag of potato chips won't cut it, nor will a handful of fat-free cookies. Snacking is only a healthful habit if you choose the right snack.

Look to complex carbohydrates when you're hungry between meals. You can save part of your breakfast, lunch, or dinner for these in-between nibbles. Instead of having whole wheat toast with your breakfast, have it with another piece of fruit at mid-morning. Or save part of your pasta salad from lunch to have with a few whole wheat crackers in mid-afternoon. Whole grain cereal is not just for breakfast. Have it with nonfat milk or soy milk for a soothing bedtime snack.

Other foods to consider: plain nonfat yogurt (add your own fruit instead of buying the kind with fruit added and save many sugar calories); instant soups; instant ramen (Japanese noodles); crunchy vegetables; leftover steamed vegetables; popcorn; whole grain breads; crackers with nonfat cheese or bean dips; or rice cakes, or lunch-box sizes of aseptic containers of soy milk.

Avoid snacking on foods that are predominantly composed of simple sugars, such as fat-free baked goods or fruit juice. Your body absorbs simple sugars quickly, causing your blood sugar to spike and then quickly fall, leaving you tired and, before long, hungry again.

## Where to Find Products

These are just a few of the companies who have products meeting the Reversal Diet guidelines.

## Beans, Rices, and Other Grains

AKPharma, Inc.
P.O. Box 111
Pleasantville, NJ 08232
1-800-257-8650
*For Beano*

Arrowhead Mills
Box 2059
Hereford, TX 79045
806-364-0730
*For a large variety of whole grain products, including specialty grains, grain mixes, flours, cereals*

Barbara's Bakery, Inc.
3900 Cypress Drive
Petaluma, CA 94954
707-765-2263
*For whole grain cereals and products*

The Bean Bag
818 Jefferson Street
Oakland, CA 94607
510-839-8988
*For dried beans, including many heirloom and organic beans, and bean mixes; hot sauces; sun-dried tomatoes; gourmet rices; specialty grains*

Burkett Mills
P.O. Box 440
Penn Yan, NY 14527
315-536-3311
*For kasha (buckwheat groats)*

Butte Creek Mill
P.O. Box 561
Eagle Point, OR 97524
503-826-3531
*For cereals, whole grains, rolled grains, stone-ground flours and meals*

Continental Mills
P.O. Box 88176
Seattle, WA 98138
206-872-8400
*For specialty whole grains, including bulgur*

Fantastic Foods
1250 N. McDowell Boulevard
Petaluma, CA 94954
707-778-7801
*For instant soups, beans, and rice in cups*

Guiltless Gourmet
3709 Promontory Point South
Suite 131
Austin, TX 78744
512-443-4373
*For fat-free chips, salsa, and dips*

Health Valley Foods
16100 Foothill Boulevard
Irwindale, CA 91706
818-334-3241
*For whole grain cereals, fat-free soups, beans products, snack foods, fat-free soy milk*

Kashi Co.
P.O. Box 8557
La Jolla, CA 92038
619-274-8870
*For kashi cereals*

Lundberg Family Farms
P.O. Box 369
Richvale, CA 95974-0369
916-882-4551
*For premium short-grain and long-grain brown rice, California basmati brown rice, organic brown rice, specialty brown rices and rice blends; also rice cakes and rice cereal*

---

Nature's Path Food
7453 Progress Way
Delta, BC, Canada V4G 1E8
604-940-0505
*For specialty whole grain cereals including millet, rice bran flakes*

Nile Spice
Box 20581
Seattle, WA 98102
no phone listing
*For instant cups of soup, beans, and grains including couscous*

Old Mill of Guilford
1340 N.C. 68 North
Oak Ridge, NC 27310
910-643-4783
*For whole wheat flour and pastry flour; cornmeal, grits, and polenta; wheat bran; and steel-cut oats*

Phipps Ranch
P.O. Box 349
Pescadero, CA 94060
415-879-0787
*For dried beans (such as cannellini, cranberry, fava, flageolet, borlotti, Wren's Egg, scarlet runner, Tongues of Fire, pinquito, and more) and dried peas; also herb vinegars, cereals, grains, herbs, and spices*

RiceTec
P.O. Box 1305
Alvin, TX 77512
*For specialty rices including brown and basmati rice*

Sokensha Co.
P.O. Box 883033
San Francisco, CA 94188
no phone listing
*For ramen, including buckwheat, and brown rice*

---

Specialty Rice Marketing, Inc.
P.O. Box 880
Brinkley, AR 72021
501-734-1234
*For specialty rices including brown and basmati rice*

U.S. Mills
4301 N. 30th Street
Omaha, NE 68111
402-451-4567
*For whole grains and cereals, including brown rice cereal*

Westbrae Natural Foods
Commerce, CA 90040
no phone listing
*For instant ramen noodles in a variety of flavors*

**Pasta Sauces**
ConAgra
Five ConAgra Drive
Omaha, NE 68102-5006
800-328-3738
*For fat-free pasta sauces, soups, and beans*

Organic Food Products
P.O. Box 1510
Freedom, CA 95019
408-685-6575
*For several varieties of fat-free pasta sauces*

**Soups and Stocks**
Campbell Soup Co.
Campbell Place
Camden, NJ 08103
609-342-4800
*For Swanson Clear Vegetable Broth*

Liberty Richter, Inc.
400 Lyster Avenue
Saddle Brook, NJ 07663
201-843-8900
*For Morga fat-free vegetable broth mix*

Real Fresh, Inc.
1211 E. Noble Avenue
Visalia, CA 93292
201-627-2070
*For Andersen's split pea soup*

The Spice Hunter
254 Granada Drive
San Luis Obispo, CA 93401
805-544-4466
*For instant soup cups including noodle, lentil*

Will-Pak Foods
1448 240th Street
Harbor City, CA 90710
310-325-3504
*For Taste Adventure instant soup cups, including bean, split pea, navy bean, instant bean flakes*

## Meat Substitutes
Boca Burger
1660 N.E. 12th Terrace
Fort Lauderdale, FL 33305
305-524-1977
*For textured soy protein products*

Harvest Direct
P.O. Box 4514
Decatur, IL 62525-4514
800-8-FLAVOR
*For fat-free texturized vegetable protein*

---

Knox Mountain Foods
5 Knox Mountain Road
Sandbornton, NH 03256
603-934-6960
*For seitan mixes including sausage*

Lightlife Foods
P.O. Box 8870
Greenfield, MA 01302
no phone listing
*For veggie hot dogs, seitan, and deli slices*

White Wave, Inc.
1990 N. 57th Court
Boulder, CO 80301
303-443-3470
*For seitan products*

Yves Fine Foods
1138 E. Georgia Street
Vancouver, BC, Canada V6A 2A8
604-251-1345
*For veggie wieners and deli slices*

## Cookware

All-Clad Metalcrafters
RD #2
Canonsburg, PA 15317
412-745-8300
*For premium nonstick cookware*

Commercial Aluminum Cookware Company
P.O. Box 583
Toledo, OH 43697-0583
419-666-8700
*For premium nonstick cookware and bakeware*

## Phyllo Dough

Athens Pastries and Frozen Foods, Inc.
13600 Snow Road
Cleveland, OH 44141-2596
216-676-8500
*For low-fat phyllo dough*


## Coffee and Tea Alternatives

Adamba Imports
585 Meserole Street
Brooklyn, NY 11237
718-628-9700
*For Inka*

Alpursa
P.O. Box 25846
Salt Lake City, UT 84125
no phone listing
*For Pero*

Bioforce Ltd.
CH-9325 Roggwil
Switzerland
*For Bambu*

Cafix of North America
15 Prospect Street
Paramus, NJ 07652
201-909-0808
*For Cafix*

Celestial Seasonings
4600 Sleepytime Drive
Boulder, CO 80301
303-530-5300
*For herb teas*

Worthington Foods
900 Proprietors Road
Worthington, OH 43085
614-885-9511
*For Kaffree Roma*

**Frozen Meals**
ConAgra
Five ConAgra Drive
Omaha, NE 68102-5006
800-328-3738
*For Life Choice frozen meals*

# Index

---

mushroom(s) (cont.)
  porcini, risotto, herbed, 270–71, **271**
  portobello, burgers of grilled onion and,
      163–64, **164**
  pudding, savory, 114–15
  and spinach lasagne, 185–86, **186**
  and spinach salad with buttermilk dressing,
      258–59
  stroganoff, creamy, 177–78, **178**
  washing, **206**
  *see also* shiitake mushrooms
mushroom-tomato sauce, rich, rigatoni with,
    194–95, **195**
mustard, 22, 23
  honey dressing, broccoli florets with, 178–79,
      **179**
  in salad dressings, 19
  tarragon, 39
mustard greens, 182, 183

National Cancer Institute, 70
Nell's southern eggplant dressing, 276–77,
    **277**
Nestle, Marion, 2
*New England Journal of Medicine,* 11
"New Year's Day Buffet," 274–79
  collard greens with tomatoes, onions, and
      peppers, 277–78, **278**
  hoppin' John, 275
  John's gingerbread, 278–79, **279**
  Nell's southern eggplant dressing, 276–77,
      **277**
nonstick spray, 61, 251
nutrient analysis:
  of beans, 42–43
  of bread, 53–54
  how to use, 61–62
  of okra, 85
nutrients, preserving, 142
"Nutritionist and the Gourmet, The" (O'Neill), 2

oat bran, 70
oatmeal, **288**
oats, **214, 288**
  rolled, 46
Oestmann, Shelly, 52
oils:
  exclusion of, 5–6
  fat in, 5, 8
  in nonstick spray, 61
  substitutes for, 23
okra, sliced, with tomatoes and onions, 85, **85**
olive oil, 5–6, 8
omega-3 fatty acids, 41, 313, 316
omega-6 fatty acids, 313–14
omelets, fresh asparagus with herbs, 107–8, **108**

O'Neill, Molly, 1–2
onions:
  braised cabbage with caraway and, 261–62,
      **262**
  collard greens with tomatoes, peppers and,
      277–78, **278**
  green, **96**
  roasted, 21–22, **117**
  roasted, Swiss chard with, 159, **159**
  sliced okra with tomatoes and, 85, **85**
onion(s), red:
  arugula salad with corn and, 135–36, **136**
  and portobello mushroom burgers, grilled,
      163–64, **164**
  spinach, beet, and cucumber salad, 79–80
  steamed chayote with lime and, 265–66, **266**
orange(s):
  -basil dressing, 102
  glazed acorn squash with ginger and, **272,**
      272–73
  juice, 21
  julienned spinach salad with jicama and,
      102–3
  sauce, baked bananas with, 259–60, **260**
  in spiced syrup, sliced, 252–53
  Sunday morning special, 289
osteoporosis, 8, 11, 314
ovens, microwave, 40, 48, 142, 144
overcooking, undercooking vs., 20, 142
overeating, 306
oxidants, 7

packaged products, miscellaneous, shopping for,
    39
pancakes:
  corn, 157–58, **158**
  potato, with warm applesauce, 250–51
  wholesome, 287–88
pans, *see* pots and pans
parchment paper, **216**
parfait, strawberry-rhubarb, 73, **73**
parsley, **95, 216**
  and bulgur salad (tabbouleh), 153–54
parsnips, roasted carrots, beets, and, 116–17,
    **117**
"Passover Seder," 112–19
  baked vanilla custard, 118–19, **119**
  cucumber salad with horseradish and dill,
      117–18, **118**
  roasted carrots, parsnips, and beets, 116–17,
      **117**
  savory mushroom pudding, 114–15
  sweet and sour red cabbage, 115–16, **116**
  vegetable broth with matzo balls, 113–14,
      **114**
pasta, 8, 299

angel hair, with fresh tomato and basil,
126–27
with creamy red pepper sauce, 150
Gary's broccoli manicotti, 201–3
mushroom and spinach lasagne, 185–86, **186**
penne with white bean and sun-dried tomato
sauce, 246–47
rigatoni with rich tomato-mushroom sauce,
194–95, **195**
selection of, 36
shells with spinach-mushroom filling, 186,
**186**
shopping list for, 31
whole wheat spaghetti marinara with
spinach, 91–92
*see also* sauce, pasta
peach(es), **157, 167**
cobbler, warm, **166,** 166–67
sherbet, quick, **141,** 141–42
spiced poached, 156–57, **157**
pear(s), **249, 274**
bread pudding, brandied, 273–74
-ginger muffins, 110–11
poached in red wine, 248–49, **249**
in sweet and sour red cabbage, **116**
vanilla poached, 187–88
pea(s), split, 41, 42, **258**
confetti rice pilaf with, 240, **240, 245**
soup, creamy, 86–88, **87, 293**
soup, leftover, **87**
peas, 27, **82,** 299, 300
peas, black-eyed, 42
hoppin' John, 275
peas, green:
baby, steamed red potatoes and, 245
guacamole, 191–92, **192**
risotto with zucchini, sun-dried tomatoes
and, 81–82, **82**
pepper mills, 22
peppers, green bell, collard greens with tomatoes, onions, and, 277–78, **278**
peppers, red bell, **156**
rice-stuffed, 219–20
risotto with corn and, 140–41
roasted, **90**
peppers, sweet bell:
marinated mushrooms and, 200–201
pizza with roasted eggplant and, 136–38
persimmons, **293**
phyllo dough, **199**
in apple-raisin strudel, 198-99
where to find, 327
phytochemicals, 7, **227**
picnics, food for, **99,** 254
pilaf, **220, 240, 245**
brown rice and shiitake, 76–77

confetti rice, with split peas, 240, **240, 245**
lentil and brown rice, 245
pineapple:
compote with candied ginger, 78, **78**
dip for, **148**
selection of, **106**
shake, frosty, 105–6
pinto beans, 70
in Greek salad, 211
pita bread, 52–53, 54
pizza on, **105**
pizza:
on pita bread, **105**
with roasted eggplant and peppers, 136–38
Southwest, 103–5, **105**
pizza dough:
white flour, 104
whole wheat, 136
planned-overs, leftovers vs., 154–55
poached dishes, 21
peaches, spiced, 156–57, **157**
pears, vanilla, 187–88
pears in red wine, 248–49, **249**
polenta, cooking of, 46
porcini mushroom risotto, herbed, 270–71, **271**
portobello mushroom and onion burgers,
grilled, 163–64, **164**
potato(es), **245**
and cucumber soup with dill, 160, **160**
hashed browns, 285, **285**
Jean-Marc's oven "fries," 216, **216**
pancakes with warm applesauce, 250–51
red, steamed baby peas and, 245–46
salad, old-fashioned, 165–66, **166**
Sunday morning special, 289
-zucchini soup, 125–26
potatoes, baked:
with herbed cheese, 88–89
new, in rock salt, 109–10, **110**
potlucks, food for, **99**
pots and pans, 91
nonstick, 39, 108–9
pre-cut vegetables, **193**
pressure cookers, 40
Preventive Medicine Research Institute
(PMRI), 24–25
produce, selection of, 35–36
protein, 314–17
in bread, 53–54
combining, 315–16
in legumes, 41, 42–43
in meat substitutes, 56
in tofu, 58
prune puree, 23
psychosocial support, 6, 11
Puck, Wolfgang, 2

pudding:
    brandied pear bread, 273–74
    savory mushroom, 114–15
    sour cherry, 101, **101**
    *see also* clafouti
pumpernickel bread, 53, 54
pumpkin:
    bars, spiced, 266–67, **267**
    bread, 290–91, **291**
puree, mango, **242**

quality of life, improvement of, 3–4
quesadillas, zucchini and cheese, 169–70, **170**
quinoa, cooking of, 46

radish(es), **103**
    lentil, and cucumber salad, 145–46
raisin:
    –apple strudel, 198–99
    -bran muffins, 294–95, **295**
raita, spinach and cucumber, **68,** 241, **241**
ramen soups, 38, 48
ranch dressing, **68,** 195–96
raspberry:
    sorbet, winter fruit platter with, 241–42
    vinegar, 23
recipes, high-fat, help for, 23
Reichler, Gayle, 310
relish, brandied cranberry, 229–30
rémoulade sauce, artichoke halves with, 67–68, **68**
Renier, Donald and Ruth, 86–87
restaurants, dining in, 303–4
Reversal Diet (Life Choice diet), 5–11,
        297–328
    cholesterol and, 7, 9–11
    commonly asked questions about, 306–19
    complex carbohydrates in, 8–9, 316–17
    dining out on, 303–5
    as plant-based, 5, 7–8
    summary of recommendations for, 5–6,
        300–302
    10 percent fat in, 9
    *see also specific recipes*
Reversal Diet Food Diary and Evaluation Form,
        302–3, 308–9
Reversal Diet Pyramid, 51, 298–99, 307, 313
rhubarb–strawberry parfait, 73, **73**
rice, **254,** 299
    leftover, 82, 155
    presentation of, **84**
    varieties of, 44
    where to find, 321–24
rice, brown, 8, **219**
    cooking of, 46, **179**
    and shiitake pilaf, 76–77
    stuffed cabbage with lentils and, 243–45, **245**

rice, long-grain white, 46
    basmati, *see* basmati rice
    salad of wild rice, baby artichoke hearts and,
        254–55
    spicy Mexican, 190–91
rice, short-grain white:
    Arborio, *see* Arborio rice
    cooking of, 46
rice, wild, 46, **219**
    salad of white rice, baby artichoke hearts and,
        254
    and white bean salad, 99, **99**
Rice Krispies, **219**
rice pilaf, **220, 240, 245**
rice-stuffed bell peppers, 219
rice vinegar, 20, 39, 57
ricotta, nonfat, 20
    herbed, baked potato with, 88–89
    in mushroom and spinach lasagne, 185–86, **186**
Riegel, Robert, 205, 289
rigatoni with rich tomato-mushroom sauce,
        194–95, **195**
risotto, 54–55
    with corn and red peppers, 140–41
    herbed mushroom, 270–71
    leftover, 82
    with peas, zucchini, and sun-dried tomatoes,
        81–82, **82**
roast(ed), roasting:
    carrots, parsnips, and beets, 116–17, **117**
    eggplant and peppers, pizza with, 136–38
    garlic toast, **93,** 93–94
    onions, 21–22, 117
    onions, Swiss chard with, 159, **159**
    of peppers, 90
    vegetables, **117**
Roe, Helen, 24–25, 51, 297
romaine lettuce, 265
    marinated artichokes with hearts of, **90,**
        90–91, **91**
Russian-style beet and cabbage borscht with
        sour cream, 251–52, **293**
rye bread, 53, 54

salad(s):
    arugula, corn, and red onions, 135–36, **136**
    broccoli, 154
    bulgur and parsley (tabbouleh), 153–54
    cabbage and green apple slaw, 193
    Caesar, with homemade croutons, 186–87
    of cold cooked greens, 159
    creamy coleslaw, 164–65, **165**
    cucumber, horseradish, and dill, 117–18, **118**
    Greek bean, 211
    honeydew or cantaloupe, 131
    hummus (creamy chickpea puree), 152–53

sugar, 6, 8, 316–17
   in bread, 52
   substitutes for, 21
   vanilla, 188
summer, 121–71
   menus for, 121–22
   recipes for, 125–71
   shopping list for, 123–24
supermarkets, **35–39**
   locating candied ginger in, 78
   panic attacks in, 4–5
   shopping list for, 25–34
sweet and sour:
   dressing, 193
   red cabbage, 115–16, **116**
sweet potato(es), **228, 261**
   baked with thyme, 260–61
   glazed holiday, 227–28
   soup with lime, 218–19
Swiss chard, 183, **258**
   white bean soup with, 255–56
   with roasted onions, 159, **159**

tabbouleh (bulgur and parsley salad), 153–54
tacos, vegetarian, 129–30
tarragon:
   carrot-cauliflower soup with, 100
   mustard, 39
   vinegar, 23, 39
tea, herbal, 39, 284, 327–28
Textured Vegetable Protein (TVP), 57
"Thanksgiving Groaning Board, A," 223–31
   apple cranberry cake, 230–31
   autumn vegetables in a squash, 226–27
   brandied cranberry relish, 229–30
   deviled eggs, 224–25
   glazed holiday yams, 227–28
   old-fashioned bread dressing, 228–29
Throckmorton, Carol, 190, 316
toast:
   French, 290
   roasted garlic, **93,** 93–94
   Sunday morning special, 289
toasting, **240**
tofu, 19, 58
   dressing, creamy, 164–65, **165**
   selection of, 35
tomato(es), fresh:
   angel hair pasta with basil and, 126–27
   baked bulgur-stuffed, 146–47
   bruschetta, **139,** 139–40
   and hummus sandwich, **153**
   peeling and seeding of, **127**
   salsa, **68,** 192
   soup, 155–56, **156**
   soup, variation of, **156**

white bean salad with zucchini, basil, and,
   149
tomatoes, canned, **277**
   balsamic vinegar and, **85**
   braising in, 20–21
   collard greens with onions, peppers, and,
      277–78, **278**
   sauce, 20, 21, 38
   sliced okra with onions and, 85, **85**
tomatoes, sun-dried, 22
   risotto with peas, zucchini, and, 81–82, **82**
   sauce, penne pasta with white bean and,
      246–47
tomato-mushroom sauce, rich, rigatoni with,
      194–95, **195**
tortillas, corn, 53
   fat in, **130**
   two-bean enchiladas, 189–90
   vegetarian tacos, 129–30
tortillas, wheat, 53
   flour, zucchini and cheese quesadillas,
      169–70, **170**
*Tufts University Diet & Nutrition Letter,* **193**
turnip greens, 182, 183
turnips, roasted, **117**
Tuscan vegetable minestrone, 69, **69**

undercooking, overcooking vs., 20, 142

vanilla, **188**
   custard, baked, 118–19, **119**
   frozen yogurt, warm whole wheat crepes with
      strawberries and, 96–98
   poached pears, 187–88
   sugar, 188
vegetable(s), 5, 8, 299, 300, 302
   autumn, in a squash, 226–27
   blanching or boiling of, 179
   broth, *see* broth, vegetable
   brunoise, consommé with, 268–69
   cutting of, **19, 69,** 142
   fiber in, 72
   leftover, 154–55
   minestrone, Tuscan, 69, **69**
   pre-cut, **193**
   quality of, 23
   ragout, 94-95
   sautéing of, 18, 23
   steaming of, 142-44
   stir-fry, 75–76
   *see also specific vegetables*
vegetable stew:
   corn lover's, 179–80, **180**
   leftover, 155
vegetarian tacos, 129–30
Villas, Jim, 2

vinegar, 20, 39
  balsamic, 20, 23, 39, 55, **85, 252**
  rice, 20, 39, 57
  in salad dressings, 19, 23
vitamin A, 7, **150, 222, 261,** 317
vitamin B$_6$, **229, 261**
vitamin B$_{12}$, 7
vitamin C, 7, 85, **136,** 143, **150,** 179, **216,**
    **228, 265,** 317
  foods high in, 318
  top greens as source of, 182
vitamin E, 7, **228, 229,** 317
  foods high in, 318–19

waffles, 286, **286**
washing:
  of leafy greens, 181
  of mushrooms, 206
  of produce, 142
water:
  blanching, use of, 179
  hard, 42
  retention of, 6
watercress, 265
watermelon salad, 130–31, **131**
Wenner, Paul, 49
wheat, cracked, 47, 154
wheat berries, cooking of, 47
whisks, wire, **291**
white bean(s):
  gazpacho with, **168,** 168–69
  penne pasta with sun-dried tomato sauce and,
    246–47
  salad with zucchini, tomato, and basil, 149
  soup with winter greens, 255–56
  and wild rice salad, 99, **99**
whole wheat, **229**
  crepes with strawberries and frozen vanilla
    yogurt, warm, 96–98
  spaghetti marinara with spinach, 91–92

whole wheat bread, 51–52
  recipe for, 133
wine, red, pears poached in, 248–49, **249**
wine vinegar, 20
winter, 233–79
  menus for, 233–34
  recipes for, 237–79
  shopping list for, 235–36
World Health Organization, 314
Wracker, Colleen, 25
Wright, Susan, 52

yams:
  glazed holiday, 227–28
  sweet potatoes vs., **228**
yeast, **138**
yogurt, nonfat, 23, **68**
  cinnamon sauce, mixed citrus compote with,
    238–39, **239**
  cucumber sauce with mint, 209–10
  frozen vanilla, warm whole wheat crepes with
    strawberries and, 96–98
  limitations of, 20, 23
  in salad dressing, 19, 23
  sauce, herbed, 147–48, **148**
  spinach and cucumber raita, **68,** 241, **241**
yogurt cheese, **210**

Ziploc bags, **201, 203**
zucchini:
  brownies, 203–4, **204**
  and cheese quesadillas, 169–70, **170**
  risotto with peas, sun-dried tomatoes and,
    81–82, **82**
  roasted, **117**
  white bean salad with tomato, basil, and,
    149
zucchini soup:
  potato-, 125–26
  with salsa, chilled, 162–63, **163**